A TIMELINE FOR ROBERT FULLER FANS

Carol A. Wirth

A Timeline for Robert Fuller Fans

Carol A. Wirth

Published by Carol A. Wirth, 2023.

A TIMELINE FOR ROBERT FULLER FANS

First edition. April 7, 2023.

Copyright © 2023 Carol A. Wirth.

ISBN: 979-8215155738

Written by Carol A. Wirth.

Table of Contents

FOREWORD 1

INTRODUCTION 2

THE LARAMIE YEARS 1959-1963 24

WAGON TRAIN YEARS 1963 - 1965 74

THE FREELANCE YEARS 1965 - 1972 96

EMERGENCY YEARS 1972 - 1979 113

OUTDOOR YEARS 1980 - 1996 148

THE LATER YEARS 1997 - 2021 158

ARTICLES / MAGAZINES 180

BOOKS MENTIONING ROBERT 182

OTHER INTERNET SITES MENTIONING ROBERT 184

ROBERT ON YOUTUBE.COM 185

YOUTUBE.COM SITES ABOUT ROBERT 188

MISCELLANEOUS 222

WESTERN LIFE 247

CONCLUSION 272

ABOUT THE AUTHOR 275

DEDICATION

This is dedicated Robert Fuller, his casts and crews for using their talents to entertain us.

FOREWORD

Carol A. Wirth has written a wonderful book on her favorite actor Robert Fuller. She has done extensive research giving very detailed information that will serve as a good reference for the many fans of this terrific actor.

She explains from the beginning how she became a fan as a young girl and continues her passion for the career of Robert Fuller. She includes a good timeline of his career that even includes his minor roles as a dancer and extra. This book is a nice tribute to Mr. Fuller.

I am amazed at the amount of information she has in this book. Carol A. Wirth worked first as a collector and then as a researcher to put this information together. It should be interesting and helpful for any fan of Robert Fuller.
Terry Swindol
Author, Film Historian, Videographer

INTRODUCTION

Front Cover is Robert with the author.

The intent of this book is to educate new and old fans about the life of actor Robert Fuller. It is written by a fan and a portion of all profits will go to Robert and Jennifer's favorite charity "Wounded Warriors". Later, if needed, proceeds will be split between this charity and maintaining Robert's official website.

Since Robert Fuller's Laramie television series, he has been receiving fan letters. Throughout his career and now in retirement, he continues to get fan mail. Fans loved him then and they love him now. He hasn't changed over time.

Since three of his television series are in reruns and on DVD's, he has gotten even more fans. Whether written yesterday to his official website or ones from the past each fan letter expresses thoughts of a moment in time. Each fan letter has its own story to tell. Each, like the one below, was sent with love.

November 6, 1999

Hi - A 12 year old girl fell in love in 1965. She wrote few words and only short sentences in her diary. Below are some I thought you would enjoy.

1/7/65 "watched Laramie & recorded Jess voice on a dictaphone" 1/21/65."Jess posed as outlaw" 2/2/65 "Laramie. Jess gets shot in shoulder" 4/11/65 "very disappointed. channel 18 is broke. Laramie is on that station. "5/9/65 "watched Wagon Train with Bob Fuller" 1/18/66 "got movie magazine with Robert Fuller "1/27/68 "watched Laramie. About Jess" 2/5/70 "went to see Bob Fuller in Boeing Boeing. Was beautiful. Talked & signed autographs after. Did a great job. Looked so handsome - the same. Nervous before seeing him".

Many things have changed over the years but Bob Fuller's work still remains magical for me and part of my life. Since 1965 I have saved anything I could find about you - TV Guide issues and ads, magazines, newspapers, books, etc. I saved the Boeing Boeing autographed program and my pen you signed it with. Since the 1980's and VCR's I have added many performances to my private video collection including my first Laramie episode recently. I have a pretty extensive list but I'd like to see how many I am missing and where I might get them.

Also have some great bio information for which I would love to be able to fill in the missing parts. I have viewed early roles via the Museum of Broadcasting in NY City and Chicago. I have memories of spoon playing and mounting a horse on the Dinah Shore show, playing Password with your kids, pheasant hunting on Wide World of Sports and hearing about your son's birth problems on Hollywood Squares.

And now the memories will continue since my sweetie found this web site for me - not only the new information that it contains but that you will be in NV in Dec. We extended our previously planned trip so this woman can once again "be nervous before seeing" you. Can't wait - it's so hard to say thanks for the hours of enjoyment your work has brought me and to wish you the very best of everything.

Carol Wirth with web address

Robert's performances and how he interacts with people creates a very special magic. People know and remember him doing things we all do - like going to school or serving in the military. Fans though have a different image of the man. They remember a particular episode of a television program or movie that impacted them. They remember seeing him playing tennis in a charity tournament. Fans remember seeing him at some event, maybe getting an autograph, hug or kiss. Some remember a particular conversation, a memory of a moment in time that continues to bring happiness. Many fans have signed photographs or photos taken with Robert. Some fans used their own skills to create musical tributes or birthday greetings. No matter what fans have done, the bottom line has been that they love him.

Fans knew Robert was busy living life rather than writing about his own life. We know he held his own memories private. As the above letter show, I am a fan. With love and respect, I created a timeline of bits and pieces of his experiences so new fans could see the whole man. Many of us fans were kids in the

1960's. Then we believed anything we read or saw. We believed those quotes, those studio or magazine photographs but now we know better. I have tried to sort out the facts and note and correct some of these inaccuracies.

Robert's official website is www.robertfuller.info[1] . Tony Gill and Robert's Fandom group worked hard to compile background on Robert. Many fans, like me, have contributed to Robert's website. I even wrote on lined paper a 63 page Laramie story. Later in high school I typed it. Remember this was a time when there weren't any correction options much less today's "cut and paste". I gave the now 26 typed pages to my English teacher to critique. Mine would be too time consuming to edit or rewrite but fans can see other stories fans have created on Robert's website.

With thousands of fans, there are many Internet sources about Robert. A Timeline for Robert Fuller Fans shares some of these sites to explore. It also includes Robert's movies, television programs, events he attended, interviews he did and awards and tributes he received. Internet searches will show hundreds of photos that for copyright reasons I could not include. Youtube choices are almost endless but some I find one day but not the next.

Over the course of Robert's lifetime, he has known or worked with names we know. His circle of friends and acquaintances is vast. Some are from the entertainment field, others are not. When possible I have shared Internet links so you can learn more. Fans, new and old, can explore links to learn about cast members, etc. Most might also be found on www.wikipedia.org[2] or www.biography.com[3] or www.imdb.com[4] or www.tvguide.com[5] or www.westernclippings.com[6] or at www.b-westerns.com[7] or www.glamourgirlsofthesilverscreen.com[8] . Each celebrity used their talents to entertain us and deserves to be remembered. Some of the names you may not recognize but you know their faces. Sadly, many are no longer with us but modern technology keeps them alive. For those living, this may be your chance to say hello and thanks. Again, these website resources above are but a few of those available. Please enjoy viewing them.

---

1. http://www.robertfuller.info

2. http://www.wikipedia.org

3. http://www.biography.com

4. http://www.imdb.com

5. http://www.tvguide.com

6. http://www.westernclippings.com

7. http://www.b-westerns.com

8. http://www.glamourgirlsofthesilverscreen.com

Using personal items I have saved over the years and my research into Robert's life, his movies, television programs and events I compiled this timeline. **I was unable to get Tony Gill's approval to be included on Robert's official website. It has not been officially 'fact checked' but to the best of my knowledge it is accurate.** I tried to present a variety of items tied to Robert's career to help both new and old fans find something new. Again sadly, due to photo ownership issues and no responses for permission from Universal Studio hundreds of photos I had hoped to include are excluded.

This timeline of Robert Fuller's life are in date order whenever possible. When dates are conflicting, I chose the one I thought was most accurate. Throughout this timeline I used the name he had on that date. For consistency I used the formal Robert although professionally and personally he goes by Bob. To many fans, he is "family" and this timeline summary is a fan's tribute.

I have included youtube (www.youtube.com[9]) story links and viewing Robert's work. Those covering many time periods or topic areas are listed after the timeline. Following the timeline fans will also find more info on celebrities and the real West. Fans can find out what was life really like in the 1800's for cowboys and Native American Indians. Fans can step back in time to visit forts, historic sites, museums and actual locations in history books. Do you want to see the Oregon Trail, ride a replica stagecoach or take a covered wagon trip?

Fans can attend annual events or go to western themed restaurants or outdoor dining musical presentations. Western lovers can go to a dude ranch to learn to ride or go on a cattle drive. The possibilities are endless and you can go in person or arm chair travel via Internet sites.

Robert, in real life and in the roles he played, has qualities to be admired. He encourages a value system, a way of life. Others, like Roy and Dale Evans, were example setters. Robert took the time and effort to make this world a better place. Most of us will never receive worldwide feedback but we all remember a moment in time when someone said or did something that impacted us. Could you show a child what fungi are? Can you encourage someone going through a divorce or comfort someone after a death? We all have something to contribute.

---

9. http://www.youtube.com

I wanted a way to honor Robert. I also wanted to create a place where his fans could support Robert's cause, The Wounded Warriors Project. A percentage of the profit from this ebook goes to this worthwhile organization and later if needed a portion of the sales will go to his official website to ensure its existence another 100 years.

Whether you are going down memory lane or this material is new, enjoy this timeline. Enjoy this mini peek into Robert's life. He is someone worth knowing and worth remembering.

Many of us loved Robert in 1959 and we love him now. Enjoy Robert's timeline and celebrate his life. He, like others before him, can be role models for your children and grandchildren. Western history and values can be passed on.

THE EARLY YEARS

8/3/1910
Betty M., Robert's mom, is born. She will have a New York social security number.

7/23/1920
Robert C. Simpson, Robert's future stepfather, is born. His Illinois social security number will be 327-14-0838.

7/29/1933
Leonard Leroy Lee was born in Troy, NY at 1:50 p.m. to Betty and "Buddy" Lee. His nickname became Buddy. *(Some sources have 1934 date and his name as Robert Cole, Jr. His step father's professional name is Robert Cole).*

Childhood and young adult photos were printed in a 110 page Japanese special Robert issue magazine during his visit there in 1961.

Buddy attends St Mary's School in New York.

1939
About this time, Buddy's parents divorce and he and his mom move to Miami, Florida. Betty supports herself and Buddy by being a chorus girl, choreographer and dancing headliner.

1940's

Buddy learns acrobatics and is a wrestling fan.

Buddy listens to the radio show Let's Pretend with Peter Brown (10/5/1935-3/21/2016 www.peterbrown.tv[10]) on the radio. (*From 1957 to 2005 Peter had over 110 roles not including three television series. Two, Lawman and Laredo, were westerns Peter gave an excellent interview introducing the release of Laredo on DVD). Robert and Peter would work together in the future and become good friends).*

9/301940 - 8/4/1941

During this time period, Robert's future stepfather, Robert C. Simpson, is a Seaman 2C in the U.S. Navy. He may have been assigned to the new ship USS Arcturus.

1943 - 1944

Buddy is in military school in Florida for 5th and 6th grades.

Betty is still dancing in Florida where there are at least four military bases. She meets Robert Simpson, Sr., born 8/23/1920, a naval officer while Buddy is in military school. He visits Buddy and they spend time together drinking cokes or at night clubs his mom is working at. Robert asks Buddy if it's ok to marry his mom. Buddy agrees and Robert Simpson became his dad, not step dad.

1944

Betty M. Lee and Robert C. Simpson marry in Broward County, Florida. Betty changes Leonard Leroy Lee's name on his birth certificate to Robert C. Simpson, Jr. voiding it. Buddy was not aware of this until he was to enter the army.

3/17/1944

Patricia Lyon, future first wife and mother to his three children, is born on St. Patrick's Day in Hammond, Indiana.

1945 - 1947

After Betty and Robert Simpson marry they move to Chicago, Illinois for one year.

Buddy is in public school for 7th to 8th grade. He is dancing.

---

10. http://www.peterbrown.tv

Buddy is spending time watching movies on Saturday afternoons. He sees stars like Gene Autry, Don "Red" Barry, Roy Rogers, Bob Steele, Randolph Scott and Throne Power. *(Later in his career, Robert will meet many of his childhood heroes).*

Gene Autry (9/29/1907-10/2/1998) started singing on radio in 1929. Known as the 'singing cowboy' from 1934 to 1953 he was in 93 movies and had his own television show (1950-1956). Gene's best known songs include Back in the Saddle Again, Rudolph, the Red Nosed Reindeer and a song he wrote Frosty the Snowman. Gene made 640 recordings writing more than 300 of them himself or with a co-author. From 1931 to 1949 he released 33 singles. In the 1950's Gene had 7 singles. He made 2 albums in 1976. Two more singles were releases in the 1990's and another two in the 2000's. His music sold over 100 million copies and his Christmas songs continue to be very popular. Gene had a weekly radio show from 1940 to 1956. In 1934 Gene made his first movie and made movies before and after his military service during World War II as a pilot. His movies were top money makers in 1937 to 1942 and were in second place from 1943 to 1952. In the 1940's and 1950's at least 133 Gene Autry comic books were published and from 1954 to 1984 a Mexican publisher put out 423 issues. Between 1942 and 1968 Gene was involved with rodeos including providing livestock. Over the years he owned recording studios, production companies, radio and television stations and a Major Baseball team. In 1968 Gene and his wife Jackie were co-owners with another couple and the four of them created the Gene Autry Museum of the American West / Western Heritage Museum (https://theautry.org). Gene has many awards including getting five stars on the Hollywood Walk of Fame. See www.geneautry.com[11].

Don "Red" Barry (1/11/1912-7/17/1980) started on stage in the late 1930's and later got his nick name "Red" while appearing on a 1940 Red Ryder film, a character he played in other movies as well. From 1933 to 1981 he appeared in over 136 roles. Red was also a movie screenwriter and director. After police were called investigating a domestic dispute with his estranged wife, sadly Don killed himself.)

Joel McCrea (11/5/1905-10/20/1990. Over 50 years starting in 1932 until 1976 Joel made over 100 movies - many were westerns. In high school he worked as a stunt double for William S. Hart (12/6/1864-6/23/1946) and Tom Mix (1/6/1880-10/12/1990 - See www.tommixmuseum.com[12]). He received several awards during his lifetime. Joel was an outdoorsman and rancher. He and his wife Frances Dee were married 57 years. After his death at least 115 acres of land he owned was donated so its wildness could be preserved. See https://www.britannica.com/biography/Joel-McCrea[13] although it contains many ads.

Roy Rogers (11/5/1911-7/6/1998) became known as 'King of the Cowboys' is also admired by the author who saw him twice in person. Roy started on radio in 1931 and traveled around in singing in The Rocky Mountaineers / Bar-O-Cowboys / Sons of the Pioneers (1934). His most popular songs included Don't Fence Me In, Tumbling Tumbleweeds and Happy Trails. From 1946 to 1991 Roy had 13 singles with My Chickashay Gal getting to #4. From 1970 to 1991 Roy had 4 albums. In 1991 he released a music video. From 1934 to 1984 Roy's had over 110 roles. In 1943, 1945, 1951 and 1952 Roy was

---

11. http://www.geneautry.com

12. http://www.tommixmuseum.com

13. https://www.britannica.com/biography/Joel-McCrea

the number one box office star. From 1946 to 1950 he was in the top 19 box office stars. In 1940 Roy got merchandising control and his family tested products with his name on them before they were sold. Roy along with his wife actress and author Dale Evans (married 51 years), promote WWII war bonds and adoptions, visited hospitals, attended many fund raising and charity events. Roy's own production company developed his television show and several others. Roy received numerous awards including 3 stars on the Hollywood Walk of Fame and 2 Country Music Awards. See www.royrogers.com[14].

Bob Steele (1/23/1907-12/21/1988). Bob came from a vaudeville family. His father went into movies, as did Bob and his twin brother Bill. From 1927 to 1967 he worked in movies and television including being a regular in several series. See www.b-westerns.com/steel1.gtm[15].

Randolph Scott (1/23/1898-3/2/1987). Robert thought he was a great cowboy. From 1928 to 1962 Randolph had over 60 of his 100 roles in westerns. In box office sales Randolph in 1950 was #10, in 1951 #7 and in both 1952 and 1953 he was #10. He invested money wisely making money in gas, oil wells, real estate and securities. Randolph enjoyed golfing and was religious. During his lifetime and afterward he received several awards. He and his wife Barbara were married for 43 years when he died of heart and lung problems.

Tyrone Power (5/5/1914-11/15/1958). Coming from a stage family back to his great grandfather born in 1795 he joined his father on stage in 1931 before he died in 12/1931. Tyrone came to Hollywood in 1936 and from 1936 to 1943 made very successful movies. Tyrone also appeared in at least 7 radio productions. He enlisted as a Marine during World War II and became a pilot and stayed in the reserves becoming a Major in 1957. Tyrone appeared in over 50 movies and in the 1950's cut back to do more stage work. He died of a heart attack while filming, donated his eyes and was buried with full military honors.

1948

When Buddy is 14 or 15 the family leaves Chicago, Illinois to move to Key West, Florida. Buddy attends Key West High School for 9th grade. In 9th grade, his last year of school, due to his lack of singing talent he couldn't be lead in a school play but instead became a Cossack. Buddy also played a sailor in a school play.

Buddy did not enjoy or do well in school and gets kicked out twice. Buddy's father tells him if he quits school, he must work. Buddy held various jobs including bellhop and bowling pin racker earning ten cents an hour.

Buddy's mom Betty convinced her husband to quit the Navy. She taught him to dance and the couple opened a dance school in Key West on Duval. Betty taught ballet to the local children and in the evenings taught adults ballroom. Hundreds of Navy personnel stationed in Key West attended their dance studio. Their professional names were Betty and Robert Cole.

---

14. http://www.royrogers.com

15. http://www.b-westerns.com/steel1.gtm

Buddy is dancing.

Buddy fishes, sees 15-foot sharks and five to six inch shrimp. He enjoys the outdoors.

A 1961 110 page Japanese magazine dedicated to Robert carries some early photos of his life.

1949 - 1951

Buddy is 15 or 16 when he and his parents move to Hollywood, California. The driving trip included their cat/cats when most trailer camps did not allow them. An escaped cat sometimes delayed their departure. They driving route was through New Orleans. In California his parents buy a home with the money from the sale of the Florida dance school. It is a duplex where the family lives in half and rents out the other half to friends.

Buddy has several jobs after moving to California including working at a gas station and at Paramount-Hollywood Theater. At one time he is earning 35 cents an hour at Grauman Chinese Theater. Here he started as doorman wearing a costume, then usher taking tickets to working his way up after about six months to Assistant Manager at age 18. Supervising a staff of 20, Robert wore a suit and tie during the day and a tuxedo in the evening. His friends encouraged him to apply for being an extra but he got many rejections.

After working about six months at Grumman's Chinese Theater he took a new job at Golden Eagle Gas station for $50 a week. He continued to apply for extra and stunt work.

Buddy's dad using his stage name of Robert Cole becomes an excellent dancer and is successful in movies. He dances in almost every musical made in Hollywood from 1950 until his retirement in 1987. His work includes Oklahoma, Jailhouse Rock, Seven Brides for Seven Brothers and Gentlemen Prefer Blonds. Buddy will eventually join his dad working as a dancer in musicals. Robert Cole also acted in The Line in 1954, Highway Patrol in 1955 and Dr. Kildare in 1961.

1950's

Betty runs a dancing studio. (Years later after getting a pinched nerve, Betty retires).

Sometime while Harry S. Truman was president (1945-1953) Betty and Robert Cole performed for him at the White House.

Some young adult photos of Robert are printed in a Japanese Magazine dedicated to Robert during his visit there in 1961.

1951

Buddy meets Chuck Courtney (7/23/1932-1/19/2000) at a party. Chuck plays Dan Reid on the Lone Ranger TV series.

1952

He is hunting and keeping meat in their freezer.

He plays the drums.

Buddy, encouraged by friends making more money than he is, changes his name when he joins the Screen Extras Guild. (SEG) There is already a Russell Simpson and Buddy didn't like Robert Simpson as a name so he used Robert Fuller. Fuller was a New York relative's name on his maternal side that traced their family tree back to the Mayflower. *See Robert Fuller Talks About His Many Names at https://www.youtube.com/watch?v=DAGSrHK62hA .*

His father already working in musicals also encourages him to work in the movies. Robert becomes a contract player with MGM. (Other MGM contract players were Rock Hudson (11/17/1925-10/2/1985) and James Drury (4/18/1934-4/6/2020 www.thevirginian.net[16]). James Drury may have introduced Robert to Jock Mahoney (2/7/1919-12/14/1989) who in turn talked to Dick Jones (2/251927-7/7/2014).

(Jock Mahoney was a pilot, flight instructor and war correspondent during World War II. During his long career he also used the names Jack Mahoney and Jock O'Mahoney. By 1947 he was doing stuntman work. Jock had over 72 credits not including two television series and two films playing Tarzan working into the 1980's. Days after a car accident Jock had a second stroke and died).

Robert's first work in the movies was as an extra. The Screen Actor's Guild extra pay was $12.05 a day including meals and stunt work was $200 a week. Dancers in musicals earned $250 a week and the typical musical had three to fours weeks of rehearsal and another 10 days of shooting. If Robert was in four or five numbers, it meant months of work.

---

16. http://www.thevirginian.net

Above and Beyond (unaccredited extra) war movie with Robert Taylor (8/5/1911-6/8/1969) and Eleanor Parker (6/26/1922-12/9/2013). It was Robert's first movie. *See Above and Beyond at https://www.youtube.com/watch?v=pw66o4nJuGEhttps://www.youtube.com/watch?v=pw66o4nJuGE .*

Come Back Little Sheba starring Burt Lancaster (11/2/1913-10/20/1994). He was an extra. Cast includes Terry Moore (1/7/1929- www.terrymoore.com[17]), Shirley Booth (8/30/1898-10/16/1992) and Richard Jaeckel (10/10/1925-6/14/1997). *See Come Back Little Sheba 1952 at https://www.youtube.com/watch?v=re8eDgidyWI .*

Death Valley Days. He was a Mexican bandit.

7/6/1952

Jennifer Alyson Savidge, Robert's second wife, is born in Alameda County, California.

1953

Calamity Jane (musical western). He is a dancer, unaccredited extra with Doris Day (4/3/1922-5/13/2019). His part includes presenting Doris Day with flowers backstage. Cast also includes Howard Keel (4/13/1919-11/7/2004).

Gentlemen Prefer Blondes (musical). He is a dancer, unaccredited in chorus line with Marylyn Monroe (6/1/1926-8/5/1962) and Jane Russell (6/21/1921-2/28/2011). He rehearsed with Marilyn for about three weeks before a one week shoot. Robert recalled she was very nervous but nice to all the dancers. According to Jane Russell's autobiography Jack Cole (shaved head, wiry, evil sense of humor) worked the dancers to death. *See Gentlemen Prefer Blondes (ErkeklerSarışınları Sever) 1953 HD at https://www.youtube.com/watch?v=Lk-zhsa6Lyw*

I Love Melvin (musical). He is a dancer, unaccredited with Debbie Reynolds (4/1/1932-12/28/2016). Robert did some acrobatics as a cheer leader. Cast includes Donald O'Connor (8/28/1925-9/27/2003 www.donaldoconnor.org[18]). *(Often incorrectly stated was Robert's first movie. While viewing a screening of a difficult dance sequence he was to do a knee slide up to Debbie Reynolds but instead fell to the floor giving everyone a laugh but obviously embarrassing Robert).*

Julius Caesar. He is an uncredited citizen of Rome. A huge cast.

---

17. http://www.terrymoore.com

18. http://www.donaldoconnor.org

Latin Lovers starring Lana Turner (2/8/1900-6/29/1995). He is an uncredited dancer. Cast includes Ricardo Montalban (11/25/1920-1/14/2009). Robert admired that Ricardo remembered everyone's name after one meeting). Via MGM he was making $125 a week in the chorus. He saw many great studio stars including Betty Grable (12/18/1916-7/2/1973) at lunch.

The Actress starring Spencer Tracy (4/5/1900-6/10/1967). He is an uncredited dancer. Cast includes Jean Simmons (1/31/1929-1/22/2010), Teresa Wright (10/27/1918-3/6/2005) and Anthony Perkins (4/4/1932-9/12/1992).

San Antone starring Rod Cameron (12/7/1910-12/21/1983), Forrest Tucker (2/212/1919-10/25/1986), Arleen Whelan (9/1/1916-4/6/1993), Bob Steele (1/23/1907-12/21/1988) and Harry, Carey, Jr. (5/16/1921-12/27/2012).

Chuck Courtney (7/23/1930-1/19/2000) teaches Robert how to ride a horse, to draw a gun, do stunt work and how to become a cowboy. In the 1950's and 1960's actors competed in fast draw competitions in places like Las Vegas, Nevada. Besides Robert, Clint Eastwood (5/31/1930-) and Peter Brown (10/5/1935-3/21/2016 www.peterbrown.tv[19]) both had fast draws.

Robert relates a story about Hugh O'Brien (4/19/1925-9/5/2016) claiming he was the best ever over WWII hero and actor Audie Murphy (6/20/1925-5/28/1971). Robert's best draw time was 28th /100th of a second.

LATE 1953

Lawless Breed. Cast includes Rock Hudson (11/17/1925-10/2/1985).and Julie Adams (10/17/1926-2/3/2019) www.julieadams.biz[20]).

Robert's last appearance as an extra was in The Sweet Smell of Success with Burt Lancaster (11/2/1913-10/20/1994) and Tony Curtis (6/3/1925-9/29/2010 www.tonycurtis.com[21]). Overall Robert had worked in about 200 movies as an extra with Columbia, Paramount and MGM studios. He also worded with Clark Gable (2/1/1901-11/16/1960) and James Cagney (7/17/1899-3/30/1986).

1953-1955

19. http://www.peterbrown.tv

20.   http://www.julieadams.biz

21. http://www.tonycurtis.com

He is drafted at 19 and spent 17 months in Korea. He is in the 19th Army Infantry Regiment. On his first day he hit his corporal and as punishment carried a gun around saying "I will never hit a corporal". He later had a serious disagreement with a captain. Robert learned discipline including being on time. Three times he was outstanding soldier (based on appearance, bearing and military knowledge) in his outfit on Guard Mount. His mother Betty Cole became a pinup for his outfit. He remained a private. He was also in Japan during this time.

Some early photos with his parents and in his military uniform appeared in a 110 page Japanese magazine dedicated to Robert during his visit there in 1961.

The first five days Robert was home he never left the house. After being in the military Robert no longer wanted just to be an extra and was thinking of leaving the business. He would have welcomed a job outdoors, like as a fish and game warden. It was something he could do with only a high school education.

1954

The Man Behind the Badge. It is a police drama and Robert is in episode titled The Portland, Oregon Story, Part 2. (This must have been made prior to Robert's military service).

5/15/1954

Man Against Crime - The episode is titled Where's Mimi. Host is Norman Rose (6/23/1917-11/12/2004). (This must have been made prior to Robert's military service). See Man Against Crime Episode 116: Where's Mimi at https://www.youtube.com/watch?v=oL48dOQPao8 .

1955

Shortly after getting out of the Army Robert purchases a 1954 T-Bird convertible for $2,200 with his ending Army pay. Robert meets future co-star, Julie London (9/26/1926-10/18/2000) when he stops in for a beer at a nightclub on Sunset Boulevard in Los Angles, (? Johnny Washes 98 Club) California she was appearing. It is her debut night as a singer with a male guitarist. Robert also meets her then boyfriend, Bobby Troup that evening. He continues to come, drink beer and enjoy her show.

Chuck Courtney along with Robert's parents (fans of Richard Boone's TV series The Medic) write a letter to Richard Boone (6/18/1917-1/10/1981) asking him to help Robert. Chuck was already attending Richard Boone's acting class. Robert sat in and Richard asked him to come up and do an improvisation which he liked. Boone's technique was individualized to each student unlike "method" used by actors like James Dean (2/8/1931-9/30/1955 www.jamesdean.com[22]). Boone's focus was to look believable on screen. Robert attends classes about one year. Class size was about ten to twelve and was two or three nights a week for up to five hours. Students paid $25 for 2 nights a week and Robert worked in film to pay for classes. Chuck also conducted strict horseback riding lessons on Saturday as part

22. http://www.jamesdean.com

of this class. *(Richard Boone tried to continue to teach the classes even after he starred on Have Gun Will Travel. Richard Boone was on Broadway in 1947, had his movie debut in 1950 and appeared in almost 75 movies and television programs not counting his four television series from 1954 to 1972. Richard later wrote, lectured and died from throat cancer).*

Robert performed in local playhouses. His father gives him Lawrence Oliver's Hamlet albums to learn a role. He performs in Romeo and Juliet. He wears boots to feel taller.

A Rebel Without a Cause. The cast includes James Dean (2/8/1931-9/30/1955 www.jamesdean.com[23]), Natalie Wood (7/20/1938-11/29/1981) and Sal Mineo (1/10/193-2/12/1976 www.salmineo.com[24]).

Highway Patrol - The episode is titled The Arsonist and he plays Arthur Bensen. Cast includes Broderick Crawford (12/9/1911-4/26/1986). See FIRE. Highway Patrol Fire at https://www.youtube.com/watch?v=U4e1u0V5uZw .

LATE 1955 OR 1956

His acting teacher Richard Boone encouraged Robert to continue his acting classes with drama coach Sanford (Sandy) Meisner at the New York Neighborhood Playhouse School of Theatre in New York City. *(Sandy was about 5'5" tall and wore thick glasses.* His teaching technique was to get students to think of their character, not themselves. Students were taught to think how they would control their body to make it believable. Some exercises might include solving one-action problems like stealing something unnoticed or a teen finding a body and creating the illusion of crying. Scenarios forced one or two students to use their own ingenuity and imagination, no scripts to complete the assignment). *Other students taught at the Playhouse Theater were Gregory Peck (4/5/1916-6/12/2003 www.gregorypeck.com[25]), Jon Voight (12/29/1938-), Robert Duvall (1/5/1931-), Edmund O'Brien (9/10/1915-5/9/1985) and Grace Kelly (11/12/1929-9/14/1982).* Afterward Robert returns to Hollywood / Los Angeles, California.

He may have appeared on the game show To Say the Least, as himself, around this time.

1956

Friendly Persuasion. Robert appears in three unaccredited roles. He plays an Amish farmer and a Confederate solider and appeared in many background scenes. He has his first speaking role playing a young Union soldier at shooting gallery. Robert was picked by director, William Wyler (7/1/1902-7/27/1981), to say one line "Bet you a dollar you can't do that again" to Gary Cooper (5/7/1901-5/13/1961 www.garycooper.com[26]). Robert's real sideburns won him the part. Cast also includes Dorothy McGuire (6/14/1916-9/13/2001) and future Laramie co-star John Smith

---

23. http://www.jamesdean.com

24. http://www.salmineo.com

25.   *http://www.gregorypeck.com*

26.   http://www.garycooper.com

(3/6/1931-1/25/1995) and Peter Mark Richman (4/16/1927-1/14/2021 www.petermanrichman.com[27]). *See friendly persuasion movies I was an extra in at https://www.youtube.com/watch?v=4PtTtKikJAs* . See Friendly Persuasion 1956 | Gary Cooper | Drama | Directed by William Wyler at https://www.youtube.com/watch?v=lApY3Bcwb9k .

Meet Me in Las Vegas starring Dan Dailey (12/14/1915-10/16/1978). His role is unaccredited and he danced with Cyd Charisse (3/8/1922-6/17/2008) and Johnny Brasher. *(Robert thought Cyd was a wonderful dancer).*

Strange Intruder is a Science Fiction series. The episode is titled Prisoner of War. He plays Judd Patterson, a prisoner of war and a bad guy killed in the third episode. This speaking role is unaccredited. Edmund Purdom (12/19/1924-1/1/2009) and Ida Lupino (2/4/1918-8/3/1995) also appear. *See Robert Fuller Strange Intruder 1956 at https://www.youtube.com/watch?v=CloMAyDhXCs and* Robert Fuller Strange Intruder 1956 at

https://www.youtube.com/watch?v=CloMAyDhXCs&list=PLHNrKWCnaFB7k0IKkBdkRz1jiYqupPAfD

.

Tea and Sympathy is his first play. It was in Santa Monica, California and also stars Eddie Byrnes (7/30/1933- 1/9/2020), Michael Landon (10/31/1936-7/1/1991), Eve Miller (8/8/1923-8/17/1973) and Jack Nicholson (4/22/1937-).

The Harder They Fall starring Humphrey Bogart (12/25/1899-1/14/1957) and Rod Steiger (4/14/1925-7/9/2002). He is an extra.

The Man in the Gray Flannel Suite starring Gregory Peck (4/5/1916-6/12/2003). He plays a solider with a Sergeant but has no dialogue and role is uncredited. Cast also includes Jennifer Jones (3/2/1919-12/17/2009) and Fredric March (8/31/1897-4/14/1975). *See The Man In The Gray Flannel Suit 1956 Full Movie at https://www.youtube.com/watch?v=-AjvayfuesY* .

The Ten Commandments. He is an uncredited extra. Movie has a huge cast.

10/5 OR 10/7/1956

Crossroads - The episode in the first season is titled The Comeback and he plays an extra, the third solider. Also starring were Don DeFore (8/25/1913-12/22/1983) and Chuck Connors (4/10/1921-11/10/1982 www.ourchuckconnors.com[28]).

---

27.   http://www.petermanrichman.com

28.   http://www.ourchuckconnors.com

1957

At about this time, Robert gets an agent.

Matinee Theater. ? extra some time before the NBC drama series ended on 6/27/1958.

Raintree County starring Elizabeth Taylor (2/27/1932-3/23/2011 www.elizaethtaylor.com[29]). He is an extra.

Teenage Thunder. He plays Maurice Weston, a teenage thug racer. It is Robert's first major movie role. He had interviewed twice but not gotten the role. Robert used his own 1954 Ford convertible to play a scene from the script with his friend and actor, Chuck Courtney (7/23/1930-1/19/2000). They staged a fight to convince director, Paul Helmick (1/24/1919-5/2/2006) and Robert gets the part over Edd Byrnes (7/30/1933-1/9/2020 www.eddbyrnes.com[30]). Cast includes Chuck Courtney (7/23/1930-1/19/2000) and Melinda Byron (10/20/1938-5/30/2018). *See TEENAGE THUNDER Chuck Courtney, Melinda Byron, Robert Fuller Full Movie at https://www.youtube.com/watch?v=s5c5dIelspU and* Teen Age Thunder - Full Movie - B&W - Juvenile Delinquent/Drama - Robert Fuller - Hot Rod (1957) at https://www.youtube.com/watch?v=XR0-94E_fm4 . Teenage Thunder movie publicity includes Robert's name. The DVD cover is a drawing.

The Brain from Planet Arous. It is the same production company as Teenage Thunder. He plays Dan Murphy. His character is killed by brain early in the film. Cast includes John Agar (1/31/1921-4/7/2002 www.johnagar.com[31]) and Joyce Meadows (4/13/1935- www.joycemeadows.net[32] and www.mmmrecordsings.com/joycemeadows[33]). The Variety review doesn't include Robert's name. The movie becomes a cult science fiction favorite. *See The Brain from Planet Arous (1957) at https://www.youtube.com/watch?v=LLHy6fWfWA8* . VHS covers are released. Two of the cover include Robert's name. DVD covers are released but one does not include Robert's name.

The movie and television industry throughout Robert's career had a script color system to denote revisions. Original script given to key cast members was white, then yellow, blue and then maybe green, again depending on the number of changes made by writers.

The Delicate Delinquent. Robert doubled for Jerry Lewis (3/16/1926-8/20/2017) in a fight scene.

11/11/1957

---

29. http://www.elizaethtaylor.com

30. http://www.eddbyrnes.com

31. http://www.johnagar.com

32. http://www.joycemeadows.net

33. http://www.mmmrecordsings.com/joycemeadows

The Gray Ghost. He was in Point of Honors, Episode 3 in the first series playing Dan Hatcher. It is a western and Angie Dickinson (9/30/1931-) also has an early role. Cast includes Tod Andrews 11/9/1914-11/7/1972) and Phil Chambers (6/16/1916-1/16/1993).

1958 - 3/1959

Robert did fifteen TV dramas.

1958

Robert is doing drag racing.

2/14/1958

Death Valley Days -The episode is titled Ten in Texas and he plays Johnny Santos, a Mexican bandit.

3/5/1958

Official Detective TV series. The episode is titled The Taxi Killers and his character Lacey is electrocuted. The show's host was Everett Sloane (10/1/1909-8/6/1965).

4/22/1958

The Californians - The episode is titled Pipeline. He plays Cobber Bannon who kills with a boomerang and gun and dies from poisoned water.

5/18/1958

No Warning / Panic! - The Episode is titled Survivors and he plays Miller, a radio operator on a life boat.

7/31/1958

Buckskin - The episode is titled The Trial of Chrissy Miller playing Gill Hargas. The town wants to lynch him but he is innocent. Cast includes Tom Nolan (1/14/1948-), Sally Brophy (12/14/1928-9/18/2007) and Mike Road (3/18/1918-4/14/2013).

9/2/1958 - 3/1959

Flight - The episode titled Outpost in Space aired sometime during this time period. Robert plays an astronaut who is killed in the third episode. Host is U.S. General George C. Kenney (8/6/1889-8/9/1977).

10/24/1958

M Squad - The episode is titled The Trap. Robert plays Danny Mitchell who thinks he killed a jeweler.

11/211958

Adventures of Rin Tin Tin - The episode is titled The Epidemic. He plays Stan, an outlaw, who dies in an epidemic. Cast includes Lee Aaker (9/25/1943-4/1/2021), James E. Brown (3/22/1920-4/11/1992) and Chuck Courtney (7/23/1930-1/19/2000). *See The Adventures of Rin Tin Tin The Epidemic 1958 at https://www.youtube.com/watch?v=3RMHJZCQRH4* .

11/28/1958

Lux Playhouse - The episode is titled Coney Island Winter with Robert starring as Andy. Kathleen Crowley (12/26/1929-4/23/2017) and Edmond O'Brien (9/10/1915-5/9/1985 www.edmondobrien.com[34]) also star.

12/7/1958

Schlitz Playhouse of Stars - The episode is titled Heroes Never Grow up. The host is James Mason (5/15/1909-7/27/1984).

12/10/1958

General Electric Theatre - The episode is titled The Castaway and he plays Till. It is hosted by Ronald Reagan (2/6/1911-6/5/2004). *(Robert and Ronald remain friends).*

12/11/1958

Death Valley Days - The episode is titled The Gunsmith. He plays Alex Derwood, a gunsmith. Anthony Caruso (4/7/1916-4/4/2003) also stars.

12/15/58

Restless Gun - The episode is titled Peligroso. He plays Bud Bardene a young bully kid who dies in the first few minutes in a gunfight. Cast includes John Payne (5/23/1912-12/6/1989). See THE RESTLESS GUN – PELIGROSO at https://www.youtube.com/watch?v=O9juswp4Lvs .

1959

By this time Robert had appeared in about 50 roles. As guest star these roles are often 'heavies' or bad guys. Robert said these types of roles were very enjoyable.

---

34.   http://www.edmondobrien.com

Alcoa Premier - The episode is titled Emergency Only.

Highway Patrol - The episode is titled Fire where he has a large role playing Judd Patterson an arsonist. Cast includes Broderick Crawford (12/9/1911-4/26/1986). *See Highway Patrol 51 in Fire at https://www.youtube.com/ watch?v=Skt2RCz30OU* .

The World of Giants - The episode is titled The Pool. It is science fiction series with Marshall Thompson (11/27/ 1925-5/18/1992 www.marshall-thompson.com[35]) and Arthur Franz (2/29/1920-6/10/2006).

Robert was producer David Dortort's second choice to play Little Joe Cartwright on Bonanza TV series. Michael Landon (10/31/1936-7/1/1991) will get the role. (*Robert later said he would not have taken the role anyhow and he had just signed up for Laramie in a better role and money*).

Robert is friends with actor Burt Reynolds (2/11/1936 - 9/6/2018. *Burt has over 160 movies and television appearances not including his reoccurring roles in several television programs. Burt also appeared on stage and was a director and producer. He was number one at the box office for five years in a row starting in 1978. Burt died of a heart attack*).

Robert met many upcoming and veteran performers early in his career. Both candid and staged publicity photos were taken. Stars Robert posed with include:

Actor Lance Fuller (12/6/1928-12/22/2001). Lance had 36 movie and television roles from 1943 to 1975.

Jayne Mansfield (4/19/1933-6/29/1967). She appeared on stage in 1951, on Broadway and in movies in 1955. Jayne later appeared in television and in a night club act singing and playing the piano and violin. Appearing in Playboy Magazine with original photos six times, photos were shown again in several later issues. Jayne was killed in an automobile accident.

Natalie Wood (7/20/1931-11/29/1981). Starting as a child in 1947 and filming as an adult in 1981 Natalie had at least 68 roles. She was nominated several times and did win an Academy Award for Best Supporting Actress. Natalie died under mysterious circumstances.

1959 - 1965

---

35. http://www.marshall-thompson.com

Germany publicity photos from 1959 to 1965 feature Robert and his work. Many photos are episode scenes and there is one of Robert holding his Germany award.

1/12/1959

The Restless Gun - The episode is titled Shadow of a Gunfighter. It was filmed in 10/1958. He plays Jim Winfield, the son of a rancher with cattle drive money who is killed. It is a bigger part than his previous role on this program. Cast includes John Payne (5/23/1912-12/6/1989). *See THE RESTLESS GUN - SHADOW OF A GUNFIGHTER at https://www.youtube.com/watch?v=-zENr6_5N6U* .

1/24/1959

U.S. Marshall - The episode is titled Pursuit. He plays Captain Eddie Wallace, a kidnapped soldier who gets beat up protecting his girlfriend. Cast includes John Russell (1/31/1921-1/19/1991 www.peterbrown/tv/johnrussell[36]), Peter Brown (10/5/1935-3/21/2016 www.peterbrown.tv[37]) and Charles Bronson (11/3/1921-8/30/2003).

2/4/1959

Wagon Train - The episode is titled Ella Lindstrom Story. He plays James Fitzpatrick. Bette Davis (4/5/1908-10/6/1989) stars. Bette was very professional and helped him as a new comer. Cast includes Robert Horton (7/29/1924-3/9/2016) and Ward Bond (4/91903-11/5/1960). *See others in Wagon Train section.* Although he had no scenes with Ward Bond, after he was outfitted, he was introduced to him. Ward was unhappy with his hat choice and threw it to the ground. Robert picked another hat to wear. *See Wagon Train section.* See Wagon Train Season 2 Episode 18 The Ella Lindstorm Story at https://www.youtube.com/watch?v=bu-7UXMy52Y .

2/7/1959

Mickey Spillane's Mike Hammer - The episode is titled I ain't Talking playing Jimmy Nelson. His character may be involved with gangsters. Cast includes Darren McGavin (5/17/1922-2/25/2006 www.darrenmcgavin.net[38]) and Bart Burns (3/31/198-7/17/2007). *See Mike Hammer 2x03 - I Ain't Talkin' at https://www.youtube.com/watch?v=ohyWhlvRaTE* .

2/21/1959

Cimarron City - The episode is titled Blind is the Killer. He plays Joe Cole who accidentally blinds the mayor, Matt Rockford. Robert gets guest star billing. Series stars George Montgomery (8/29/1916-12/12/2000) as the mayor. Patrick Kelly, talent studio head, saw Robert in this role and decided to offer him a co-staring role. John Smith (3/6/1931-1/25/1995) stars in this series *(see him in Laramie section)*. See CIMARRON CITY - BLIND IS THE KILLER - Episode Twenty at https://www.youtube.com/watch?v=_QybP0oiGJk .

---

36.   http://www.peterbrown/tv/johnrussell

37.   http://www.peterbrown.tv

38.   http://www.darrenmcgavin.net

3/31/1959

The Life and Times of Wyatt Earp - The episode is titled The Judas Goat. He plays Deputy Marshall Hank Drew who works undercover but turns out to be a bad guy. Cast includes Hugh O'Brien (4/19/1925-9/5/2016) and Jimmy Noel (5/15/1903-1//31/1985). *See The Life and Legend of Wyatt Earp S04E29 The Judas Goat https://www.youtube.com/watch?v=fXU5YvgRgQI* ,

4/1959

By this time Robert has had ten lead parts.

4/2/1959

Mickey Spillane's Mike Hammer - The episode is titled Park the Body. He plays Roy Barlow who is a killer hit by car. *See Mike Hammer 2x09 - Park the Body at https://www.youtube.com/watch?v=pcnw9XGMKAY* .

4/5/1959

Lawman - The episode is titled The Souvenir. He plays Davey Carey who is killed in a gunfight. Cast includes John Russell (1/31/1921-1/19/1991) and Peter Brown (10/5/1935-3/21/2016 www.peterbrown.tv[39]). *He and Peter remain lifelong friends.*

It was about this time that Robert bought a horse. *(Robert used his own horses in both Laramie and Wagon Train).*

5/6/1959

Wagon Train - The episode is titled Kate Parker Story. He plays Chris Finley, a married man on the run. Cast included Ward Bond as Major Seth Adams (4/9/1903-11/5/1960) and Ruta Lee Ruta Lee (5/30/1935-www.rutalee.com[40]). *See WT THE KATE PARKER STORY at https://www.youtube.com/watch?v=Zl0gcNDuBC4* .

5/7/1959

The Lawless Years - The episode is titled Cutie Jaffy Story. He plays Cutie Jaffy, a small town hoodlum who is machine gunned down. Cast includes James Gregory (12/23/1911-9/16/2002) and Robert Karnes (6/19/1917-12/4/1979). *See The Lawless Years - The Story of Cutie Jaffe, S1E04 * Classic TV show at https://www.youtube.com/watch?v=Lp4fRV9RXsU* .

6/28/1959

---

39.   http://www.peterbrown.tv

40.   http://www.rutalee.com

Lawman - The episode is titled The Friend and he plays Buck Harmon. He is part of a gang set to rob the bank in the town his religious father lives in. His character gets killed after switching sides. This television series was set in Laramie, Wyoming. Cast includes John Russell (1/31/1921-1/19/1991) and Peter Brown (10/5/1935-3/21/2016 www.peterbrown.tv[41]). This episode was written by Clair Huffaker (9/26/1926-4/3/199), produced by Jules Schermer (9/9/1908-3/23/1996) and directed by Mark Sandrich, Jr. (1/2/1928-12/2/1995). A 33 page script for this episode includes John Russell's preview of this episode from Lawman's previous episode. There were three correction pages. Robert's schedule for this shoot was 6:30 a.m. until 5:55 p.m. *Actors' Call Sheets detail the number of extras and animals needed and filming locations.*

LATE 1950's

Robert doubled for Steve McQueen (3/24/1930-11/6/1960).

41.   http://www.peterbrown.tv

THE LARAMIE YEARS 1959-1963

1959 - 1963

Robert is summoned to Vice President of Talent, Patrick Kelly's office fearing he was going to be fired. Patrick Kelly said liked Robert's work and wanted him for a one half hour TV detective series starring Ray Milland (1/31/1907-3/19/1986). Robert was offered the second lead but refused saying he wanted to do westerns.

A few weeks later Patrick Kelly offered him a part in a 30 minute western called Laramie. Robert loved script but was offered Slim Sherman role and he wanted role of Jess Harper. John Smith had been given Jess role so Robert refused the role of Slim. Later that day, Robert's agent calls and said he can test for the role of Jess Harper. The next day he got role Jess and John got recast as Slim. John Smith didn't like switch in beginning but after about three episodes he was fine with switch. *(Robert tells how he got the part of Laramie many times - www.youtube.com/watch?v=UHYnLojmyBc[1] and www.youtube.com - Laramie - Robert Fuller Created Jess Harper and LARAMIE - Robert Fuller says "I wanna do a Western!" on A WORD ON WESTERNS and https://www.youtube.com/watch?v=Ap9yqLLziJ4 and Robert Fuller talks about how he got the part of Jess Harper https://www.youtube.com/watch?v=5NGJg7_4bOM and Laramie Valentin Robert Fuller talks about how he got the part of Jess Harper https://www.youtube.com/watch?v=5NGjg7_4bOM).*

Jess Harper would become Robert's favorite role of all time. Jess has characteristics like honesty and the importance of friendship that is the real Robert Fuller. He is proud of Laramie's good story lines, characters and its good camera and direction work.

Creator John C. Champion (10/13/1923-10/3/1994) wrote 36 episodes and produced many of the Laramie episodes.

Robert learned a lot on Laramie from two older directors. One was Lesley Selander (5/28/1900-12/5/1979) *who directed 45 Laramie episodes from 1959 to 1963. Robert remembers that Les wore the same gray flannel outfit for years. Once while Robert was doing a scene in Laramie when "cut' was called unexpectedly he turned and his ¼ blank load went off into Les. Seconds later his gun went off again hitting Les again. (Les worked as a teenager at a studio as a lab technician he worked his way up to directing his first film, a western, in 1936.* Over his career Les directed at least 107 times until he retired in 1968).

The other older director was Joseph Kane (3/19/1894-8/25/1975) who directed 30 Laramie episodes from 1960 to 1963. *Robert remembers Joe smoked a cigar and when unhappy with a scene would remove his hat, throw it on the ground and stomp on it. Robert could calm him down and reassure him the scene would be redone the way he wanted.* (In 1934 Joe switched his career from cellist to co-direct his first serial in 1935. He worked for Republic studios until it closed in 1958. Becoming a top western film director from 1935 to his death in 1975 Joe directed 119 films and many television episodes. His talents also included being assistant producer / producer on over 60 films. He was also film editor or

---

screenwriter on over 20 films. A few of the stars he directed are Gene Autry, Walter Brenan, Edgar Buchan, Smiley Burnette, Rod Cameron, Lee Van Cleef, Jim Davis, Paul Fix, George "Gabby" Hayes, Fred MacMurray, Ann Rutherford, Roy Rogers, Barbara Stanwyck and John Wayne).

Ray Rennahan (5/1/1896-5/19/1980) was director of photography for Laramie and helped Robert get more comfortable with cameras. Ray won a jointly with Ernest Haller the 1940 Academy Award for Cinematography for Gone With The Wind and another Academy Award jointly with Ernest Palmer for 1942 Blood and Sand. Ray was also nominated six more times between 1940 and 1945. Ray has a star on the Hollywood Walk of Fame for cinematography.

Early Laramie musical scores were framed by Leigh Harline (3/26/1907-12/10/1969. Leigh was a composer, songwriter with television and movie scores including several Walt Disney movies and died of throat cancer), Albert Sendrey (12/26/1911-5/18/2003). Albert Richard was an arranger, composer and conductor with over 170 television and movie credits who died at age 91) and Harry Sukman (12/2/1912-12/2/1984. Harry was a composer, Oscar winner who died from a stroke at age 72.

Other behind the scenes people involved in Laramie over the full four years included:

Alex Quiroga (5/14/1919-1/5/1980) as Color Consultant.

David Ullman (10/18/1918-10/23/1979) wrote 22 episodes and by 4th years was Associate Producer.

Earl Crain, Jr. (6/12/1915-2/3/1986) worked on 31 episodes as part of the Series Sound Department.

John C. Fuller worked on 56 episodes and Ray DeVally (4/7/1914-2/27/1993) worked on 49 episodes as part of Film Editing.

John McCarthy, Jr. did 70 episodes. Perry Murdock (9/18/1901-4/19/1988) did 60 Laramie episodes. Perry worked with Bob Steele in silent and talkie movies. By 1930 Perry and Bob were sharing an apartment. He also wrote from 1927 to 1937. Thirty year old Perry married 19 year old Erma Purviance on 6/8/1932 and remained married. By the late 1930's Perry moved behind the camera and did set direction for many programs including Wagon Train. Ralph Sylos (6/17/1902-6/9/1981) worked on 24 Laramie episodes. All three worked in Set Direction.

Loyd S. Papez (6/27/1921-11/10/1998) with 45 episodes, George Patrick with 23 and Russell Kimball (11/1/1903-6/29/1975) with 22 all worked in Art Direction.

Stanley Wilson (11/25/1917-7/12/1970) with 124 episodes worked in the Series Music Department.

Vincent Dee was in 124 episodes as Costume Supervisor.

Robert on Laramie had a five day shoot starting at 7:30 or 8 a.m. to 7 at night earning $600 a week. They worked 11 months a year and often the other month was spent doing publicity. They worked on set and on location using no fill in scenes from other movies or TV programs. Robert's work was done in one or two takes. There were two stables, each with hundreds of horses, supplying the studios with animals. *(Robert stated western can't be done today since there are no horses trained to deal with gunshot or do tricks, etc. and that studios today don't know what to do save time).*

Publicity magazines say Robert is 5'11" and weights 175 to 180 pounds. Except for the very first hat he wore, Robert dressed himself. He used his own hat, 45 gun, gun belt, spurs and boots. He rode his own quarter horse, maybe named Hute / Hoot. His NBC Laramie arm chair was made of hand tooled leather. Robert said his often seen very dirty hat was because he was a working cowboy.

Robert and John's dressing rooms included a dressing area, living room, make-up area and a kitchen. Their dressing rooms were across from Tony Curtis (6/3/1925-9/29/2010 www.tonycurtis.com[2]) and Rock Hudson (11/17/1925-10/2/1985) whose areas were three times the size of everyone else. Lee Marvin (2/19/1924-8/29/1987) also had a dressing room nearby. John and Robert shouted back and forth between their dressing rooms disturbing others. One evening, a hole was broken between their two dressing rooms. After the studio heads saw the damage a slider type door was put in between their rooms. Other pranks included shooting out light bulbs with a BB gun. *(Robert talks about this many times).*

On accident that occurred was a runaway stage down hill past the ranch filmed via an overhead boom camera. Robert tried to stop but knew he couldn't. It pasted parked cars hidden behind house and continued down street to studio main gate. The driver jumped but John's stand in also on board (his first time) and lost a leg. *See www.youtube.com/watch?v=69gRh00UBW4[3] - Accidents on Western TV Show Sets Virginian and Laramie with James Drury (4/18/1934- 4/6/2020) – See www.thevirginian.net[4] or www.youtube.com/playlist?list=PL2YPNORBEDacHOOhmmdXp4c3390FKLf[5] or www.youtube/playlist?list=PLD23A4ABA[6] .*

---

2. http://www.tonycurtis.com

3. http://www.youtube.com/watch?v=69gRh00UBW4

4. http://www.thevirginian.net

5. http://www.youtube.com/playlist?list=PL2YPNORBEDacHOOhmmdXp4c3390FKLf

6. http://www.youtube/playlist?list=PLD23A4ABA

Robert and John Smith spend some off time fishing together.

During Laramie time, Robert and Chuck Courtney (7/23/1930-1/19/2000) did a 15 minute act at fairs making $8,500 a week. Chuck played guitar and they did gunfights, fist fights, etc. Robert and Chuck Courtney wearing cowboy outfits also visited kids in hospitals.

Laramie cast included:

John Smith as Slim Sherman. (3/6/1931-1/25/1995). John was 6'1 inches, 185 pounds with blue eyes. John's knick name of Smitty. John and Robert agreed not to have any fighting and not ask for raise but instead ask for a bonus. Which they did get. John was born in Los Angeles, California and his real name was Robert Van Orden. At Dorsey High School John played basketball football and sang with a dance band. He then attended UCLA's engineering program. He also worked at MCM's mail room working up from mail boy to being its head until he was fired for attending acting classes on company time. John also sold cars. Before being on Laramie John had 80 television appearances. John enjoyed boating and water sports. John's acting career was from 1950 until 1975 where he had over 30 roles in movies plus reoccurring television roles in 1954's That's My Bow, 1958's Cimarron City and Laramie. He experienced some type casting after being Slim in Laramie and it appears the director of Circus World in 1964 may have tried to sabotage John's future acting work. John became a rancher raising horses and enjoyed traveling. John died at 63 years old from heart and liver problems and his ashes were scattered at sea. There are many sites you can see John on www.youtube.com[7] . Two examples are John Smith: A Tribute to Smitty at www.youtube.com/watch?v=wRVPB3jJJMo[8] and Sunset Carson interview at www.youtube.com/watch?v=wDp7Yxq6PpA[9] .

Hoagy Carmichael as Jonesy (11/22/1899-12/27/1981 www.hoagy.com[10]). He was on the first season only and lived on the 9th hole of the Thunderbird Golf Course in Palm Springs. Cast had a 7:30 a.m. call and Hoagy was often on the golf course rather than at work which was a two hour drive each way. *(Robert relates story about him dismantling a piano in the episode with Eddie Albert and Nanette Fabray).* Hoagy decided the drive was too much and left after the first season. His doorbell chime played Stardust, a song he wrote in 1927. Hoagy was well known since the 1930's both as a singer, songwriter and composer. At least 50 of his several hundred songs became hits. He also started singing and acting in films in 1937. Hoagy, in 1971, was inducted into the Songwriters Hall of Fame. Hoagy wrote two autobiographies and died of a heart attack at age 82.

Robert Crawford, Jr. as Andy Sherman (5/13/1944-). Robert Crawford, Jr.'s father was a film editor and actor and his brother Johnny (3/26/1946-4/29/2021) was also an actor, best known for his role on The Rifleman. Robert Jr. started acting at age 13. In the 1970's after acting Robert Crawford, Jr. went behind the scenes into production. Robert

---

7.   http://www.youtube.com

8.   http://www.youtube.com/watch?v=wRVPB3jJJMo

9.   http://www.youtube.com/watch?v=wDp7Yxq6PpA

10. http://www.hoagy.com

became Associate Producer, Producer, Dialog Coach and a singer. He attends celebrity shows and on 9/30/2019 attend Silver Spur Awards (hosted by the Reel Cowboys) given for Lifetime Achievement. See ww.silverspsurawards.com and *www.youtube.com/watcdh?tv=R0eyrgQGOMbw*[11] and *www.youtube.com/watch?v=QKZs484l4Ag*[12] . Also see www.robertcrawfordjr.com[13] . One magazine article has an article with photos of his double date with Robert Fuller.

Dennis Holmes as Mike Williams (10/3/1950-). Robert may have taught Dennis to drink, smoke and swear. He also almost let him get tattooed. (See DVDs). Dennis was born in California and was first seen on screen at age six months. He returned to the screen at age 7 ½. By Laramie time, he had acted in almost 100 roles and enjoyed swimming and reading science books. Dennis was living in Woodland Hills, California, was blue eyed and weighed 70 pounds. NBC data gave an incorrect birth date in their Fall 1962 data. Dennis acted from 1950 to 1964 before he retired and became a computer expert. Dennis attends celebrity shows and on 9/30/2019 attended Silver Spur Awards (hosted by the Reel Cowboys) and was given Lifetime Achievement. See ww.silverspsurawards.com and *www.youtube.com/watcdh?tv=R0eyrgQGOMbw*[14] and *www.youtube.com/watch?v=QKZs484l4Ag*[15] .

Spring Byington as Daisy Cooper (10/17/1886-9/7/1971). Spring joined cast in the third season. Spring was fun to be with and could out swear her male cast members. She was born in Colorado Springs, Colorado. After her father died she, at age 14, worked with the Elitch Garden Stock Company. At 17 years old she toured with them earning $35 a week. Spring worked in the theater from 1903 to 1935 and in New York she appeared in over 30 plays. Starting in silent films from 1930 to 1938 and also appeared on radio. She switched to television in 1954 and became known in the December Bride television program. Spring was 77 yrs old when Laramie ended and retired in 1968. Spring died at 84 years old from cancer and donated her body for medical research.

Stuart Randall as Sheriff Mort Corey (7/24/1909-6/22/1988). He acted in over 70 movies and television programs from 1950 to 1971.

Eddy Waller as Mose Shell (6/14/1899-8/20/1977). He was born in Wisconsin and in college starting acting. In the 1920's he started on stage and by 1923 he was well known, acting, directing and producing. Eddy came to Hollywood in 1929 but made more movies starting in 1936. Eddy had more than 250 roles in movies and television from 1929 to 1963. He retired in the early 1960's and died at age 88 from a stroke.

Jack Coffer (4/1/1938-2/18/1967) is stunt double in Laramie. He died in an auto accident.

---

11. *http://www.youtube.com/watcdh?tv=R0eyrgQGOMbw*

12. *http://www.youtube.com/watch?v=QKZs484l4Ag*

13. http://www.robertcrawfordjr.com

14. *http://www.youtube.com/watcdh?tv=R0eyrgQGOMbw*

15. *http://www.youtube.com/watch?v=QKZs484l4Ag*

Hal Needham (3/6/1931-10/25/2013) doubled for guests who Robert fought with. *Via Hal's autobiography Stuntman!: My Car-Crashing, Plane-Jumping, Bone-Breaking, Death-Defying Hollywood Life some of his stunt crew were uncomfortable working with Robert so Hal was there often.*

The program aired on Tuesday nights at 6:30 p.m. Central Standard time and its competition was Warner Bro.' Sugarfoot / Bronco and the Dennis O'Keefe Show. They filmed at Revue Studios (later taken over by Universal Studio). Filming locations included Lone Pine, California and Kanab and St. George in Utah. Robert also lived with Sheriff John Maples in Camilla, Georgia while there filming. Robert helped get started the Georgia Sheriffs Boys Ranch in Hahira, Georgia - www.georgiasheriffsyouth.org[16] . Robert appears as Grand Marshall in about seven of the areas or Atlanta's 4th of July parades.

As script writers became more aware of Robert's talents, scripts could be created with more action scenes. Robert sometimes insisted on doing stunts that he was advised against doing like riding a bucking horse or riding a horse across a deep stream. Special effects used electronic squibs or air guns to effectively create realistic action scenes.

When the program changed from filming in black and white to color, the characters changed their costumes. Color filming is a warmer process so previous costume material choices (buckskin) are now too hot to wear. As the years passed, due to pressure from the P.TA. and the government, shooting action scenes decreased.

Other places to hear Robert talk about Laramie are at *Laramie Robert Fuller Created Jess Harper(with Beverly Garland) are https://www.youtube.com/watch?v=HkGCQcpJC8M&list=PLF683D699AC8A04E4&index=6 and Bob Fuller about Television show Laramie at https://www.youtube.com/watch?v=UHYnLojmyBc and www.toyguntown.com*[17] .

Episode details can be found at www.wikivisually.com/wiki/Laramie-(TV-Series[18]*.) There are also websites where they can be viewed like www.youtube.com/watch?v+S4aaJMCZdok*[19] *) or cable television channels like www.grittv.com*[20] .

Some guest stars appeared in more than one episode. A few key guest stars are listed below:
    Adam West (9/19/1928-6/9/2017) www.adamwest.com[21]
    Alan Hale, Jr.(3/8/1921-1/2/1990) www.gilligansisle.com[22]
    Alex Cord. (5/3/1933-). This was his first acting part.

---

16. http://www.georgiasheriffsyouth.org

17. http://www.toyguntown.com

18. http://www.wikivisually.com/wiki/Laramie_(TV_Series

19. http://www.youtube.com/watch?v+S4aaJMCZdok

20. http://www.grittv.com

21.   http://www.adamwest.com

22.   http://www.gilligansisle.com

Anthony Caruso (4/7/1916-4/4/2003)
Barton MacLane (12/25/1902-1/1/1969)
Ben Cooper (9/30/1933-2/24/2020)

Ben Johnson (6/13/1918-4/8/1996). There is a Ben Johnson Cowboy Museum in Pawhuska, Oklahoma.

Beverly Garland (10/17/1926-12/5/2008)
    Bing Russell (5/5/1926-4/8/2003)
    Brian Keith (11/4/1921-6/24/1997)
    Bruce Gordon (2/11/1916-1/22/2011)
    Charles Bronson (11/3/1921-8/30/2003)
    Charles Drake (10/2/1917-9/10/1994)
    Charles McGraw (5/10/1914-7/30/1980)
    Claude Akins (5/25/1926-1/27/1994)
    Cloris Leachman (4/30/1926-1/27/2021)

Clu Gulager (11/16/1928-) www.clugulager.com[23] . Clu retired in 2012 after 60 years of acting.

Chuck Courtney (7/23/1930-1/19/2000)
    Constance Moore (1/18/1920-9/16/2005)
    Dabbs Greer (4/2/1917-4/28/2007)

Dan Duryea. (1/23/1907-6/7/1968). Dan was friends with Laramie's creator John C. Champion. When Dan was on Laramie the first time he took Robert to his first lunch in the green room - vs. the black room for extras where Dan knew the name of every one of the wait staff. Dan gave Robert some financial advice about not buying a new car. (Three days later Robert bought a new white 2 door, 4 seater 1959 Thunderbird with blue interior). Dan's wife had died 1/21/1967 from heart trouble and although cancer was official cause of Dan's death, he really missed his wife.

Dawn Wells (10/18/1938-12/29/2020)
    DeForest Kelley (1/20/1920-6/11/1999)
    Dennis Patrick (3/14/1919-10/13/2002)
    Denny Miller *(see him in Wagon Train section)*
    Denver Pyle (5/11/1920-12/25/1997)

---

23. http://www.clugulager.com

Dick Foran. (6/18/1910-8/10/1979). He gave Robert his first shotguns, a Winchester 12 and 16 gauge. The Model 1897 shotguns were made from 1897 until 1957. They shot together.

Don "Red" Barry (1/11/1912-7/17/1980)
    Don C. Harvey 12/12/1911-4/23/1963)
    Don Durant (11/20/1932-3/15/2005)
    Dub Taylor (2/26/1907-10/3/1994)
    Earnest Borgnine (1/24/1917-7/8/2012)
    Ed Nelson (12/21/1928-8/19/2014)
    Ed Prentiss (9/19/1908-3/19/1922)
    Eddie Albert (4/22/1906-5/26/2005)
    Edgar Buchannan (3/20/1903-4/4/1979)

Edmond O'Brien (9/10/1915-5/9/1985). He didn't pull a punch and Robert got loose teeth and a swollen lip.

Edward Platt (2/14/1916-3/19/1974)
    Elisha Cooke, Jr. (12/26/1930-5/18/1995)
    Fay Spain (10/6/1932-5/8/1983)
    Francis de Sales (3/231912-9/25/1988)
    Frank DeKova (3/17/1910-10/15/1981)
    Frank Ferguson (12/25/1899-9/12/1978)
    Frank Wilco (5/18/1914-3/28/1989)
    Gary Clarke (8/16/1933-)
    George Kennedy (2/18/1925-2/28/2016)
    George Keymas (11/18/1925-1/16/2008)
    George Tobias (7/14/1901-2/27/1980)
    Gloria Talbott (2/7/1931-9/19/2000). She is a serious actress.
    Grandon Rhodes (8/7/1904-6/9/1987)
    Hal Smith (8/24/1916-1/28/1994)
    Harold J. Stone (3/13/1913-11/18/2005)
    Harry Carey, Jr. (5/16/1921-12/27/2012)
    Harry Harvey (1/10/1901-11/27/1985)
    Harry Townes (9/18/1914-5/23/2001)
    Helen Corby (6/3/1911-4/14/1999)
    Herbert Lytton (12/4/1897-6/26/1981)
    Howard McNear (1/27/1905-1/3/1969)
    Jack Elam (11/13/1920-10/20/2003)
    Jacqueline Scott (1/1/1932-7/23/2020)
    James Best (7/26/1926-4/6/2015). He enjoyed fishing.
    James Brown (3/22/1922-4/11/1992)

James Coburn (8/31/1928-11/18/2002)
James Gregory (12/23/1911-9/16/2002)
James Westerfield (3?22/1913-9/20/1971)
Jan Merlin (4/3/1925-9/20/2019)
Jan Shephard (3/19/1928-)
Jason Evers (1/2/1922-3/13/2005)
Jason Robards (7/26/1922-12/26/2000)
Jay Silverheels (5/26/1912-3/5/1980
Jean Byron (12/10.1925-2/3/2006)
Jeanette Nolan (12/30/1911-6/5/1998)
Jim Davis (8/26/1909-4/26/1981) www.ultimatedallas.com[24]
Joanna Barnes (11/15/1934-)

Jock Mahoney (2/7/1919-12/14/1989). *Jock observed Robert as he worked on a complicated fight scene. Wanting to impress Jock he continued on to a door busting down scene. Rather than choosing the special effects option of making the kick easier, Robert instead tried to do it himself and wound up five feet back with his wind being knocked out.*

John Anderson (10/20/1922-8/7/1992)
John Dehner (11/23/1915-2/4/1992)
John Intire - *See him in Wagon Train section.*
John Larch (10/4/1914-10/16/2005)
Julie London - *See her in Emergency section.*
John Lormer (5/7/1906-3/19/1986)
John Mitchum (9/6/1919-11/29/2001)
Karl Swenson (7/23/1908-10/8/1978)
Kathie Browne (9/19/1930-4/8/2003) www.darrenmcgavin.net[25]
Kenneth MacDonald (9/8/1901-5/5/1972)
Kent Taylor (5/11/1907-4/11/1987)
Kevin Hagen (4/3/1928-7/9/2005)
King Donovan (11/25/1918-6/30/1987)
Lee Van Cleef (1/9/1925-12/16/1989)

Leonard Nimoy (3/26/1931-2/27/2015) www.theofficialleonardnimoyfanclub.com[26]

LQ Jones (8/19/1927-)
Lloyd Nelson (6/10/1927-7/25/2007)

---

24.   http://www.ultimatedallas.com

25.   http://www.darrenmcgavin.net

26. http://www.theofficialleonardnimoyfanclub.com

Lloyd Nolan (8/11/1902-9/27/1985)

Lori Nelson (8/15/1933-8/23/2020)

Lyle Bettger (2/13/1915-9/24/2003)

Maurice Manson (1/31/1913-9/20/2002)

Michael Pate (2/26/1920-9/1/2008)

Monica Lewis (5/5/1922-6/12/2015)

Mort Mills (1/11/1919-6/6/1993)

Nanette Fabray (10/27/1930-2/22/2018)

Nestor Paiva (6/30/1905-9/9/1966)

Paul Carr (1/31/1934-12/17/2006)

Paul Fix (3/13/1901-10/14/1983)

Phyllis Avery (11/14/1922-5/19/2011)

Rafael Campos (5/13/1936-7/9/1985)

Rand Brooks 9/21/1918-9/1/2003)

Ray Teal (1/12/1902-4/2/1986)

Raymond Bailey (5/6/1904-4/15/1980)

Richard Farnsworth (9/1/1920-10/6/2000)

Richard Kiel (9/13/1934-9/10/2014)

Robert Blake (9/18/1933-) www.robertbobbyblake.com[27]

Robert J. Wilke (5/18/1914-3/28/1989)

Robert Vaughn (11/22/1932-11/11/2016) www.manfromuncle.org[28]

Roberta Shore (4/7/1943-)

Rod Cameron (12/7/1910-12/21/1983). Rod was friend of creator John Champion and appeared several times. Robert thought he was a great western cowboy. Rod, like Robert started as a stuntman. From 1939 to 1977 Rod had almost 100 roles not including starring in three TV series. He worked at Paramount, Republic, Universal Studios and Monogram Pictures and died of cancer.

Ron Harper (1/12/1936-)

Ron Hayes (2/25/1929-10/1/2004)

Rory Calhoun (8/8/1922-4/28/1999). He was friends with Laramie's creator John C. Champion.

Ross Elliot (6/18/1917-8/12/1999)

Ross Martin (3/22/1920-7/3/1981)

Roy Bancroft (9/7/1902-11/28/1969)

Roy Engel (9/13/1913-9/29/1980)

---

27.   http://www.robertbobbyblake.com

28.   http://www.manfromuncle.org

Roy Roberts (3/19/1906-5/28/1975)
Russ Conway (11/25/1913-1/12/2009)
Russell Johnson (12/10/1924-1/16/2014) www.gilligansilse.com[29]
Ruta Lee (5/30/1935-) www.rutalee.com[30]
Ryan O'Neil (4/20/1941-) www.ryanoneil.com[31]
Simon Oakland (8/28/1915-8/29/1983)
Susan Oliver (2/3/1932-5/10/1990)
Thomas Mitchell (7/11/1892-12/17/1962)
Tom Fadden (1/6/1895-4/14/1980)
Tom Skerritt (8/25/1933-)
Tommy Sands (8/27/1937-)
Vera Miles (8/23/1929-)
Vince Edwards (7/9/1928-3/11/1996)
Warren Oates (7/5/1928-4/3/1982)
Warren Stevens (11/2/1919-3/27/2012)
Will Wright (3/26/1894-6/19/1962)
William Bryant (1/31/1924-6/26/2001)
William Fawcett (9/8/1894-1/25/1974)
Willis Bouchey (5/24/1907-9/27/1977)
Vinton Hayworth (6/4/1906-5/21/1970)
Yvonne Craig (5/16/1937-8/7/2015)

Behind the scenes photos were printed included John and Robert in their set chairs.

Laramie was on Tuesday evenings during its four years of 124 episodes. Laramie was in local television ads and TV Guides.

The series had Promo Photos, NBC Fact Sheet and press releases. Area TV guides like Milwaukee, Wisconsin had both photo ads and drawings.

Coloring book by Whitman is introduced in 1959.

A Laramie cork pistol was made. A drawing of Jess and the name Laramie appeared on the handle.

---

29.   http://www.gilligansilse.com

30.   http://www.rutalee.com

31.   http://www.ryanoneil.com

Laramie toy gun and holster set by Leslie-Henry Company is introduced in 1959.

Laramie Posters are also created in 1959.

Photo shoot variations occurred with cast changing positions in the photo. Some were released to magazines, others as posters and post cards. Postcards were also created in the United Kingdom. One was Picturegoer, S Series of Film/Music Stars. The photo chosen was used for many years and appeared in U.S. and foreign magazines.

Besides fans in the U.S. it gained millions of fans around the world. The series ran in over 70 countries. It was especially popular in Australia, Canada, England, Germany, Italy, Japan and Spain. Foreign articles, photos and publicity were created.

Laramie was the number one program in both Germany and Japan. Robert wins 5 consecutive Otto Awards in West Germany. The Bravo Otto is a German honor first started in 1957 and readers of the Bravo magazine choose the winners. The awards are in gold, silver and bronze and given out in the beginning of the year. In Japan they think Jess is like a samurai or underdog and Robert also receives awards in Japan.

Foreign puzzles are created and included French and Spanish speaking countries.

Germany has 2 ½ x 3 ¾ inch cards being made with Laramie characters on each.

In Germany Laramie was called 'At the Foot of Blue Mountains'. Laramie episode books were published by Alex Gifford. Between the books and television program at least 19 different Laramie press photos are also created.

Autograph cards were created. Japanese cards about 1 ½ x 2 ½ inches are created.

Laramie Friends Club in Japan later created a CD-ROM Scrapbook Collection - No. 2.

When the series started Robert lived with his parents and he bought a Ford T Bird car for $2,200. Later he bought ten suits and rented a house with Chuck Courtney (7/23/1930-1/20/2000). Sometimes co-star Dennis Holmes (10/3/1950-) came to spend the weekend.

Studio or magazine publicity has him dating actress Connie Stevens (8/8/1938-) www.conniestevens.com[32] . It also states Robert is against animal experimentation and supports Cat Care Club and the Pet Assistance League. Magazines say Robert dated Kathy Nolan (9/27/1933-) from Real McCoys for 3 years. (*Kathy was born into an acting family she was on the stage at 13 months. It is said that while working as an usher at the Palace Theater where Judy Garland performed Judy saw her perform and helped get her on stage as Wendy in Peter Pan in 1954. Kathy was also working in television during this time and from 1967 to 1962 she was a regular on The Real McCoys. On 2/23/1961 Kathy was thrown from a horse while filming The Real McCoys and injured her back, was in a wheel chair and didn't return to work until 6/15/1961. She was President of the Screen Actors Guild for 2 terms from 1975 to 1979 and also was a member of the SAG board*).

Fan magazines have Robert's free time activities as fencing, hunting mountain lion with a bow and arrow, judo, jumping off cliffs and wrestling sharks. Saturday night dates were often dancing with four other couples at someone's house. Sundays were spent skin diving or at the beach.

1959 articles include:
Unknown magazine titled Guess the Secrets of the Stars profiles John and Robert.

Hollywood Secrets Annual Magazine. He is not on cover. He may be listed in "Hollywood's Most Exciting Bachelors" section.

TV Yearbook Magazine. He is not on cover.

In the early 1960's The P.T.A. (Parents Teachers Association) complained to Bobby Kennedy and the FCC that Westerns had too much violence. They didn't want cowboys wearing
guns or shooting them. As regulations increased, each year cut back on how many shots could occur and how Indians were portrayed. This continued into the Wagon Train years. (*For kids growing up in the 1950's and 1960's we were wearing our cowboy hats and boots playing cowboys and Indians. We have toy holsters, guns and bows and arrows. We were glued to dozens of TV westerns with the bad guys getting shot, no blood and just falling over*).

Laramie DVD's. The first season photo cover was on the 2/1962 comic book and was also used on Germany's DVD volume 2.

UK / Europe DVD version of Laramie Series with seven volumes in English is created. Each one contains two DVDs.

Laramie fans might also enjoy checking out Television's New Frontier: The 1960s , Sunday, July 30, 2017, Laramie (1961)[33] at http://tvnewfrontier.blogspot.com/search/label/Laramie and Television's New Frontier: The 1960s [34] at http://tvnewfrontier.blogspot.com/2012/06/laramie-1960.html and

Laramie TV Show Word Search Word Search at https://thewordsearch.com/puzzle/287907/laramie-tv-show-word-search/ .

8/26/1959

NBC publicity is material sent out publicity about a new action filled 1870's western called Laramie.

9/12/1959

TV Guide with Arthur Godfrey (8/31/1903-3/16/1983) on the cover includes Laramie debut.

9/15/1959

Laramie Episode - Stage Stop[35]

Jess Harper meets Slim Sherman and then Andy and Jonesy when Sherman house is taken over by bad men.

9/22/1959

Laramie Episode - Glory Road[36]

Female preacher and man who once saved Jess's life arrive. Jess unsuccessfully tries to avoid him and Jonesy gets involved too.

9/29/1959

Laramie Episode - Circle of Fire[37]

Indians attack ranch after female stage coach passenger shots and injures the son of Indian chief. With her is ex-major accused of being a coward.

10/6/1959

Laramie Episode - Fugitive Road[38]

Jess's Army deserter brother-in-law wants help getting to Canada. He is being followed by two Army men. Slim discourages Jess from getting involved but later follows them. *(His sister is dead in this one).*

---

33. http://tvnewfrontier.blogspot.com/2017/07/laramie-1961.html

34. http://tvnewfrontier.blogspot.com/

35.   https://www.imdb.com/title/tt0624761/?ref_=ttep_ep1

36.   https://www.imdb.com/title/tt0624729/?ref_=ttep_ep2

37.   https://www.imdb.com/title/tt0624715/?ref_=ttep_ep3

38.   https://www.imdb.com/title/tt0624728/?ref_=ttep_ep4

10/13/1959

Laramie Episode - The Star Trail[39]

Jess travels to help a friend, is hired as a deputy with a sheriff tempted by a woman he loves to become a criminal.

10/20/1959

Laramie Episode - The Lawbreakers[40]

Jess goes undercover to guide outlaws trying to retrieve stolen money.

10/27/1959

Laramie Episode - The Iron Captain[41]

Slim and Jess capture outlaw but gang recaptures outlaw and takes Slim and Jess as hostages. Slim must bring outlaw's girlfriend to him but she doesn't want to come.

11/1959

Movie Life Magazine. He is not on cover and sells for 25 cents.

11/3/1959

Laramie Episode - General Delivery[42]

Hired killer arrives in Laramie. After an animal trap accident he heals at ranch with Slim and Andy and decides he won't kill Slim.

11/10/1959

Laramie Episode - The Run to Tumavaca[43]

Jess's goes to Mexico after a woman who left her husband for another man.

11/17/1959

Laramie Episode - The General Must Die[44]

Slim's former Civil War soldier friend arrives to kill General Sherman who will be traveling through on the stage.

39.   https://www.imdb.com/title/tt0624805/?ref_=ttep_ep5

40.   https://www.imdb.com/title/tt0624785/?ref_=ttep_ep6

41.   https://www.imdb.com/title/tt0624779/?ref_=ttep_ep7

42.   https://www.imdb.com/title/tt0862223/?ref_=ttep_ep8

43.   https://www.imdb.com/title/tt0624801/?ref_=ttep_ep9

44.   https://www.imdb.com/title/tt0624777/?ref_=ttep_ep10

11/24/1959

Laramie Episode - Dark Verdict[45]

Jess and Slim try to save a man from being hung. An illegal trial occurs and an innocent man is lynched. Jess returns with the real criminal and he and Slim both seek justice in court.

12/1959

TV & Radio Mirror Magazine titled Inside View of the "Fuller Life". His parents are shown.

12/1/1959

Laramie Episode - Man of God[46]

Jess guides a Father on way to meet Sitting Bull to prevent further violence.

12/8/1959

Laramie Episode - Bare Knuckles[47]

Jonesy earns extra money as promoter for a traveling crooked boxer.

12/15/1959

Laramie Episode - The Lonesome Gun[48]

Jonesy visits a man who sent a letter threatening to kill Slim's dad not knowing he is dead. His revenge turns to wanting to kill Slim instead.

12/22/1959

Laramie Episode - Night of the Quiet Men[49]

Slim rents part of his land unknowingly to outlaws. A retired sheriff is trying to help them start a new crime free life. Towns people are angry and don't want them around.

12/25/1959

For Christmas Robert gave cast members a leather director chair with their name engraved on it.

12/[50]29/1959

45.   https://www.imdb.com/title/tt0624717/?ref_=ttep_ep11

46.   https://www.imdb.com/title/tt0624740/?ref_=ttep_ep12

47.   https://www.imdb.com/title/tt0624709/?ref_=ttep_ep13

48.   https://www.imdb.com/title/tt0624788/?ref_=ttep_ep14

49.   https://www.imdb.com/title/tt0624745/?ref_=ttep_ep15

50. https://www.imdb.com/title/tt0624794/?ref_=ttep_ep16

Laramie Episode - The Pass[51]

Indian trouble and Slim helps the Army dynamite a snowy mountain pass to keep Sioux and Cheyenne Indian tribes from joining up. Jess is with Armstrong Custer cavalry.

1960'S

Many studio publicity photos were created. Robert might be dressed as a cowboy with his saddle or guns or in Japanese outfits.

Movie exhibit cards were made including a penny arcade card.

Two different styles of Japanese playing cards are created. Each was with a different revolver.

Polydor in Europe creates Laramie postcards.

German post cards are created. Robert is wearing a suit jacket and with a horse.

Latin American Laramie Poster is created. Robert is crunched down with gun in hand.

Magic Ink trading cards are made with a drawing of .Jess.

Early TV / Movie Magazines had many photos of Robert alone or with his wife Patty Lyon. He was also photographed with cast like John Smith (3/6/1931-1/25/1995), John's wife Luan Patten (7/6/1938-5/1/1996), Robert Crawford (5/13/1944-) and Dennis Holmes (1-/3/1950-).

Early TV / Movie Magazine included photos of Robert with other celebrities like Clint Eastwood (5/31/1930- - http://www.clinteastwood.net/ . *His 1959-1965 Rawhide television character helped launch his career. From 1954 until at least 2020 Clint has acted, produced and directed over 50 times. Clint won numerous awards including Academy Awards for acting and directing).*

TV Times with Laramie is on cover.

---

51.   https://www.imdb.com/title/tt0624794/?ref_=ttep_ep16

The Wyatt Earp Story #21 in Germany. He is on cover.

Japanese Magazine - 25 Favorites from Foreign TV Shows. He is not on cover.

Japanese Magazine – The cover has the English words "TV Film Section with Robert on half of the cover: Photos include Laramie with second cast.

Japanese Magazine. The cover has the number 12 in the lower left corner. Robert is wearing a striped white shirt, holding a revolver with two hands with a Jess Harper wanted poster on the wall behind him. Variations of from this photo shoot also appear in this magazine.

1960 OR 1961

When translating from English to Japanese Robert's performances usually were recreated by actors with similar looks and voices vs. some other countries that did not match up well.

During one visit to Japan 500,000 fans were waiting for him at Osaka. Japan aired Laramie episodes followed by five minute segment updating fans on what was new. *(During one of his Japan visits his hand is wrapped in a bandage).*

Magazine Article titled The Private World of Robert Fuller: Wonder Dolls, a T-Bird, and all that Jazz.

1960

For Laramie's second season Cyril Mockridge (8/6/1896-1/18/1978 was hired to work on musical scores and he did 124 Laramie episodes. *Between 1934 and 1963 Cyril worked on over 90 movies).*

Local TV Guide ad features Slim and Jess on more than half of the page. It is about 5 x 7 inches in size.

Laramie board game by Lowell Toy in Long Island, New York is being sold.

Wagon Train, (Robert had earlier roles on and his next job) is currently airing and board games by Milton Bradley and Revue Productions are being sold.

Johnny Midnight. ? extra - sometime between 1/30/1960 to 9/21/1960. It is a crime drama starring Edmond O'Brien (9/10/1915-5/9/1985).

Articles Robert was in include:
Movieland & TV Time Yearbook Magazine. He is not on cover and sells for 35 cents.

Movie Life Yearbook Magazine by Ideal. He is not on cover and sells for 35 cents.

Photoplay Annual Magazine. He is not on cover and sells for 35 cents.
TV Annual Magazine
TV Radio Annual Magazine. He is not on cover.
TV Star Annual Magazine #8.

TV Yearbook No. 8 Magazine - Robert and Kathy Nolan (9/27/1933-). Article tells Kathy told Robert about getting role in Real McCoys. Robert is bachelor also shown with Ruta Lee at archery range.

Western Film and TV Annual Magazine. He is not on cover.

Who's Who in Television, Radio & Records #10 Magazine. Western Stars (Laramie). His bio is included in Westerns section and photo is with John Smith (3/6/1931-1/25/1995). Magazine is sells for 35 cents.

Publicity included photos with Robert using a bow and arrow at sea appeared in article titled "Everyone's Happy - Except the Sharks" taken off Catalina Island in California and Mexico. Kathy Nolan was with him.

1/1960
Movieland and TV Times. Article is titled I Want to be a Bad Guy.

1/12/1960
Laramie Episode - Trail Drive
Needing money, Jess and Slim go on cattle drive with strangers.

1/19/1960

Laramie Episode - Day of Vengeance[52]
Jess takes a prisoner to Laramie. Wife of murdered man wants revenge.

1/26/1960

Laramie Episode - Laramie Episode - The Legend of Lily[53]
Jonesy is long time fan and meets singer Lily Langford. She has a crooked husband.

2/2/1960

Laramie Episode - Death Wind[54]
Passengers, one with hit man after him, want to continue on despite tornado coming.

2/9/1960

Laramie Episode - Company Man[55]
Horses are stolen. New stage line manager, known for killing people, demands Jess be fired. Slim refuses.

2/14/1960

This Week Magazine (England publication).

2/16/1960

Laramie Episode - Rope of Steel[56]
Criminal is interrupted during murder and robbery. A neighbor finds and keeps money and then puts blame on Slim for taking missing money.

2/23/1960

Laramie Episode - Laramie Episode - Duel at Alta Mesa[57]
In Slim's absence Jess agrees to search secretly for stage line's stolen money.

3/1960

TV Star Parade Magazine. He is not on cover.

52.   https://www.imdb.com/title/tt0624718/?ref_=ttep_ep18

53.   https://www.imdb.com/title/tt0624787/?ref_=ttep_ep19

54.   https://www.imdb.com/title/tt0624720/?ref_=ttep_ep20

55.   https://www.imdb.com/title/tt0624716/?ref_=ttep_ep21

56.   https://www.imdb.com/title/tt0624755/?ref_=ttep_ep22

57.   https://www.imdb.com/title/tt0624724/?ref_=ttep_ep23

3/1/1960

Laramie Episode - Street of Hate[58]

Slim is responsible for paroled man but his family and the town doesn't want paroled man to stay.

3/8/1960

Laramie Episode - Ride or Die[59]

Slim searches and finds the bank robber who killed a deputy in the desert. Slim forces a couple the outlaw befriended to help bring robber back to be identified.

3/15/1960

Laramie Episode - Hour After Dawn[60]

Criminal is caught and Slim and Jess must take over trial and hanging after the sheriff is wounded.

3/22/1960

Laramie Episode - The Protectors[61]

Slim and Jess try to prevent a fight between ranchers and nesters who hired men with other motives.

3/29/1960

Laramie Episode - Saddle and Spur[62]

With low cattle prices, Slim and Jess need money and take jobs as marshal and deputy. Parts of this episode were filmed at Iverson Ranch. This cave was also Walt Disney's Zorro cave. To see more great television programs and movies filmed at Iverson Ranch see http://iversonmovieranch.blogspot.com/2014/11 .

4/1960

Robert had been asked to come to Japan with expenses paid because Laramie was the number one show there. The studio arranged time off for a 10 day visit but it was extended to 30 days. An engine caught on fire on the way to Hawaii so the plane returned to California delaying his scheduled 10 p.m. arrival in Japan. People with children had already left by the time he arrived at 2 a.m. When deplaning last he saw banners and was greeted by 10,000 people still waiting for him. There were also parades during his visit. (*After seeing Robert in a parade, Atsuko Yamoguchi became friends with Robert and she continues to travel to U.S. to see Robert*). He had police security and one evening raised money for the Red Cross.

58.   https://www.imdb.com/title/tt0624764/?ref_=ttep_ep24

59.   https://www.imdb.com/title/tt0624751/?ref_=ttep_ep25

60.   https://www.imdb.com/title/tt0624732/?ref_=ttep_ep26

61.   https://www.imdb.com/title/tt0624797/?ref_=ttep_ep27

62.   https://www.imdb.com/title/tt0624757/?ref_=ttep_ep28

In Tokyo thousands see him and he receives numerous gifts. He visits hospitals too.

Publicity marketing items include:

Laramie Game with cover that does not include Jess.

Laramie Holster.

Laramie pads of 26 sheets. Robert on his horse is on cover.

Articles include:

Movie Life Magazine. His name is on front cover with article titled Bob Fuller and Kathy Noland Weekend Lovers. There are nine photos including two of both Robert and Kathy (9/27/1933-). (*Robert was upset with lies*).

TV Star Parade Magazine. His picture is on the cover with article, Battle of the Bobs / Danger Stalks My Footsteps with his dancing parents and talking about skin diving and sharks. It tells about him using arrow to shot mountain lion, about Edmund O'Brien (9/15/1915-5/9/1985) not pulling punch giving him a lose tooth and swollen lip and about his New York arrest. Magazine sells for 25 cents.

4/5/1960

Laramie Episode - Midnight Rebellion[63]

Jess poses as a sheriff killer to join a private army.

4/12/1960

Laramie Episode - Cemetery Road[64]

Taking Jonesy to doctor in town, Slim runs into trouble stopping an argument between local craftsman and someone in a wagon train.

4/19/1960

Laramie Episode - Men of Defiance[65]

Jess is hurt when he and marshal try to escape outlaws by going to a private fort. This episode has Fort Defiance beginning vs. Laramie.

4/23 - 4/29/1960

63.   https://www.imdb.com/title/tt0624743/?ref_=ttep_ep29

64.   https://www.imdb.com/title/tt0624714/?ref_=ttep_ep30

65.   https://www.imdb.com/title/tt0624742/?ref_=ttep_ep31

TV Guide Cover with original cast. Article includes Robert getting permission to do his own stunt riding a bronco horse. *See www.tvguidemagazine.com/archive/suboffer/1960's*[66] .

5/1960

Star Parade Magazine with article titled I Adopted Bob Fuller.

TV Radio Mirror Magazine. He is not on cover.

5/19 - 5/25/1960

Sydney TV Week television guide with Robert and Robert Crawford, Jr. (5/13/1944-) on cover.

6/1960

"Marty" Young Adult United Kingdom Magazine. He is on 3 of the 19 pages.

? SUMMER OF 1960

Bravo German Magazine. He is on the cover which also announces the Beatles are coming. *The Beatles toured from 8/17 to 10/3/1960.*

7/1960

Screen Spotlight Magazine. He is not on cover.

TV Star Parade Magazine. Debbie Reynolds (4/1/1932-12/28/2016) is on cover.

8/1960

Dell Comic Book Laramie #1125 August to October 1960 issue costs ten cents. The cover is the first year Laramie cast at a fence rail. (In 2016 reprints of all four issues are published consisting of 156 pages).

Dell Comic four color book titled Turok Son of Stone #12 - Into Los Valley came "The Conqueror issue contains a Laramie section. Cover does not contain any reference to Laramie TV program storyline.

TV Screen Life Magazine.

66.   http://www.tvguidemagazine.com/archive/suboffer/1960's

9/1960

Bravo German Magazine. He is on cover.

9/20/1960

Laramie Episode - Queen of Diamonds[67]

Slim and Jess disagree on motives of woman they meet. She uses Slim to get out of a jam and protect her husband.

9/27/1960

Laramie Episode - The Track of the Jackal[68]

Bounty hunter who usually kills men vs. taking them in wants a friend of Jess.

10/4/1960

Laramie Episode - Three Rode West

Stage driver with Slim takes stage line money and Slims try to find location of man and missing money from his girlfriend.

10/7/1960

Spartacus. For fun while doing Laramie and wearing a beard Robert plays a solider with stuntman Red West (3/8/1935-7/18/2017). They have a fight together. Unaccredited. Huge cast.

10/11/1960

Laramie Episode - Ride the Wild Wind[69]

After being angry with Slim, Andy runs away, is hurt and is found by outlaws. Slim follows to bring Andy home.

10/18/1960

Laramie Episode - Ride into Darkness[70]

Jess's prospector friend writes for help but when he arrives everyone denies knowing him.

10/25/1960

Laramie Episode - The Long Riders[71]

67.	https://www.imdb.com/title/tt0624749/?ref_=ttep_ep1

68.	https://www.imdb.com/title/tt0624808/?ref_=ttep_ep2

69.	https://www.imdb.com/title/tt0624752/?ref_=ttep_ep4

70.	https://www.imdb.com/title/tt0624750/?ref_=ttep_ep5

Slim and Jess rescues a man in Sioux territory but his questions about Slim's past make Jess suspicious.

10/29/1960

Local TV Guide with Danny Kaye (1/18/1911-3/3/1987) cover has shark article.

11/1960

Movie Star TV Close-ups Magazine. He is not on cover.

11/1/1960

Laramie Episode - The Dark Trail[72]

To get bonus money Jess travels to get horses for the stage line and runs into horse thieves.

11/15/1960

Laramie Episode - Laramie Episode - .45 Calibre[73]

After Laramie marshal is killed Jess doesn't want to cooperate with new deputy.

11/22/1960

Laramie Episode - License to Kill[74]

Jess is taken by bounty hunter who often kills vs. taking men in for trial. Slim goes along to make sure Jess arrives alive.

11/29/1960

Laramie Episode - Drifter's Gold[75]

Phony gold strike leaves town almost empty when Slim arrives. He pretends to be a prisoner when he finds bank robbers are in town.

12/6/1960

Laramie Episode - No Second Chance[76]

Woman blames Slim and the stage line for her father's suicide. She sets out to destroy the stage line by starting another.

71.	https://www.imdb.com/title/tt0624789/?ref_=ttep_ep6

72.	https://www.imdb.com/title/tt0624769/?ref_=ttep_ep7

73.	https://www.imdb.com/title/tt0624702/?ref_=ttep_ep8

74.	https://www.imdb.com/title/tt0624737/?ref_=ttep_ep9

75.	https://www.imdb.com/title/tt0624723/?ref_=ttep_ep10

76.	https://www.imdb.com/title/tt0624747/?ref_=ttep_ep11

12/13/1960

Laramie Episode - Duel at Parkison Town[77]

Accidental shooting and death of a neighbor boy leads to opening up old feud with Slim's family.

12/27/1960

Laramie Episode - A Sound of Bells[78]

Gold on the stage and Indian attacks leave passengers at ranch on Christmas eve. *See Trailer for "Laramie: A Sound of Bells" at https://www.youtube.com/watch?v=IcyWiBaSXvY .*

1961

Laramie cast change. *See new introduction at "Laramie" US TV series (1959—63) intro / lead-in https://www.youtube.com/watch?v=Xt1YtA7RG5E or laramie intro at https://www.youtube.com/ watch?v=Y376o68Ihgg&list=PLzVEuYNZIlJ4V3dxyfRAM-wsDVH06XYu8 .*

Sometime during the last two years of Laramie, Robert moved from his parent's house into a house with Chuck Courtney. David Nelson, son of Ozzie and Harriet Nelson, secretly kept his dirt bike there and the three of them used nearby Columbia's 30 acres to ride in. It was also during this time that co-star Dennis Holmes (10/3/1950-) would visit for the weekend.

Robert's future first wife, Patty Lyon, after winning the Indiana Jr. Miss competition goes to Mobile, Alabama to compete for America's Jr. Miss. (Patty was active in school theatre productions and studied dance while at school. She modeled in Chicago, Illinois. After high school Patty had moved to Los Angeles, California to attend Mount St. Mary's College but was offered a contract with MGM studios to appear in a pilot Andy Hardy TV series. The pilot did not sell and Patty acted in The Donna Reed Show, My 3 Sons and appeared multiple times on A Queen for a Day. During this time Patty studied with Bob Bush who was Sanford Meisner's assistant in Los Angeles. She continued to do commercials until shortly after the birth of her first son in 4/1967).

Germany - Best Actor Award. *(Robert visited Germany several times).*

Comic books like Dell #1223 issued in 1961 has Jess and Slim on the cover. A foreign version Domingos Alegres #449 issued in Spain has the same cover but with lighter yellow color background. A second English version has a green background color.

---

77.   https://www.imdb.com/title/tt0624725/?ref_=ttep_ep12

78.   https://www.imdb.com/title/tt0624704/?ref_=ttep_ep13

Four Color Comics Laramie #1273 is printed.

Aventura #200 is a Spanish comic book. The cover is of first year Laramie cast at fence rail. (The English version of Dell Comics had this photo on its cover in 8/1960).

Japanese notebook and memo cards were created. The photo is Robert by himself at the fence rail. Penny arcade postcards were also created from this photo minus the Laramie title.

Wagon Train (Robert had appeared on and will be his next series) issues a tray puzzle by the Whitman Publishing Company. Wagon Train is number one show via Nielson ratings for 1961-1962.

Studio publicity or magazines have Robert dating Kathy Perry. He was also dating dancer and 1959 Grammy Award singer Keely Smith (3/9/1928-12/16/2017) while separated before her 1961 divorce. An early 1962 magazine article says Robert spent Christmas eve and New Years Day with Keely and New Years Day with Patty Lyon (his future first wife).

Robert has many articles and photos with Ruta Lee (5/30/1935- www.rutalee.com[79]) but wasn't dating vs. publicity (via Ruta in the 2000's). Articles also had him engaged to an actress who loved sports, Kathy Nolan (9/27/1933-). Magazines, like Photoplay, pay for celebrity photo shoots and articles.

One magazine article title was 'Spring Joins Laramie'.

Magazines say Robert went diving with sharks off Mexico's coast.

Articles Robert appeared in include:
    Modern Screen Yearbook No. 4. He is not on cover. It sells for 35 cents.

Movie Mirror Yearbook No. 2 Magazine - Excuses! Excuses! Always Excuses contains two photos, one with Ruta Lee *(5/30/1935- . In high school Ruta was studying acting and appearing in school plays. Ruta has appeared in 25 films and almost 110 television programs. Ruta also voiced Hidea Frankenstone in 18 episodes of The Flintstones Comedy Hour. She is also a dancer and singer. In 1964 after speaking with Soviet leader Nikita Khrushchev she got a pardon for her grandmother in an interment camp in Siberia since World War II. In 1987 she got her 18 year old Lithuanian cousin released. Ruta has been a member of various youth and mental health organizations. Ruta has been married to Lester B. Lowe, Jr. since 1976. See www.rutalee.com[80]).* Magazine sells for 35 cents.

Movie Mirror Yearbook #3 Magazine. Kathy's Desperate Battle (Kathy Nolan (9/27/1933-).

Star Album Magazine #2. He is not on cover.

Teen Stars Album No. 1 Magazine. Robert is under Western Favorites has one photo on ¼ page and sells for 35 cents.

Teen Stars Album No. 2 Magazine - They Ride the Range has one photo and sells for 35 cents.

Teen Stars Album No. 3 titled Kathy's Desperate Battle has a photo with Robert.

TV Annual #12 Magazine. Shared page with John Smith (3/6/1931-1/25/1995) with photos.

TV-Radio Album Magazine. He is not on cover and sells for 50 cents. Summer Fun has photo of him dancing with his dad and with Kathy Nolan (9/27/1933-).

TV-Radio Mirror Magazine. He is not on cover.

TV Star Annual No. 11 Magazine. He is not on cover. Article is titled Late For the Wedding and includes photos telling about Kathy Nolan 99/27/1933-)'s accident, Robert's trip in Japan and Robert Crawford, Jr. (5/13/1944-). It sells for 35 cents.

TV Star Annual No. 12 Magazine has three photos and sells for 35 cents.

TV Yearbook No. 10 - Giant All Star Western Roundup Magazine. Laramie and Kathy Nolan (9/27/1933-) with two photos, one is with John Smith (3/6/1931-1/25/1995). It sells for 35 cents.

---

80. *http://www.rutalee.com*

TV's Top Stars. He is not on cover.

This year is a busy one for Robert. Laramie is very popular in Japan and many special edition magazines are printed. One cover is Robert leaning against wood log holding a rife against a blue sky. Inside photos include Robert mainly as a cowboy, riding a horse. There is one photo of him behind the wheel of a car that appeared in many magazines. Photos also feature Laramie's two new cast members and show Robert playing 'spoons'.

Japanese Screen Western No. 2 Japanese magazine. Robert is on cover and it is 172 pages. Two pages titled Robert Fuller's Gun Play shows his pistol drawing techniques.

A 76 page Japanese No. 12 issue has Ty Hardin (1/1/1930 - 8/3/2017) and Troy Donahue (1/27/1936 -9/2/2001) on cover.

Another Ty Hardin (1/1/1930 – 8/3/2017) cover Japanese TV Film section magazine is issued. It is 174 pages. A photo included in this magazine appeared in many magazines and can be seen on a 9/9/1962 TV Guide.

Japanese TV Film Section #6 Magazine. He is not on cover and is 174 pages. This is another one where he is in a sports car.

Japanese Magazine – TV Film Section with John Wayne (5/26/1907-6/11/1979) with Comancheros cover. Article title is Robert Fuller and His Lover Kathy Nolan (9/27/1933-). *(This is another article that may have angered Robert).*

Japanese Western Magazine. He is not on cover and is 174 pages. Photos include a Laramie shot with guest Julie London and riding a motor bike.

Japanese Western Magazine with Burt Lancaster (11/2/1913-10/20/1994) on the cover. The popular photo chosen was used many times.

1/1961
   Movieland Magazine. He is not on cover.

Screenland Magazine. Rock Hudson (11/17/1925-10/2/1985) is on cover.

1/3/1961

Laramie Episode - The Passing of Kuba Smith[81]

Slim and Jess get bounty money and spend part of it only to find they must repay because person shot wasn't the real criminal.

1/10/1961

Laramie Episode - Man from Kansas[82]

Robin Hood character saves Jess but then robs some on stage. Slim is angry no one will testify against this guilty accused man.

1/24/1961

Laramie Episode - Killer Without Cause[83]

Slim's Indian hand is murdered by a neighbor and Slim pursues justice in court. Many locals want murderer set free.

1/31/1961

Laramie Episode - Stolen Tribute[84]

Jess is forced to help brother of man who buried stolen money.

2/14/1961

Laramie Episode - The Lost Dutchman[85]

Slim and Jess travel to buy cattle to find man sold them. Slim gets mad and when cattle owner is killed, Slim is jailed. Jess tries to clear Slim.

2/21/1961

Laramie Episode - Cactus Lady[86]

Old female friend of Jess fakes being sick to get Jess's help after getting him jailed before. Slim is willing to help her despite her outlaw family.

81.   https://www.imdb.com/title/tt0624795/?ref_=ttep_ep14

82.   https://www.imdb.com/title/tt0624739/?ref_=ttep_ep15

83.   https://www.imdb.com/title/tt0624734/?ref_=ttep_ep16

84.   https://www.imdb.com/title/tt0624762/?ref_=ttep_ep17

85.   https://www.imdb.com/title/tt0624783/?ref_=ttep_ep18

86.   https://www.imdb.com/title/tt0624713/?ref_=ttep_ep19

2/26/1961

St. Louis TV Magazine with article titled Buddies Feud Time.

3/7/1961

Laramie Episode - Riders of the Night[87]

Slim and vet thought by outlaws to be a doctor, are kidnapped to tend to wounded outlaw.

3/14/1961

Laramie Episode - Mark of the Manhunters[88]

A wounded marshal asks Slim for help to get man to testify in Cheyenne. They are trapped at ranch by one group wanting to kill him and another wanting him to get there to testify.

3/21/1961

Laramie Episode - Rimrock[89]

Jess chases a pinto horse involved in one death and wounding Slim. The pinto belongs to sheriff.

4/4/1961

Laramie Episode - Run of the Hunted[90]

Half Cheyenne man wants to let his tribe move on his ranch. Relatives try to prevent this. Slim helps the half Indian rancher.

4/11/1961

Laramie Episode - Two for the Gallows[91]

Slim is hired to be a guide to find an old gold strike. Man is really killer.

4/18/1961

Laramie Episode - Laramie Episode - The Debt[92]

Bounty hunter's prisoner saved Jess's life in past so Jess let him go but goes to the town to see if he is really innocent.

4/23 - 4/29/1961

87.   https://www.imdb.com/title/tt0624753/?ref_=ttep_ep20

88.   https://www.imdb.com/title/tt0624791/?ref_=ttep_ep21

89.   https://www.imdb.com/title/tt0624754/?ref_=ttep_ep22

90.   https://www.imdb.com/title/tt0624756/?ref_=ttep_ep23

91.   https://www.imdb.com/title/tt0624822/?ref_=ttep_ep24

92.   https://www.imdb.com/title/tt0624771/?ref_=ttep_ep25

Laramie on local TV Guide cover and sells for 15 cents.

4/25/1961

Laramie Episode - Killers' Odds[93]

Starving drifter comes to ranch and is hired. He keeps to himself fearing hired guns will find him again. They do.

5/2/1961

Laramie Episode - Bitter Glory[94]

Jess helps find old Army friend who saved his life who is now AWOL and payroll money is missing.

5/9/1961

Laramie Episode – The Tumbleweed Wagon

Father and son needing the bounty money, Slim is substituted as prisoner in transit when real prisoner is killed.

5/16/1961

Laramie Episode - Trigger Point[95]

Army payroll money is robbed with help of stage driver. Jess is riding shotgun and all passengers are left in desert.

5/23/1961

Laramie Episode - Badge of the Outsider[96]

Known outlaw who saved Slim's life as a child, asks for his help in proving he didn't kill a deputy found on his land.

5/30/1961

Laramie Episode - Men in Shadows[97]

The man who saved Jess's life in past now wants his help as a fugitive. Jess finds out he is not the same man he once knew.

6/6/1961

Laramie Episode - Strange Company[98]

93.   https://www.imdb.com/title/tt0624735/?ref_=ttep_ep26

94.   https://www.imdb.com/title/tt0624711/?ref_=ttep_ep27

95.   https://www.imdb.com/title/tt0624821/?ref_=ttep_ep29

96.   https://www.imdb.com/title/tt0624708/?ref_=ttep_ep30

97.   https://www.imdb.com/title/tt0624741/?ref_=ttep_ep31

98.   https://www.imdb.com/title/tt0624763/?ref_=ttep_ep32

After Indian attacks Slim helps men repair another old route before stage can use it. Men are being mysteriously killed.

6/11 - 6/17/1961

Local TV Guide.

6/13/1961

Laramie Episode - Widow in White[99]

Stage line wants Slim's help to renew a right of way. Woman's dead husband is rumored to have robbed payroll money buried on ranch.

SUMMER OF 1961

Japan - Japan's Best Actor Award. - Konga Award.

Japanese notebook and memo cards were created. Robert wearing cowboy working and dressy attire and modern clothing.

Robert goes to Japan with his parents.

Like his previous trip, thousands greet him and follow his visit. (In 1961 or 1962 his visit is 22 days). Coverage of Robert's trip to Japan via local TV Guides. The Japanese consider his Jess Harper character to be like a Samurai, helping the underdog.

On his previous trip, Robert had helped raise $100,000 one evening for Japan's Red Cross for physically challenged and orphaned Japanese children. He went to Japan to receive the Golden Order of Merit / Red Cross which was presented by the Empress of Japan. He was the first American to receive. He also met the Emperor and had lunch at the Prime Minister's home.

During Robert's visit thousands of photographs were taken. Several total magazines were dedicated to his visit. A few are included below.

Chuck Conners (4/10/1921-11/10/1992) is on cover - All Westerns Magazine. It includes Robert's visit to Japan.

---

99.   https://www.imdb.com/title/tt0624825/?ref_=ttep_ep33

Japanese Magazine with Sandra Dee (4/23/1942-2/20/2005) on cover. It includes many photos from Robert's visit.

Several whole magazines were devoted to Robert and his visit. One is 76 pages and has photos of Robert, his parents, speaking appearances and places he visited (like fawn park).

Japanese magazine dedicated to Robert has him on the cover holding his rifle down with blue sky background. It is 86 pages with solo photos and many first year Laramie action shots. Both cast and guest stars are also shown. Several pages show Robert and his pistol draw. Other photos show Robert using his rifle or with his horse. There are also photos of Robert wearing a suit and tie along with other photos taken during his Japan visit. Robert also appears in drawings. The back cover is Robert with his horse.

Japanese Laramie special magazine is created with a cover showing Robert holding an Japanese doll / ?award. Photos inside include Robert with a Jess Harper figure about three feet tall, signing autographs and many with kid and adult fans.

A 188 page Japanese Laramie special edition is made. The cover is Robert on Laramie including a photo sitting on a fence rail in front of the SR on the barn wall. Robert plays the drums and attends events with his parents meeting people.

A 240 page magazine dedicated to Robert is also created. Some photos in here also appear in a 188 page special edition magazine. Besides Robert's visit, this issue has Laramie scene photos like Jess talking to Slim while he shaves.

Japan Magazine #7 - TV Film Section. He is not on cover. Photos include his visit with his parents including sights he was taken to.

Japanese Special Edition magazines #38 is made. The new Laramie cast is on the cover. Robert is seen sailing, in hospitals, with his pistol, with fans and with his parents.

Japanese Western Magazine. Tom Tryon (1/14/1926-9/4/1991) and Harry Carey (5/16/1921-12/27/2012) are on cover. It is 174 pages long and includes Robert visit.

7/1961

Japanese Magazine (Eiju No Tomo). Laramie Special Edition. The whole magazine was about Robert and is 110 pages. A section is titled All About Jess has Laramie action shots with cast and guest stars. Photos also include childhood and young adult photos and first year cast with wagon wheel. Kathy Nolan (9/27/1933-) is also pictured. There are many photos of his visit including arrival crowds and visiting Japanese dignitaries. Robert is shown playing the drums, looking Japanese, practicing judo, playing spoons, swimming and receiving awards. There is even a drawing of him wearing a tie.

Movie Mirror Magazine. He is not on cover.

7/9/1961

Bravo German No. 28 Magazine. He is not on cover.

9/1961

Missouri Local TV Guide.

9/9/1961

TV Guide with Checkmate cover. Article is titled He is Hot in Tokyo and has three photos. *See www.tvguidemagazine.com/archive/subofer/1970's[100]* .

9/26/1961

Laramie Episode - Dragon at the Door[101]
Japanese travelers have child, Mike, whose parents were killed by Indians. Men try several times to rob Japanese group.

10/3/1961

Laramie Episode - Ladies' Day[102]
Jess and Slim need to hire woman and make good impression to judge in order to keep Mike. Daisy arrives thinking she owns property there. Bounty hunter and fake doctor arrive.

10/6/1961

Robert appeared on NBC's thirty minute afternoon talk show, Here's Hollywood, in its second season.

---

100.   *http://www.tvguidemagazine.com/archive/subofer/1970's*

101.   https://www.imdb.com/title/tt0624722/?ref_=ttep_ep1

102.   https://www.imdb.com/title/tt0624736/?ref_=ttep_ep2

10/8 - 8/14/1961

Local Sunday TV News Guide. Second Laramie cast on cover with Slim and Jess seated at table with Daisy and Andy looking on.

10/10/1961

Laramie Episode - Siege at Jubilee

Daisy and Jess with toothache go to Cheyenne. They return with bank robber who hid money from gang.

10/15/1961

Japanese Screen Movie Magazine. This special issue is all about Robert Fuller's visit and is 116 pages. Photos include Robert in his room, in the park, with his parents, with an anchor, car and motorcycle.

10/17/1961

Laramie Episode - The Mountain Men[103]

Mountain man and his sons disagree with court sentence and try to lynch a man going to jail for killing another son.

10/24/1961

Laramie Episode - Laramie Episode - The Fatal Step[104]

Jess is hurt while riding shotgun for payroll. Robbery was done by someone Jess knows.

10/31/1961

Laramie Episode – The Last Journey

Slim helps wounded marshal and criminal return money he stole.

11/7/1961

Laramie Episode - Deadly Is the Night[105]

Jess with lame horse stops at a former relay station to find bank robbers want to use it as a hide out.

11/14/1961

Laramie Episode - Laramie Episode - The Accusers[106]

Daisy sees a man leave a murdered woman's room. It is Slim's boss and she is determined to testify. Some try to convince her she didn't see what she did.

103.　　https://www.imdb.com/title/tt0624793/?ref_=ttep_ep4

104.　　https://www.imdb.com/title/tt0624774/?ref_=ttep_ep5

105.　　https://www.imdb.com/title/tt0624719/?ref_=ttep_ep7

106.　　https://www.imdb.com/title/tt0624765/?ref_=ttep_ep8

11/15/1961

Robert is in New York dressed as Jess Harper for the Jerry Lewis telethon. (Bobby Van 12/6/1928-7/31/1980 was one of the many celebrities present). This was a time before hijacking, etc. when wearing a .45 Colt studio gun, being in western costume was acceptable even on airplanes. While on a break from the Jerry Lewis Telethon about 10 p.m., Robert, his date Keely Smith and her brother decide to go to the Copra for dinner and see the Tony Bennett show. Not wanting to leave his gun with stage staff and having no problems in past, Robert kept his gun. He was in costume when the three of them were heckled by two men upon arriving at the restaurant. The bouncer stopped these two men. When leaving about midnight these 2 men were back and came right for Robert so he pulled his full load prop gun and fired at the man twice, once in the stomach. The noise was heard from police station around the corner and they immediately respond. Robert tried to explain but was thrown to the ground. Robert hit the officer. He was handcuffed and taken to the 3rd precinct station. The police had taken his gun but now couldn't figure out how to unload it. They returned the gun to Robert to do and then took gun back and took him into the interrogation room. Robert shouting Laramie, studio names, etc. to get them to listen to him. He was charged with having an illegal weapon and firing it which could have resulted in 20 years in jail and a $200,000 fine. Robert is arrested, finger printed and put into drunk tank. Robert is moved to four different police precinct locations delaying his bail. Robert was held in jail for three days and later had to appear before a grand jury. In court Robert said was an accident and charges are removed from his record. The incident received nationwide publicity. Fearing he would be fired, Robert is surprised when studio heads suggest he do something similar before next season's opening episode. *Robert has spoken about incident several times.*

(Keely Smith (3/9/1928-12/16/2017. By the time Keely is 11 years old she was singing. Keely was separated from her husband at this time and later this year divorced. Keely sang often until about 1966 when she took a break returning in 1985. She was still singing in 2011. Keely had 10 albums involving a former husband Louis Prima and 20 solo albums. She died of heart failure).

11/21/1961

Laramie Episode - Wolf Cub[107]
Jess rescues crippled Indian boy from scalp hunter. They get boy operated on and he and Mike become friends.

12/5/1961

Laramie Episode - Handful of Fire
Slim as Army scout rushes to get orders to stop attack to commanding officer. He refuses to look at and a court trial follows after many Indians are killed.

12/12/1961

Laramie Episode - The Killer Legend[108]

107.	https://www.imdb.com/title/tt0624826/?ref_=ttep_ep9
108.	https://www.imdb.com/title/tt0624781/?ref_=ttep_ep11

Jess tries to help man recently released from jail but finds he may be seeking revenge by trying to kill the sheriff he blames for unjustly convicting him.

12/19/1961

Laramie Episode - The Jailbreakers[109]

Sheriff kills a woman and blames it on former criminal, Slim's friend. Slim wants his friend to turn himself in.

12/26/1961

Laramie Episode - The Lawless Seven[110]

Jess is framed for murder and escapes posse to show up at another outlaw's hideout.

1962

Cain's Hundred - The crime drama episode is titled The Debasers.

Die Leute von der Shilo Ranch (Freundschaftsdienst fur einen Toten). Possible connection to Robert or via translation may pertain to a Virginian episode.

Robert attended some event at the Shrine Auditorium in Los Angeles, California where girl scouts were present.

Robert went to New York to appear as a guest on the Tonight Show hosted by Jack Paar. (Episode #5-235).

The Dinah Shore (2/29/1916-2/24/1994) Show. He played spoons, jumping over back end of horse, wearing tux. (Tim Reid from The Lone Ranger, actor Chuck Courtney may have taught him to play spoons).

Sunday TV News Guide in Lancaster / Philadelphia, Pennsylvania with Joey Bishop cover has an article about shark fishing.

Articles Robert appeared in include:

TV Album Magazine. He is not on cover. It costs 35 cents.

109.   https://www.imdb.com/title/tt0624780/?ref_=ttep_ep12

110.   https://www.imdb.com/title/tt0624786/?ref_=ttep_ep13

TV Radio Album Magazine. He is not on cover. Talks about 22 day tour to Japan.

TV Radio Annual Magazine. Horse Opera Heroes with ¼ page and photo has him hold an album. Magazine is selling for 50 cents.

TV Star Annual #13 Magazine. He is not on cover. Heroes on Horseback has two photos on him sailing on ¼ page.

TV World Album #1 Magazine. Keyhole Close ups has his bio on ¼ page with one photo. Magazine sells for 35 cents.

TV Yearbook Magazine. He is not on cover.

An article titled Let's Get Married Again is printed early this year. It says Robert was in New York and spent Christmas Eve and New Year's Day in 1961 with Kelley Smith and New Years Eve with Patty. It goes on to say Robert, a non-Catholic and Patty Lyon, a Catholic, were married in Las Vegas but kept it a secret and future possibility of remarrying in a church.

Japanese Magazines. Scenes include Laramie action shots.

Japanese Western Magazine. Ty Hardin (1/1/11930-8/3/2017) is on cover. It is 174 pages and includes Robert and Laramie cast and guest photos.

Dell Comic Books are created and sell for 15 cents. Both Jess and Slim are on cover.

Danish gum cards E113 Robert Fuller – Laramie - are released.

1/1962
    Movieland TV Time Magazine. He is not on cover.

1/2/1962
    Laramie Episode - The Perfect Gift[111]

---

111.   https://www.imdb.com/title/tt0624796/?ref_=ttep_ep14

Slim is part of trial involving Indian woman's acquittal. He then saves her life and she is given to him despite the fact she is in love with someone else. Afterward Slim begins to fall in love with her.

1/9/1962

Laramie Episode - The Barefoot Kid

A young Mexican teen steals Jess's horse and his trial leads to hanging verdict by prejudiced judge. Jess releases boy and gets jailed himself. This episode was produced by John Champion with Dan Ullman as *Associate Producer,* Joe Kane is *Director,* Dick Nelson is *Writer* and instrumental music theme was created by Cyril Mockridge. For a more detailed summary, cast and crew *see LARAMIE: THE BAREFOOT KID (TV) - Paley Center at https://www.paleycenter.org/ collection/item/?q=nbc&p=265&item=T80:0071 .*

1/16/1962

Laramie Episode - Shadows in the Dust[112]
Slim find women cattle rustler and is wounded. She saves his life.

Alcoa Premier - The episode is titled Hour of the Bath. He plays Henry Detweilder (Dienst in Vietname: Fronturlaub), an agricultural graduate in South Vietnam. Other cast includes Barbara Luna (3/2/1930- www.barbaraluna.com[113]).

1/23/1962

Laramie Episode - The Runaway

Daisy tries to teach a boy living with his uncle to read. Jess also tries to prevent him from running around with two drifters.

1/27/1962

Indianapolis, Indiana TV Guide. He is not on cover.

1/30/1962

Laramie Episode - The Confederate Express

Neighbor's secret husband returns to his family trying to cash a bank draft for fresh start. He saves Jess's life and both Slim and Jess help him get to bank. He is really a bank robber.

TV Magazine - Confederate Express - *See episode above.*

---

112.   https://www.imdb.com/title/tt0624759/?ref_=ttep_ep16

113. http://www.barbaraluna.com

2 - 4/1962

Dell Comic Book #1284 is issued. (The cover photo of Slim and Jess both firing will later appear on Europe's DVD Volume 2 of the series).

2/1962

Hollywood Tattler Magazine. He is not on cover.

2/6/1962

Laramie Episode - The High Country[114]
Slim finds a partly tamed horse for Mike. It is stolen and Slim searches for it and gets involved in range war.

2/13/1962

Laramie Episode - A Grave for Cully Brown
Jess helps a stranger out and is later is shot. Thinking Jess is dying he's switches places with him. Jess escapes jail to clear his name and get money man stole from him.

2/20/1962

Laramie Episode - The Runt[115]
Neighbor's family comes and holds his wife hostage to force neighbor's help in a robbery. Slim is acting sheriff.

3/6/1962

Laramie Episode - The Dynamiters[116]
Jess is on stage with money when stage is robbed. Jess tracks wounded outlaw.

3/13/1962

Laramie Episode - Day of the Savage[117]
Indians uprising. A stranger shows up and Jess, Slim and this man search for his fiancé on a missing stage.

3/20/1962

Laramie Episode - Justice in a Hurry[118]

114.	https://www.imdb.com/title/tt0624778/?ref_=ttep_ep19

115.	https://www.imdb.com/title/tt0624803/?ref_=ttep_ep21

116.	https://www.imdb.com/title/tt0624773/?ref_=ttep_ep22

117.	https://www.imdb.com/title/tt0624770/?ref_=ttep_ep23

118.	https://www.imdb.com/title/tt0624733/?ref_=ttep_ep24

A girl asks Slim to alibi her father but finds her father was quickly hung. Slim helps the daughter find out what happened.

3/27/1962

Laramie Episode – The Replacement

New deputy was in charge of Jess's old POW camp. Other former prisoners come to kill him. Jess and Slim differ on how to handle and if revenge killing is the answer.

4/3/1962

Laramie Episode - The Turn of the Wheel[119]

Slim's old love comes to Laramie and she is messed up with illegal operations. Slim goes undercover at saloon to help sheriff recover counterfeit money plates.

4/10/1962

Laramie Episode - Trial by Fire[120]

Jess takes break from fire fighting to get neighbor's mail order possible bride. Man' step son doesn't want her around and finds out she is not who she claims to be.

4/17/1962

Laramie Episode - Fall into Darkness[121]

Slim helps rescue a woman who fell in a well. To force help of her outlaw husband's gang, Slim throws money in well with her.

5/10/1962

Canal TV - Argentina TV Guide says that Robert rented a house in Toluca Lake with Chuck Courtney (7/23/ 1930-1/19/2000) and Bill Battersby for $500 a month. A caretaker was hired but Robert works on his own new sports car and new motorcycle. Article also states Robert wants to buy more horses, is doing less night clubbing and that he has a New York job and is then looking forward to 30 day vacation. Article also says he is dating Ruta Lee (5/30/1935- www.rutalee.com[122]) and that they were engaged for two years *(untrue)*.

5/13/1962

Bravo German Magazine No. 19. He is not on cover.

---

119.   https://www.imdb.com/title/tt0624810/?ref_=ttep_ep26

120.   https://www.imdb.com/title/tt0624820/?ref_=ttep_ep27

121.   https://www.imdb.com/title/tt0624727/?ref_=ttep_ep28

122.   http://www.rutalee.com

7/1962

TV Star Parade Magazine. He is not on cover. Article is titled "How Broken is a Broken Engagement".

8/5/1962

Bravo German Magazine No. 31. He is not on cover. Robert's photo is him using both hands to hold a pistol.

9/6/1962

NBC Publicity is released.

9/7/1962

NBC Laramie 4th season publicity is released.

9/9 - 9/15/1962

Philadelphia, Pennsylvania TV Guide. It contained two photos. (One sailing photo sitting at the wheel may have also appeared in a 1961 Lancaster, Pennsylvania TV Guide).

Laramie promotion photos of Robert alone were adapted to be used on Wagon Train. Some appeared as a part of a TV guide ads.

9/25/1962

Laramie Episode - Among the Missing[123]
Jess and the sheriff hunt bank robbers who shot Mike. Dying person reveals guess of where money may be. Jess goes on alone to find.

10/2/1962

Laramie Episode - War Hero[124]
Slim's former commander is running for President. Jess guards stage he is on but when candidate is wounded he stays at ranch to heal.

10/9/1962

Laramie Episode - The Fortune Hunter[125]

123.   https://www.imdb.com/title/tt0624705/?ref_=ttep_ep1

124.   https://www.imdb.com/title/tt0624824/?ref_=ttep_ep2

Slim's girlfriend wants more attention and flirts with a man to make Slim jealous. Man is after her money.

10/16/1962

Laramie Episode - Shadow of the Past[126]

Jess's sister that he thought was dead, shows up wanting to bury her outlaw husband. Her husband is really wounded. (His same sister is now alive and different background reason now vs. 10/6/1959 one).

10/23/1962

Laramie Episode - The Long Road Back[127]

Slim is searching for money stolen from stage and finds someone who may be involved.

10/30/1962

Laramie Episode - Lost Allegiance[128]

After Jess is hurt from a falling tree he runs into former friend, now an outlaw. Jess is nursed in area where rustling is occurring.

11/1962

TV Life Magazine. He is not on cover and sells for 25 cents.

11/13/1962

Laramie Episode - The Sunday Shoot[129]

Shooting contest is won by young country (vs. town) man. Slim and Jess try to get him not to let win go to his head as he is being set up to lose money he won.

11/20/1962

Laramie Episode - Double Eagles[130]

To tempt and get posse (sheriff, Jess and others) to fight amongst themselves bank robbers leave gold coins behind.

11/27/1962

Laramie Episode - Beyond Justice[131]

125.   https://www.imdb.com/title/tt0624775/?ref_=ttep_ep3

126.   https://www.imdb.com/title/tt0624758/?ref_=ttep_ep4

127.   https://www.imdb.com/title/tt0624790/?ref_=ttep_ep5

128.   https://www.imdb.com/title/tt0624738/?ref_=ttep_ep6

129.   https://www.imdb.com/title/tt0624807/?ref_=ttep_ep7

130.   https://www.imdb.com/title/tt0624721/?ref_=ttep_ep8

Slim is deputy trying to keep a murder suspect alive.

12/4/1962

Laramie Episode - Bad Blood[132]

Jess promises dying woman to get her son to his father. His father turns out to be an outlaw.

12/11/1962

Laramie Episode - Time of the Traitor[133]

An accident occurs and a passenger on stage helps save young man's life but he loses arm. Young man's father is angry and blames doctor who turns out to be now released Dr. Samuel Mudd (convicted for being involved with the Abraham Lincoln assassination).

12/20/1962

Publicity articles previously mention that Robert was already secretly married. Robert did marry the sister of Kathy Nolan's roommate, 19 year old Patricia (Patty) Lee Lyon. She is an actress making at least two movies and one television appearance) and a dancer. *Later on Patty sells saddles to help support their family.*

Robert and Patty have a home in San Fernando Valley. Argentina TV magazine on 5/10 stated Robert owns a $60,000 mansion on a hill with a view overlooking Revue Studios in the San Fernando Valley. It has living room, kitchen, patio and 40-foot pool. His parents buy a house near his. *(This might have been a ranch style home in North Hollywood).*

12/25/1962

Laramie Episode - Gun Duel[134]

Jess is deputy with only one prisoner and an eager want-a-be deputy. Trouble arises and deputy proves not to be helpful.

EARLY 1960'S

Yakima, Washington fundraiser. Robert attended with James Drury (4/18/1934 - 4/6/2020).

1963

Bravo Otto Award Silver for best male TV actor in Germany. It's like U.S.'s Emmy Award.

---

131.   https://www.imdb.com/title/tt0624710/?ref_=ttep_ep9

132.   https://www.imdb.com/title/tt0624706/?ref_=ttep_ep10

133.   https://www.imdb.com/title/tt0624816/?ref_=ttep_ep11

134.   https://www.imdb.com/title/tt0624730/?ref_=ttep_ep12

Robert and James Drury (4/18/1934-4/6/2020 www.thevirginian.net[135]) are both under contract with MGM.

Local TV Guide ads include Chicago, Illinois TV Guide. It is one half page ad with a drawing of Robert telling that Laramie is on Channel 7 at t 5 p.m.

Local TV Guide ad 'Look what's happening on Monday on the new ABC' features three shows of 14 new ones on channels 7-13. Lying on the ground action photo of Robert promotes Wagon Train's 1 ½ hour color season.

Detroit / Flint's WJMT Channel 12 in Michigan is advertising Laramie in its TV Guide.

TV Top Stars Magazine. He is not on cover.

Who's Who in the Movies #1 Magazine. It contains his bio and sells for 35 cents.

Japanese trading cards are created. Both Jess and Slim appear.

1/1963
Screenland Magazine - Rock Hudson (11/17/1925-10/2/1985) is on cover. Article is titled "Kathy Nolan and Bob Fuller: Will They or Won't They? Get married, that is what everyone is wondering about steady-dating Kathy and Bob....
It may have been around this time an article appeared titled The Untold Truth About Our Romance by Kathy where she might have spoke about her relationship with Robert.

1/1/1963
Laramie Episode - Naked Steel[136]
Slim comes back from cattle drive to learn the man with the money, the son, was killed. Slim returns to town to find out what happened and get money back.

1/8/1963
Laramie Episode - Vengeance[137]

---

135. http://www.thevirginian.net

136.   https://www.imdb.com/title/tt0624744/?ref_=ttep_ep13

137.   https://www.imdb.com/title/tt0624823/?ref_=ttep_ep14

In self defense Jess shoots man as he turns so bullet is in his back. His girlfriend contacts his outlaw brothers to take revenge on Jess.

1/15/1963

Laramie Episode - Protective Custody[138]

One of the stage bosses is looking for his daughter. Jess knows she is saloon girl and Slim and Jess must decide what to do. The daughter hates her father and is involved with outlaws.

1/22/1963

Laramie Episode - The Betrayers[139]

A former friend of Jess involves him in a robbery. He first invites him to join the gang and then when Jess tells sheriff what he knows, gang changes plans. Jess is arrested and is to be hung. *See Adam West On Laramie As Kett Darby An Outlaw (Season 4 Ep. 16) at https://www.youtube.com/watch?v=9Dolj_2ZkOo .*

1/29/1963

Laramie Episode - The Wedding Party[140]

Slim and Daisy go to a wedding where the former husband wants to prevent marriage.

2/1963

Teen Life Magazine has his photo on the inside cover.

2/5/1963

Laramie Episode - No Place to Run[141]

Jess tries to help former outlaw being framed and forced into another bank robbery.

2/12/1963

Laramie Episode - The Fugitives[142]

Slim is missing and outlaw admits to shooting him but he wants to go free in exchange for details on where Slim is. Jess tries to get him and his sister to reveal location before Slim freezes too death. Chicago, Illinois NBC TV Guide ad is a drawing of mountains with episode title and 7:30 p.m. time.

138.   https://www.imdb.com/title/tt0624748/?ref_=ttep_ep15

139.   https://www.imdb.com/title/tt0624767/?ref_=ttep_ep16

140.   https://www.imdb.com/title/tt0624814/?ref_=ttep_ep17

141.   https://www.imdb.com/title/tt0624746/?ref_=ttep_ep18

142.   https://www.imdb.com/title/tt0624776/?ref_=ttep_ep19

2/19/1963

Laramie Episode - The Dispossessed[143]

Slim and Jess see a damaged wagon and try to help but people are very unfriendly. At their destination, ranchers think family is Comancheros and search for them.

2/26/1963

Laramie Episode - The Renegade Brand[144]

Slim, Daisy and Mike find Jess and stage line officer shot. Slim goes after robbers and kills one who is son of wealthy ranch owner. Everyone initially denies the son could have been involved.

3/1963

Bravo German Magazine No. 11. He is on the cover.

Movie Life Magazine. He is not on cover. Article is titled Bob Fuller - My 9 Hours in Jail.

3/5/1963

Laramie Episode - The Violent Ones[145]

Son angry that Jess shot his outlaw father five years earlier, tries to get him to draw. Jess refuses to accept challenge many times but when revengeful son hurts Slim, Jess takes action.

3/12/1963

Laramie Episode - The Unvanquished[146]

Ranch hand is murdered and Indians may be involved. Murdered man's brothers seek revenge.

3/19/1963

Laramie Episode - The Sometime Gambler[147]

Jess and Slim are in charge of wounded former outlaw who was forced to be part of a bank robbery. The gang thinks he took money and Slim helps him see his daughter before he dies.

4/2/1963

Laramie Episode - Edge of Evil[148]

143.   https://www.imdb.com/title/tt0624772/?ref_=ttep_ep20

144.   https://www.imdb.com/title/tt0624798/?ref_=ttep_ep21

145.   https://www.imdb.com/title/tt0624813/?ref_=ttep_ep22

146.   https://www.imdb.com/title/tt0624812/?ref_=ttep_ep23

147.   https://www.imdb.com/title/tt0624804/?ref_=ttep_ep24

Jess visits a couple he knows. They find mule with gold on a burro and the husband wants to keep money. Jess survives being driven off. He rejoins the couple and others and must determine who real gold owner is.

4/13 - 4/19/1963

Chicago, Illinois TV Guide ad for Laramie on from 7:30 to 8:30 p.m. has photo of Slim and Jess.

4/9/1963

Laramie Episode - Broken Honor[149]

Jess warms sheriff and stage line of a bribery attempt for him not to ride shotgun. Stage line doesn't trust Jess and forbids him to travel with stagecoach but Jess secretly rides along anyhow to ruin robbery plans. *See it in English with subtitles. Laramie / Série clássica de Tv at https://www.youtube.com/watch?v=R2PrrxUP5fU&list=PLSjObr0dIeIimmFm8eGXaaK_PAisBth9J .*

4/13/1963

Local Philadelphia, Pennsylvania TV Guide. Richard Egan (7/29/1921-7/20/1987) is on cover.

4/16/1963

Laramie Episode - The Last Battleground[150]

Jess finds old wagon wheel and Slim goes with Army to find real story of Civil War missing money that involves Slim's father.

4/23/1963

Laramie Episode - The Stranger[151]

A mountain climbing outlaw is hiding nearby. He is taking Sherman beef but paying for it and saves Mike's life. Mike and Jess are convinced he is not dangerous and Jess is injured climbing the mountains to help him.

4/30/1963

Laramie Episode - The Marshals[152]

Jess warns a Marshal in charge of a tumbleweed wagon carrying criminal. When Jess is shot the only doctor is where the rest of the gang hangs out.

---

148.   https://www.imdb.com/title/tt0624726/?ref_=ttep_ep25

149.   https://www.imdb.com/title/tt0624712/?ref_=ttep_ep26

150.   https://www.imdb.com/title/tt0624782/?ref_=ttep_ep27

151.   https://www.imdb.com/title/tt0624806/?ref_=ttep_ep28

152.   https://www.imdb.com/title/tt0624792/?ref_=ttep_ep29

5/1963

Movieland and TV Time Magazine. He is not on cover.

5/7/1963

Laramie Episode - Badge of Glory[153]

Former bounty hunter and now preacher accepts money to build a church from dying outlaw he knows. Other gang members want money endangering preacher and town.

5/14/1963

Laramie Episode - Trapped[154]

Slim finds injured girl who had escaped kidnappers. When Slim is found with her, her father thinks he is involved.

5/21/1963

Laramie Episode - The Road to Helena[155]

A woman saves Slim from robbery and asks him to help her and her father to a town to return stolen money. Others want the money.

6/20 OR 6/21/1963

Robert and Patty attend a movie premier in California. This may be first time public found out they were married in December. *(Could this have been for Cleopatra held at the Pantages Theater at 6233 Hollywood Boulevard?).*

This photo was with magazine article that says that couple kept marriage a secret and had a December 1962 wedding in Las Vegas, Nevada.

6/24/1963

Local TV Guide.

153.   https://www.imdb.com/title/tt0624707/?ref_=ttep_ep30

154.   https://www.imdb.com/title/tt0624819/?ref_=ttep_ep31

155.   https://www.imdb.com/title/tt0624800/?ref_=ttep_ep32

WAGON TRAIN YEARS 1963 - 1965

1963 - 1965

In 1957 the series syndication title was Major Adams, Trail Master. Better known as Wagon Train it was broadcast by NBC for the first five years. Marketing included a Flint McCullough and Seth Adams Holster Sets, Official Wagon Train Play Set made by Marx (original and facsimile made). Playset Magazine #42 promoted these Marx Playsets. (In 4/1994 Plastic Figure & Playset Collector's Magazine #30 had info about this Marx playset). Sears sells the Official Wagon Train On-the-Trail set which includes wagon with tailgate that opens and closes, two horses on wheels (so it can be pulled), driver, lanterns, whip and 10 inch high figure of Seth Adams with guns, hat and rope and a horse. In 1958 Toys & Games in London, England has a Wagon Train Board Game and in 1960 Milton Bradley also has a Wagon Train board game. A Wagon Train Little Golden Book is also made. The last three years Wagon Train is shown on ABC.

Later VHS tape releases can be confusing since here they combined an early episode with a later day cast cover.

In Spain, Wagon Train is 'Caravan" and here again a DVD set from Part One Season 1 with 19 episodes, has wrong cast on cover. Cover includes John, Andy and Coop.

Robert Horton (7/29/1924-3/9/2016) who played original scout in seasons one through five. Duke Shannon played by Scott / Denny Miller (4/25/1944-9/9/2014) joined the cast as a scout in 1961 for seasons five through seven. Robert's contract with the studio ended but due to his popularity in Laramie in U.S. and oversees, the studio offered him a new seven year contract. Robert moved right from Laramie to Wagon Train in its seventh season playing scout Cooper Smith. He met William Smith 93/24/1933-7/5/2021) here. Some filming took place in California's San Fernando Valley.

Robert, again uses his own horse.

The show aired on Monday evening (later time slot than Laramie had) and had four programs to compete with. They are The Lucy Show, Danny Thomas Show, The Andy Griffith Show and Hollywood and the Stars.

They made 32 episodes each season or 5 days of shooting for each show. *(By 2016 one hour shows took eight to nine days).* Wagons used were exact replicas of originals and that meant no padded seats. They worked 11 months a year and often the other month was publicity. The cast might travel to five different cities and really only have ten days off each year.

Virgil W. Vogel (11/29/1919-1/1/1996) directed 80 episodes of Wagon Train from 1958 to 1965. *Virgil started out as an assistant editor in 1940 and directed for the first time in 1956. Other westerns Virgil directed include Big Valley, Bonanza and the Centennial mini series. Over almost sixty years he directed in at least 13 different television series.*

One director on seven episodes, William Witney (5/15/1915-3/17/2002), who Robert had problems with in Laramie, also directed some Wagon Train episodes. Since Robert still enjoyed and missed stunt work he snuck on the set dressed as an Indian. But when William found out about it, he came up and shouted at a real Indian, not Robert. Robert corrected William and later that evening both Robert and William had a fistfight at the motel.

All seasons were black and white and one hour long except for the seventh which was extended to one and one half hour and made in color. The last season returned to one hour and black and white format. Like Robert's series Laramie pressure from the P.TA. and the government meant less shooting action scenes in Wagon Train too.

Wagon Train was in local television ads and TV Guides.

The series probably had Promo Photos and NBC Fact Sheet and press releases.

To see opening and closing Wagon Train themes *see*

Wagon Train 1957 - 1965 Opening and Closing Theme – YouTube at [1]*https://www.youtube.com/watch?v=BESu7Ly18uY* [2].

Cast included:

John McIntire as Christopher Hale (6/27/1907-1/30/1991). He had joined cast in 1961 after Ward Bond dies and two years before Robert. John and his wife actress Jeannette Nolan lived on a ranch in Montana and John flew in for filming. John was born in Washington State and grew up on a Montana ranch where his father was an Indian Affairs Commissioner. At 16 John won a bronco competition. By high school John was living in California. While working in radio in 1935 he met Jeanette Nolan who he was married to for 56 years. At age 40 John went into movies and until he retired in 1989, he was in over 100 films. After Laramie John worked on Virginian and he and his wife also voiced Disney movie characters. John died from emphysema and lung cancer at 83 years.

Frank McGrath as Charlie Wooster (2/2/1903-5/13/1967). Frank was born in Missouri. Between1932 and 1968 he appeared in almost 50 roles including Tammy and Don Knotts movies. Frank and Terry Wilson did rodeos together. Even at age 53 he was still doing stunt work. Frank died of a heart attack at age 64.

1.   *https://www.youtube.com/watch?v=BESu7Ly18uY*

2.   *https://www.youtube.com/watch?v=BESu7Ly18uY*

Terry Wilson as Bill Hawks (9/3/1923-3//30/1999). Terry was born in California and did stunt work first and doubled for John Wayne (5/26/1907-6/11/1979), Ward Bond (4/9/1903-11/5/1960) and Forrest Tucker (2/12/1919-10/25/1986). Terry remained good friends with John Wayne working with him in several films over the years. From 1942 to 1981 Terry had over 35 roles. Terry and Frank McGrath did rodeos together. He died at age 75.

Denny / Scott Miller as Duke Shannon (4/25/1944-9/9/2014). He was born in Indiana. He played basketball and was in Los Angles on a college scholarship. He made a Tarzan movie. The studio changed his name and he appeared in over two hundred roles from 1959 to 1981. After Wagon Train Scott also appeared in Groton's commercial playing a fisherman. Scott retired in 1996 and wrote an autobiography. In 2014 Scott was diagnosised with ALS (Amyotrophic Lateral sclerosis) and died later that year at age 80.

Michael Burns (12/30/1947-) as Barnaby West. Michael was an actor from 1960-1973 before becoming a history professor in 1980. He is author of three books and retired in 2002.

Robert had the same dressing room he had during Laramie. The dressing room section was nicknamed Whiskey Row. Other stars in this area were Frank McGrath, Terry Wilson and Lee Marvin (2/19/1924-8/29/1987).

Some guest stars appeared in more than one episode. Some are listed here:
    Alfred Ryder (1/5/1916-4/16/1995)
    Andrew Prine (2/14/1936-)
    Ann Blyth (8/16/1928-)
    Anne Bancroft (9/17/1931-6/6/2005)
    Anne Helm (9/2/1938-)
    Annette Funicello (10/22/1942-4/8/2013) www.annetteconnection.com[3]
    Arthur O'Connell (3/29/1908-5/18/1981)
    Arthur Space (10/12/1908-1/13/1983)
    Audrey Dalton (1/21/1934-)
    Barbara Bain (9/13/1931-)

Barbara Stanwyck (7/16/1907-1/20/1990). She had several appearances and her nickname is Missy. John McTire introduced Robert to her after he joined the cast.

Barry Atwater (5/16/1918-5/24/1978)
    Bethel Leslie (8/3/1929-11/28/1999)

Betsy Hale (4/18/1922-1/26/2017)

Beverly Owen (5/13/1937-2/21/2019)

Beverly Washburn (11/25/1943-)

Bobby Darin (5/14/1936-12/20/1973) www.bobbydarin.net[4]

Bobby Diamond (8/23/1943-5/15/2019)

Bradford Dillman (4/14/1930-1/16/2018)

Brian Keith (11/4/1921-6/24/1997)

Brooke Bundy (8/8/1944-)

Burgress Meredith (11/16/1907-9/9/1997)

Caesar Romero (2/15/1907-1/1/1994)

Carol Lawrence (9/5/1932-)

Carolyn Jones (4/28/1930-8/3/1983)

Cathy Lewis (12/27/1916-11/20/1968)

Charla Doherty (8/6/1946-5/29/1988)

Charles Drake (10/2/1917-9/10/1994)

Charles Ruggles (2/8/1886-12/23/1970)

Cheryl Holdridge (6/20/1944-1/6/2009)

Chris Robinson (11/5/1938-)

Clu Gulager. (11/16/1928-) www.clugulagher.com[5]

Cynthia Pepper (9/4/1940-)

Dabbs Greer (4/2/1917-4/28/2007)

Dan Duryea (1/23/1907-6/7/1968)

Dana Wynter (6/8/1931-5/5/2011)

Debra Walley (8/12/1941-5/10/2001)

Diana Hyland (1/25/1936-3/27/1977)

Diane Baker (2/25/1938-)

Diane Brewster (3/11/1941-11/12/1991)

Dick Sergeant (4/19/1930-7/8/1994)

Dick York (9/4/1928-2/20/1992)

Don Collier (10/17/1928-)

Don Galloway (7/27/1937-1/8/2009)

Dwayne Hickman (5/18/1934-) www.dwaynehickman.com[6]

Ed Begley, Sr. (3/25/1901-4/28/1970)

Eddie Little Sky (8/15/1926-9/5/1997)

Ernest Borgnine (1/24/1917-7/8/2012)

Fabian Forte (2/6/1943-) www.fabianforte.net[7]

Frances Reid (12/9/1914-2/3/2010)

Frank deKova (3/17/1910-10/15/1981)

George Keymas (11/18/1925-1/17/2008)

Guy Stockwell (11/16/1933-2/6/2002)

---

4.   http://www.bobbydarin.net

5.   http://www.clugulagher.com

6.   http://www.dwaynehickman.com

7.   http://www.fabianforte.net

Hari Rhodes (4/10/1932-1/15/1992)

Hugh Beaumont (2/16/1909-5/14/1982)

Jack Bighead (4/23/1930-4/28/1993)

Jack Kelly (9/16/1927-11/7/1992)

Jack Lord (12/30/1920-1/21/1998)

Jack Warden (9/18/1920-7/19/2006)

Jay North (8/3/1951-)

Jeanne Cooper (10/25/1928-5/8/2013)

Jeanette Nolan(12/30/1911-6/5/1998)

Jena Engstrom (6/30/1942-)

Jennifer Billingsley (5/14/1942-)

Jim Davis (8/26/1909-4/26/1981) www.ultimatedallas.com[8]

Joan Blondell (8/30/1906-12/25/1979)

Joanna Moore (11/10/1934-11/22/1997)

Joe DeSanis (9/24/1957-2/14/1936)

Joel McCrea (11/5/1905-10/20/1990)

John Archer (5/8/1915-12/3/1999)

John Doucette (1/21/1921-8/16/1994)

John Hoyt (10/8/1905-9/15/1991)

John War Eagle (6/8/1901-2/7/1991)

Joseph Wiseman (5/15/1918-10/19/2009)

Joyce Bulifant (12/16/1937-) www.joycebulifant.com[9]

Karl Swenson (7/23/1908-10/8/1978)

Katharine Ross (1/29/1940-)

Kathleen Freeman (2/17/1919-8/23/2001)

Kathy Browne (9/19/1930-4/8/2003) www.darrenmcgavin.net[10]

Ken Lynch (7/15/1910-2/13/1990)

Kevin Cochran (6/10/1949-10/6/2015)

Kim Darby (7/8/1947-)

Larry Pennell (2/21/1928-8/28/2013)

Leif Erickson (10/27/1911-1/29/1986)

Leslie Neilsen (2/11/1926-11/28/2010)

Linda Evans (11/18/1942-)

Lisa Eilbacher (5/5/1956-)

Lola Albright (7/20/1924-3/23/2017)

Loraine Day (10/18/1920-11/10/2007)

Marilyn Maxwell (8/3/1921-3/20/1972)

Marjorie Maine (2/24/1890-4/10/1975)

Marta Kristen (2/28/1945-) www.martakristen.com[11]

Michael Parks (4/24/1940-5/9/2017)

---

8.   http://www.ultimatedallas.com

9.   http://www.joycebulifant.com

10.   http://www.darrenmcgavin.net

11.   http://www.martakristen.com

Michael Rennie (8/25/1909-6/10/1971)

Morgan Woodward (9/16/1925-2/22/2019) www.morganwoodward.com[12]

Myrna Fahey (3/12/1933-5/6/1973)

Naomi Stevens (11/26/1926-1/13/2018)

Neville Brand (8/13/1920-4/16/1992)

Noah Beery, Jr. (8/10/1913-11/1/1994)

Patricia Lyon. Robert's wife appeared in one episode in 1963 and another in 1964.

Paul Fix (3/13/1901-10/14/1983)

Peter Brown (10/5/1935-3/21/2016) www.peterbrown.tv[13]

Peter Falk (9/16/1927-6/23/2011)

Pippa Scott (11/10/1935-)

Randy Boone (1/17/1942-)

Ray Danton (9/19/1931-2/11/1992)

Reta Shaw (9/13/1912-1/8/1982)

Rhonda Fleming (8/10/1923-10/14/2020). *One scene was reshot and Robert talks about it several times including www.youtube.co,/watch?v=nkzuTZz720 and Rhonda Fleming Story or The Rhonda Fleming Story and* We're Here With Favorite Moments My Life in TV-1. Other guests include Charlene Tilton 12/1/1958-). Robert tells the Rhonda Fleming Story - *See https://www.youtube.com/watch?v=yNAJK_sGiQA . (Rhonda is a third generation performer, singer and actress. Rhoda was in almost 50 roles from 1943 to 1990. Starting in 1957 Rhoda also performed in Las Vegas, Nevada. She works for charities and took an active part (with other celebrities) to try to keep school prayer giving it first amendment rights in the early 1960's. See www.rhondafleming.com[14]) .*

Richard Carlson (4/29/1912-11/25/1977)

Richard Long (12/17/1927-12/21/1974)

Robert Emhardt (7/24/1914-12/26/1994)

Robert Hogan (9/28/1933-)

Robert Ryan (11/11/1909-7/11/1973)

Ron Hayes (2/25/1929-10/1/2004)

Ronald Reagan (2/6/1911-6/5/2004)

Rory Calhoun (8/8/1922-4/28/1999)

Ross Martin (3/22/1920-7/3/1981)

Ryan O'Neal (4/20/1941-) www.ryanoneal.com[15]

---

12.   http://www.morganwoodward.com

13.   http://www.peterbrown.tv

14. *http://www.rhondafleming.com*

15.   http://www.ryanoneal.com

Sharon Farrell (12/24/1940-) www.sharonfarrell.com[16]
Sherry Jackson (2/14/1942-)
Susan Seaforth Hayes (7/11/1943-)
Suzanne Pleashette (1/31/1937-1/19/2008)
Tom Ewell (4/29/1909-9/12/1994)
Tom Skerritt (8/25/1933-)
Tommy Sands (8/27/1937-)
Vera Miles (8/23/1929-)
Virginia Christine (3/5/1920-7/24/1996)
Virginia Gregg (3/6/1916-9/15/1986)

Robert broke his leg and ankle in three places while redoing a stunt to make it better. It was the last scene of the day and he fell on the only non-breakaway chair during a fight scene. A stand-in had to cut off his boot.

During this time Robert appeared in a dive suit with Doug McClure (5/11/1935-2/5/1995). Other guests include Don Rickles (5/8/1926-4/6/2017) Hugh Hefner (4/9/1926-9/27/2017). *See Robert Fuller After Dark. www.youtube.com/waqtch?v=Kw6E6Ro-ZO4*[17].

Local TV ads are created. One in Chicago, Illinois for ABC, Channel 32 includes photo the cast of five.

Newspaper articles like one from Milwaukee, Wisconsin contained inaccurate information confusing fans. It states his name was Robert Cole, Jr. As kids many of us believed anything we read in newspapers and fan magazines had to be true.

VHS tapes and DVD's are later created.

Studio marketing includes:
    Dell Comic Books.

Gold Key Comic Books. There were several Wagon Train editions. Comics cost 12 or 13 cents.

At least two versions of Wagon Train fan cards are created.

---

16.   http://www.sharonfarrell.com

17. *http://www.youtube.com/waqtch?v=Kw6E6Ro-ZO4*

Cooper Smith 8 inch tall action figure is created. Western Heroes box cover has good photo of Coop.

Publicity photos are created with five cast members.

Trading cards are being made. One is of John Intire and Robert in Wagon Train.

Magazine articles include article titled Back at the Ranch.

Wagon Train article titled Wagon Train Too Much Temperament?

Publicity occurs via fan magazines, photos, etc. around the world including in England, Germany and Japan.

Some German publicity photos include action shots of John and Robert.

Japanese Cards were created. One is with both John Smith and Robert.

Canal Tv Spanish magazine includes signed 9 x 11 inch poster of John and Robert- Caravana (Wagon Train). The stamped dedication reads "Best hopes to Canal Tv" John Mc Intire - Robert Fuller. It was signed and the reverse side has a biography of John Mc Intire and history of the series.

Spanish TV Cards were made. Card #127 is 2 inches x 2 ½ inches. The back of the card is numbered with his name and the name of the set - Artistas De La T.V. in Spanish.

8/5/1963
German Bravo Magazine No. 31. He is not on cover. Popular two hands on pistol shot is shown.

8/22 - 8/28/1963
Mexican TV Guide. Cover shows Robert in front of a sailing shop model.

9/1963

Guns Magazine. Article is titled Fast Draw Grows Up!

9/16/1963

Wagon Train Episode - The Molly Kincaid Story is from Season 7 and is about two freed white Comanche captives trying to adapt. This season is in color. See Wagon Train Season 7 Episode 1 The Molly Kincaid Story HD 1080p at https://www.youtube.com/watch?v=2s7u2a-tTpA .

9/23/1963

Wagon Train Episode - The Fort Pierce Story is about the fort refusing to give the wagon train an escort. *See Wagon Train Sea 07 Epis 02 The Fort Pierce Story at https://www.youtube.com/watch?v=JrOvtTGLlGg* .

9/30/1963

Wagon Train Episode - The Gus Morgan Story is about Chris Hale guiding railroad man and his son into mountains to scout out a route. *See Wagon Train Season 7 Episode 3 The Gus Morgan Story at https://www.youtube.com/watch?v=uiMmEn94k9Q* .

10/1963

Bravo German Magazine No. 40 in Germany. He is not on cover.

10/5/1963

TV Guide - *See www.tvguidemagazine.com*[18] . *Phil Silvers (5/11/1911-11/1/1985) is on cover.* Robert's duo role airing on Wagon Train on 10/7 is topic.

10/7/1963

Wagon Train Episode - The Widow O'Rourke Story. Robert plays a duo role of Cooper Smith and Captain Terrence O'Rourke using his first accent. His O'Rourke character is via a flashback. *See Wagon Train Sea 07 Epis 04 The Widow O'Rourke Story at https://www.youtube.com/watch?v=hb1Tii3JRzI* .

10/11/1963

Bravo German Magazine No. 42 in Germany. He is not on cover.

10/14/1963

Wagon Train Episode - The Robert Harrison Clarke Story is about Cooper Smith and Chris Hale along with a British journalist party and others dealing with Indian attacks. *See Wagon Train Season 7 Episode 5 The Robert Harrison Clarke Story at https://www.youtube.com/watch?v=B_hy-FCdGqg* .

10/21/1963

Wagon Train Episode - The Myra Marshall Story is about Cooper Smith taking a woman to visit her sister and brother-in-law in a rough town. *See Wagon Train s07e06 The Myra Marshall Story 21 Oct. 1963 at https://www.youtube.com/watch?v=jUA2H5s8ee8* .

10/28/1963

Wagon Train Episode - The Sam Spicer Story is about Barnaby West being taken hostage. *See Wagon Train s07e07 The Sam Spicer Story 28 Oct. 1963 at https://www.youtube.com/watch?v=0OPoVMeG2-U or* Wagon Train Season 7 Episode 7 The Sam Spicer Story at https://www.youtube.com/watch?v=5aXA75uu1J4 .

11/4/1963

Wagon Train Episode - The Sam Pulaski Story is about Cooper Smith re-meeting unsavory characters (via flashback in Brooklyn, New York) in the present on wagon train. *See Wagon Train s07e08 The Sam Pulaski Story 4 Nov. 1963 at https://www.youtube.com/watch?v=pR8CK9by6NU or Wagon Train Season 7 Episode 8 The Sam Pulaski Story at https://www.youtube.com/watch?v=8cWZrR_B1zU* .

11/11/1963

Robert's daughter, Christine Ann is born.

Wagon Train Episode – The Eli Bancroft Story is about Cooper Smith and other wagon train members being attacked and left stranded by a revenging family. Robert's wife Patricia Lyon guest stars as Rose Mason on this episode. *See Wagon Train Sea 07 Epis 09 The Eli Bancroft Story at https://www.youtube.com/watch?v=ICLjRiaBNyQ* .

Bravo German Magazine No. 46. He is not on cover. This article also appears in No. 50 and No. 52.

11/18/1963

Wagon Train Episode - The Kitty Pryor Story is about a woman joining the wagon train pretending to be married to someone else until man she loves gets a divorce. *See Wagon Train s07e10 The Kitty Pryer Story 18 Nov. 1963 at https://www.youtube.com/watch?v=VKpqJoUUhmw* .

11/25/1963

Bravo No. 48 German Magazine. He is on the back cover holding a rifle.

12/2/1963

Wagon Train Episode - The Sandra Cummings Story is about Cooper Smith meeting a Union woman responsible for his brother's execution and seeking revenge. *See Wagon Train s07e11 The Sandra Cummings Story 2 Dec. 1963 at https://www.youtube.com/watch?v=Tw_lqztiLiY or* Wagon Train Season 7 Episode 11 The Sandra Cummings Story at https://www.youtube.com/watch?v=XEJr0I5_a-0 .

12/7-12/13/1963

TV Guide. He is on cover with John McIntire (6/27/1907-1/30/1991). Article is titled The Gentle Brawler and photo and tells about being in jail after stuntman needled him, newspaper misquotes saying it occurs in bar vs. coffee shop. *See www.tvguidemagazine.com/archive/suboffer/1960's*[19] .

12/9/1963

Wagon Train Episode - The Bleeker Story is about a family gang joining the wagon train to hide their weapons and eventually rob a fort of gold. *See Wagon Train Sea 07 Epis 12 The Bleecker Story at https://www.youtube.com/watch?v=Mc-hl1CX3Bk .*

12/12/1963

Bravo German Magazine No. 50. He is not on cover. *See 11/11/1963 Bravo issue No. 46.*

12/16/1963

Wagon Train Episode - The Story of Cain is about Cooper Smith finding a man near death in the desert who found gold. Afterward both recover, Cooper Smith becomes blind. *See Wagon Train Sea 07 Epis 13 The Story Of Cain at https://www.youtube.com/watch?v=UXBorQv0rJs or See Wagon Train Season 7 Episode 13 The Story Of Cain at https://www.youtube.com/watch?v=5RKyWW7F-E4 or See Wagon Train – The Story of Cain P1 at*
https://www.youtube.com/watch?v=jeU4A1-YsMg&list=PL2YYPNORBEDbIszOzoPrJwc7u1Qi1TRN4 and P2 at https://www.youtube.com/watch?v=bdZiRj-2owY and P3 at https://www.youtube.com/watch?v=eNC4XbE7fF4&list=PL2YYPNORBEDbIszOzoPrJwc7u1Qi1TRN4&index=9 and P4 at https://www.youtube.com/watch?v=q0vm1NHt9kY&list=PL2YYPNORBEDbIszOzoPrJwc7u1Qi1TRN4&index=6 and P5 at https://www.youtube.com/watch?v=Et9OqrJedRc&list=PL2YYPNORBEDbIszOzoPrJwc7u1Qi1TRN4&index=12 and P6 https://www.youtube.com/watch?v=8gI3_buSNCQ and P7 at https://www.youtube.com/watch?v=qTKbO-hBrFc&list=PL2YYPNORBEDbIszOzoPrJwc7u1Qi1TRN4&index=4 .

12/23/1963

---

19.   *http://www.tvguidemagazine.com/archive/suboffer/1960's*

Wagon Train Episode - The Cassie Vance Story is about a woman falsely accused of robbery after her criminal past is revealed. *See Wagon Train Sea 07 Epis 14 The Cassie Vance Story at https://www.youtube.com/watch?v=TvokAxTtrz0 .*

12/29/1963 - 1/4/1964

Bravo German Magazine No. 52. He is not on cover. *See 11/11/1963 Bravo issue No. 46.*

12/30/1963

Wagon Train Episode - The Fenton Canaby Story is about a scout of an earlier wagon train who was unable to find water to save the people in his care. He is forced to try to help Chris Hale's wagon train survive. *See Wagon Train s07e15 The Fenton Canaby Story 30 Dec. 1963 at https://www.youtube.com/watch?v=rUAp4P0MAp0 .*

1964 - 1965

Unnumbered Danish gum card about 1 ¾ x 2 ¾ is released. (Another source has 1965 - 1967). Photo is pistol drawn action shot.

Who's Who in Movies Magazine - photo with John McIntire (6/27/1907-1/30/1991). Magazine sells for 35 cents.

Who's Who in Television #4 Magazine. Westerns (Wagon Train) sells for 35 cents. Typical format in this and many magazines is for a photo, name, height, color of eyes and hair and when they first started in movie / TV business.

1964

Destry promo trailer as his Wagon Train character, Cooper Smith. He appears with John Gavin (4/8/1941-2/9/2018).

Bravo Otto Award Gold for best male TV actor in Germany. It's like U.S.'s Emmy Award. Publicity photos are released including one showing John McIntire his award.

Wagon Train lunch box and thermos by King-Seeley Thermos are being sold.

Some articles Robert was in include:

TV Radio Annual Magazine. He is not on cover. It is 96 pages and sells for 50 cents.

TV Radio Mirror Magazine. What's New? - With John Smith (3/6/1931-1/25/1995) and his fiancé Luana Patten (7/6/1938-5/1/1996), Burt Reynolds (2/11/1936-9/6/2018). *Robert had previously met Burt Reynolds on a hayride magazine photo shoot. Another evening at Johnny Mathis' home for a photo shoot Burt and Robert seeing Fabian (3/6/1943-) surrounded by girls pretend to kidnap him. Fabian thought it was real until they explain.*

TV Star Annual #17 Magazine. Robert and Patty's lovesick photo includes their son Robert John. Magazine sells for 35cents.

Western Television & Film Annual magazine in the United Kingdom. He is on cover.

Who's Who in the Movies #35 Magazine. He is under Western Stars and bio has his name as Robert Simpson, Jr. Magazine sells for 35 cents.

Who's Who in Television - 1964-1965 #14 Magazine. He is in Westerns - Wagon Train and photo also includes John McIntire (6/27/1907-1/30/1991). Magazine sells for 35 cents. Article states Patty is 21 and that they kept their marriage a secret for 3 years.

1/1964

Gold Key #1 Wagon Train comic book issued. One story is titled Miracle at Devil's Gorge. Cover shows John, Michael and Robert on wagon side. Inside photo is Michael shooting a rifle and Robert his pistol.

1/6/1964

Wagon Train Episode - The Michael Malone Story is about a former minister hiding his past and a young girl falling in love with him. *See Wagon Train Season 7 Episode 16 The Michael Malone Story at https://www.youtube.com/watch?v=k6TJmOXDVZ4 .*

1/13/1964

Wagon Train Episode - The Jed Whitmore Story is about a former outlaw becoming a sheriff and his brothers, now out of jail, searching for him. *See Wagon Train Sea 07 Epis 17 The Jed Whitmore Story at https://www.youtube.com/watch?v=xBlVRX0H8fA .*

1/20/1964

Wagon Train Episode - Wagon Train Episode - The Geneva Balfour Story is about a woman passenger destroying supplies they are desperate for and her husband taking the blame. Archie Moore (12/13/1916-2/9/1998), a real life light weight boxing champion, is one of the guest stars. *See Wagon Train Season 7 Episode 18 The Geneva Balfour Story at https://www.youtube.com/watch?v=AozjHv1Qgcg* . A photo of Robert and Archie practicing twirling a pistol is created.

1/27/1964

Wagon Train Episode - The Kate Crawley Story is about Chris Hale's romance with a freight line operator. See Wagon Train Season 7 Episode 19 The Kate Crawley Story at https://www.youtube.com/watch?v=bl1_Qm0L8PY . A publicity photo of Robert, Barbara and John is created.

2/3/1964

Wagon Train Episode - The Grover Allen Story is about a detective searching for a man who set a bomb killing his boss. *See Wagon Train Season 7 Episode 20 The Grover Allen Story at https://www.youtube.com/watch?v=DRbQIPMhfrc* .

2/10/1964

Wagon Train Episode - The Andrew Elliott Story is about Duke Shannon being arrested by the Army to explain and retrace the incident. See Wagon Train Season 7 Episode 21 The Andrew Elliott Story at https://www.youtube.com/watch?v=7UP8zNOtnYI ,

2/17/1964

Wagon Train Episode - The Melanie Craig Story is about a woman who becomes a widow on the wagon train and the men wanting to protect and court her. See Wagon Train Season 7 Episode 22 The Melanie Craig Story at https://www.youtube.com/watch?v=DWPdDOQdHcw .

2/24/1964

Wagon Train Episode - The Pearlie Garnet Story is about a woman thief thrown off the wagon train. *See Wagon Train Season 7 Episode 23 The Pearlie Garnet Story at https://www.youtube.com/watch?v=bsfOWr9spVs* .

3/2/1964

Wagon Train Episode - The Trace McCloud Story is about a strangler loose in a town the wagon train passes through. *See Wagon Train Season 7 Episode 24 The Trace McCloud Story at https://www.youtube.com/watch?v=chHXy4HmemM* .

3/7/1964

Bravo German Magazine No. 9. He is not on cover.

3/9/1964

Wagon Train Episode - The Duncan Melvor Story is about Duke Shannon and Bill Hawks being rescued by a man who turns out to be an Army officer who stole supplies. *See Wagon Train Season 7 Episode 25 The Duncan McIvor Story at https://www.youtube.com/watch?v=pWquc7rWorw or Wagon Train Season 7 Episode 25 The Duncan McIvor Story at https://www.youtube.com/watch?v=uwwYfE4eFTM* .

3/16/1964

Wagon Train Episode - The Ben Engel Story is about a former Civil War soldier who plots the murder of the man who paid him to substitute for him. *See Wagon Train Season 7 Episode 26 The Ben Engel Story at https://www.youtube.com/watch?v=JGGjQBhV770* .

3/23/1964

Wagon Train Episode - The Whipping is about Bill Hawks punishing Barnaby West and Barnaby breaking his leg.

3/30/1964

Wagon Train Episode - The Santiago Quesada Story is about a woman in love with an Indian who is murdered. *See Wagon Train Season 7 Episode 28 The Santiago Quesada Story at https://www.youtube.com/watch?v=jQZAwiK7amE* .

4/1964

Gold Key Wagon Train #2 comic book sells for 12 cents. The three photo cover includes wagon trains, Robert shooting pistol and Michael and John shooting their pistols.

4/6 - 4/12/1964

Bravo German Magazine No. 15. He is on cover.

4/6/1964

Wagon Train Episode - The Stark Bluff Story is about Duke Shannon visiting a town to find his male friend dead. His widow is working in a saloon where the owner is trying to force her to marry him. Duke is framed for killing a deputy. *See Wagon Train Season 7 Episode 29 The Stark Bluff Story at https://www.youtube.com/watch?v=vTYdbdDErDg* .

4/13/1964

Wagon Train Episode - The Link Cheney Story is about Cooper Smith trying to help a wounded professional gambler. A woman falls in love with the gambler but fears he can't stop gambling. *See Wagon Train Sea 07 Epis 30 The Link Cheney Story at https://www.youtube.com/watch?v=aeAeLmShQYE .*

4/20/1964

Wagon Train Episode - The Zebedee Titus Story is about an aging legendary mountain man with now poor eye sight joining the wagon train to help Cooper Smith and Duke Shannon scout. *See Wagon Train Season 7 Episode 31 The Zebedee Titus Story at https://www.youtube.com/watch?v=IcLuBW38VRA .*

4/21/1964

First son Robert John (Rob) is born. They are living in the San Fernando Valley in California. (In 1999 Robert John lives in Florida and may be a marksman like his dad. He may also have lived near James Garner (4/7/1928-7/14/2014) and been friends with Patrick Duffy 3/17/1949-).

4/27/1964

Wagon Train Episode - The Last Circle Up is about passengers splitting up at the end of the trail. *See Wagon Train Season 7 Episode 32 The Last Circle Up at https://www.youtube.com/watch?v=jk-kU-QpUNs&list=PLzbySc9FI5LephOkZXZBE-mJWQ0DmRLNk .*

5/7/1964

Bravo No. 27 German magazine. He is not on cover.

7/1964

Gold Key Wagon Train #3 is issued. Cover includes three action shoots and one of John.

7/19 - 7/25/1964

Wisconsin TV Guide sold at druggist stores. Cover shows popular publicity photo of John on horseback shaking Robert's hand.

8/15 - 8/21/1964

TV Guide. Cast of four (no Barney) is on cover.

FALL OF 1964

The Players Vol. 1, No. 1 Magazine. He is not on cover.

9/20/1964 SUNDAY

TV Guide ad and Wagon Train episode summary. Photo is John and Robert along with episode description and guest stars Robert Ryan, Vera Miles, Tommy Sands, Andrew Prime, Bill Smith. (See them all in earlier guest star list).

Wagon Train Episode - The Bob Stuart Story is Season 8 and about Cooper Smith escorting a man who had previously shot him in the back to the wagon train. *See Wagon Train Season 8 Episode 1 The Bob Stuart Story HD 1080p at https://www.youtube.com/watch?v=a8NiUls5agA* .

9/27/1964

Wagon Train Episode - The Hide Hunters is about Cooper Smith and Barnaby West joining buffalo hide hunters to find food for the wagon train passengers. *See wagon train s08e02 The Hide Hunters at https://www.youtube.com/watch?v=10q9kB_JtxU* .

10/1964

Golden Key Wagon Train Comic Book #4 is issued. He is not on cover.

10/4/1964

Wagon Train Episode - The John Gillman Story is about an orphan girl helping a wounded criminal. *See wagon train s08e03 The John Gilman Story at ttps://www.youtube.com/watch?v=Wt4Bca8Heto* .

10/11/1964

Wagon Train Episode - The Race Town Story is about Bill Hawks and Barnaby West in a tent city. Barnaby had followed a girl he likes there and Bill tries to keep Barnaby out of trouble. *See wagon train s08e04 The Race Town Story at https://www.youtube.com/watch?v=kxYKq3C0gXU* .

10/18/1964

Wagon Train Episode - The Barbara Lindquist Story is about Cooper Smith riding in on a stagecoach robbery. Later Cooper gets wounded and thinking he is dying gets serious about one of the female stagecoach passengers. *See wagon train s08e05 The Barbara Lindquist Story at https://www.youtube.com/watch?v=mspBtJqu-Kc* .

10/25/1964

Wagon Train Episode - The Brian Conlin Story is about a delirious and ill Irishman arriving into their camp. Once he is better Cooper Smith joins him to find the rest of the immigrants and their broken wagons. Robert's wife, Patricia Lyon, guest stars as Mary. *See wagon train s08e06 The Brian Conlin Story at https://www.youtube.com/watch?v=BLSLTLvuxWw* .

11/1964

Bravo German Magazine No. 46. He is not on cover.

11/1/1964

Wagon Train Episode - The Alice Whitetree Story is about Cooper Smith finding a half Indian girl alone in the wilderness and falls for her. The girl may have been captive for ten years and a sheriff says she has killed two people. *See wagon train s08e07 The Alice Whitetree Story at https://www.youtube.com/watch?v=qErROk0NRdI* .

11/8/1964

Wagon Train Episode - Those Who Stay Behind is about an former convict hunted by his former partner. Chris Hale can't take everyone on the next leg of the trip and is told he must stay behind. *See wagon train s08e08 Those Who Stay Behind at https://www.youtube.com/watch?v=WMglVsagXGg* .

11/22/1964

Wagon Train Episode - The Nancy Styles Story is about a woman claiming to be daughter of company that owns wagon train. Due to early snow Chris Hale tells her they are by-passing town she wants to go to. *See wagon train s08e09 The Nancy Styles Story at https://www.youtube.com/watch?v=e4xrqihT2rk* .

11/23 - 11/29/1964

Bravo German Magazine No. 48. He is on cover with photo on right side with drawing on left.

11/29/1964

Wagon Train Episode - The Richard Bloodgood Story is about a blind man joining the wagon train who turns out to be Cooper Smith's blood brother. He want to kill Coop. *See wagon train s08e10 The Richard Bloodgood Story at https://www.youtube.com/watch?v=WT7iRncVWGE* .

12/6/1964

Wagon Train Episode - The Clay Shelby Story is about troops telling Chris Hale and Cooper Smith a relief column will help them fight Comanches. *See wagon train s08e11 The Clay Shelby Story at https://www.youtube.com/watch?v=yXmXm8m4RS0* .

12/13/1964

Wagon Train Episode - Little Girl Lost is about Charlie Wooster and other passengers hearing a little girl crying. She may be a ghost from The Donner Party. *See wagon train s08e12 Little Girl Lost at https://www.youtube.com/ watch?v=4zrxlvYKkfI .*

12/20/1964

Wagon Train Episode - The Hector Heatherington Story is about Charlie Wooster and an inventor working on a flying machine. *See wagon train s08e13 The Story Of Hector Hearthington at https://www.youtube.com/ watch?v=5A9moOz9siw .*

1965

Bravo Otto Award Gold for best male TV actor in Germany. It's like U.S.'s Emmy Award.

Canal TV Guide in Uruguay. Cover has him holding a rifle.

Dutch Film / TV set of ten numbered bubble gun cards are created. Robert is a cowboy on the cover.

Television Age Magazine - TV & Pop - Special Features - The Spy Shows with David McCallum (9/19/1933-) cover - 2 pages of 76 including cover. This issue also includes a photo of John Smith and another with both Spring Byington and Dennis Holmes along with Robert alone and another with him on his horse.

Japan's magazine TV Pop #4. He is not on cover. Photos include action shots with cast and guest stars along with photos alone.

TV Star Parade Magazine. He is not on cover. It sells for 25 cents.

1/1965

While The War Lord movie is being filmed, on a cold and rainy night, Robert in make up and wearing a tunic like the rest of the cast brought liquor to warm up the extras. He got chosen to be the first guy to cross a bridge and get an arrow. As the scene progressed Robert got climbed over and then went into the moot. He guessed they knew who he was.

1/2/1965

Local TV Week Guide with Robert on cover.

1/3/1965

Wagon Train Episode - The Echo Pass Story is about Cooper Smith and Charlie Wooster looking for water and finding a gang of robbers and killers. Cooper is forced to guide them through a mountain pass. *See wagon train s08e14 The Echo Pass Story at https://www.youtube.com/watch?v=odnOYBCiGWA* .

1/10/1965

Wagon Train Episode - The Chottsie Gubenheimer Story is about Chris Hale finding an old girlfriend working in a saloon. *See Wagon Train Chottsie Gugenheimer Story at ttps://www.youtube.com/watch?v=ayE4T0mNqeU* .

1/17/1965

Wagon Train Episode - The Wanda Snow Story is about a woman who can see things before they happen and is called a witch. A traveling medicine show peddler hopes to use her talents. *See wagon train s08e16 The Wanda Snow Story at https://www.youtube.com/watch?v=8zYwkjzOaLE* .

1/31/1965

Wagon Train Episode - The Isaiah Quckfox Story is about Cooper Smith and Charley Wooster finding a deserted town expect for several people, one a woman, looking for her father in a cave filled with bats. *See wagon train s08e17 The Isaiah Quickfox Story at https://www.youtube.com/watch?v=jS-js2ia0x8* .

2/14/1965

Wagon Train Episode - Herman is the story of a 3,000 Belgian horse that is slowing down the wagon train. *See wagon train s08e18 Herman at https://www.youtube.com/watch?v=YNyfm_vPjzg* .

2/21/1965

Wagon Train Episode - The Bonnie Brooke Story is about a man with an ill pregnant wife seeking money from a bank for her medical care. See wagon train s08e19 The Bonnie Brooke Story at https://www.youtube.com/watch?v=GbN8xJMtGuo .

2/28/1965

Wagon Train Episode - The Miss Mary Lee McIntosh Story is about a school teacher who refuses to pay to join the train but instead follows behind. Once her wagon overturns she will need Chris Hale's help. *See wagon train s08e20 The Miss Mary Lee McIntosh Story at https://www.youtube.com/watch?v=SrhoVuIK_6U* .

3/13/1965

Bravo German Magazine. He is on cover.

3/21/1965

Wagon Train Episode - The Captain Sam Story is about a female ferryboat captain traveling to California so she can take a Pacific voyage. Her family has not told her she is ill and must seek a dry climate. See Wagon Train Sea 08 Epis 21 The Captain Sam Story at https://www.youtube.com/watch?v=wUrYYfvc3Kc .

3/28/1965

Wagon Train Episode - The Betsy Blee Smith Story is about Cooper Smith looking for a former girlfriend and instead finding her twin sister. He is asked to pretend to be her missing husband and father to her baby girl. *See Wagon Train - s08e22 The Betsy Blee Smith Story at https://www.youtube.com/watch?v=cEXtFNI_CcA .*

4/1965

TV Star Parade Magazine. Donna Reed (1/27/1921-1/14/1986) is on cover. It sells for 25 cents.

4/11/1965

Wagon Train Episode - The Katy Piper Story is about Barnaby West killing a boy his own age and dealing with guilt. *See Wagon Train - s08e23 The Katy Piper Story at https://www.youtube.com/watch?v=NpCT87bC_Iw .*

4/18/1965

Wagon Train Episode - The Indian Girl Story is about Bill Hawks capturing an Indian girl he knows is being mistreated and will be tortured and killed for killing a chief's son. *See Wagon Train Sea 08 Epis 24 The Indian Girl Story at https://www.youtube.com/watch?v=8XaCIoddBXw .*

4/22/1965

Kraft Suspense Theatre - The episode is titled Jungle of Fear. Robert plays Rory O'Rourke, an adventurer. It is a series pilot. Cast includes Robert Loggia (1/3/1930-12/4/2015) and Ann Blyth (8/16/1928-). See Robert Fuller Kraft Suspense Theatre Jungle of Fear at https://www.youtube.com/watch?v=qU2piIJu0eU .

4/25/1965

Wagon Train Episode - The Silver Lady is about Cooper Smith telling Bill Hawks a story about a woman in a coffin of silver coins. *See Wagon Train Sea 08 Epis 25 The Silver Lady at https://www.youtube.com/watch?v=93QWGwO_sAs .*

5/2/1965

Wagon Train Episode - The Jarbo Pierce Story is the series final episode as Charlie Wooster and Bill Hawks tell stories. *See Wagon Train Season 8 Episode 26 The Jarbo Pierce Story at https://www.youtube.com/watch?v=lKR1bL89hcw* .

6/1965

Spanish #387 Wagon Train comic book titled Aventura presenting La Caravana is created. Cover photo has everyone with guns drawn, John McIntire (6/27/1907-1/30/1991) and Scott Miller (4/25/1944-9/9/2014) are by a wagon where Michael Burns (12/30/1947-) is inside.

6/1/1965

Bravo German Magazine No. 23. He is on cover.

6/7/1965

Bravo German Magazine No. 24 of 1965. He is not on cover.

6/21/1965

Bravo German Magazine No. 25 of 1965. He is not on cover.

6/27/1965

Bravo German Magazine No. 26 of 1965. He is not on cover. Article photo has Robert with riffle and bird hunting dog.

10/1965

Bravo German Magazine No. 42. He is not on cover.

10/1965

Gold Key Wagon Train's Legend of the Million-Dollar Mountain comic book is issued and costs 12 cents. It contains the same photo as in the 6/1965 Spanish version. Using the same photo there are two different English text cover variations. One back cover contains the same photo as the front but with only the words Wagon Train near top left corner.

12/1965

Bravo German Magazine.

THE FREELANCE YEARS 1965 - 1972

1965 OR 1966

Robert turned down a role in The Rounders.

Wild World of Sports. Robert hunts pheasant or white tail deer in Texas.

1966

For a few years Robert made movies in Germany, Israel and the U.S.

Incident at Phantom Hill - He plays Matt Martin with Dan Duryea (1/23/1907-6/7/1968 who had been on Laramie several times). He is a soldier who recovers Civil War gold after war ends. The premier took place in Munich. Germany. Other cast include:

    Claude Akins (5/25/1926-1/27/1994)

    Denver Pyle (5/11/1926-12/25/1997)

    Jocelyn Lane (5/16/1937-)

    Noah Berry, Jr. (8/10/1913-11/1/1994)

    Paul Fix (3/13/1901-10/14/1983)

    Tom Simcox (6/17/1937-)

See Incident at Phantom Hill Western 1966 Robert Fuller, Jocelyn Lane & Dan Duryea at *https://www.youtube.com/watch?v=dAw09qx8tTM* or O Pistoleir Sem Alma - Dublado (movie in Portuguese) at *https://www.youtube.com/watch?v=Q0WafdBgHwc* or INCIDENTE EM PHANTOM HILL 1966 - Faroeste complete legendado com Robert Fuller (movie in English with Spanish subtitles) at *https://www.youtube.com/watch?v=iMIp5z6PPS4&list=PLG_3yhX9FRiVH5RNLFfgwRhBOPFHCI4ho* (it is in English). Also *See Incident at Phantom Hill Western 1966 Robert Fuller at www.youtube.com/watch?v=dAw09qx8tTM*[1] *and at https://video.search.yahoo.com/search/ video?fr=yfp-t&p=robert+fuller+interviews#id=14&vid=f7860f5a98ff085003a86b536ee4a797&action=view*[2] .

Showman's Manual Press Book for Incident at Phantom Hill is released in Europe. Cover has drawings.

---

1. *http://www.youtube.com/watch?v=dAw09qx8tTM*

2. *https://video.search.yahoo.com/search/ video?fr=yfp-t&p=robert+fuller+interviews#id_43ec3e5dee6e706af7766fffea512721_14_6cff047854f19ac2aa52aac51bf3af4a_vid_43ec3e5dee6e706af7766fffea5127 21_f7860f5a98ff085003a86b536ee4a797_6cff047854f19ac2aa52aac51bf3af4a_action_43ec3e5dee6e706af7766fffea512721_view*

Many variations using different photos from the movie were used as lobby cards and in magazines. Popular photos are a close up of Robert fighting someone with a knife, long shot of knife fight, Robert with Jocelyn near wagon, Robert in water with two dead and wagon scene.

A 11 x 14 lobby card of Jocelyn, Robert and Dan was also made into a poster.

A #3 poster is created focusing on an Indian water charging scene.

Another poster, 27 x 41, features Robert on the top right with two action drawings superimposed over mountains.

Danish Movie Poster included a photo of Jocelyn Lane and a drawing of Robert holding rifle along with movie title, Indians and other characters.

Danish Movie Program included action shots from the movie.

French publicity includes a 24 x 32 inch poster with photos of Robert, Jocelyn and the back of Denver Pyle, a three photo with Robert and Dan, one of Jocelyn and another a running wagon.

Another French poster is a drawing of two men fighting.

Mexican Lobby Card is created as a combination of many images with running water Indian scene in front.

Another Mexican Lobby card features top left drawing of Robert and Jocelyn on other half.

Several French DVD versions are released. One has both Robert and Dan on left side of cover. Another has Robert in front of wagon and mountain drawings and yet another is a photo of Robert, Dan and another man in a hotel room.

A German DVD and Blue Ray cover has Robert on left side and action horse shot below and to the right.

A United Kingdom DVD releases several different versions. One cover is two action shots drawings.

There may have been a European premiere in Munich, Germany.

Japanese publicity is created. There are photos of Robert and Jocelyn, the popular close up knife shot along with others.

More Japanese Magazines include Robert. One example has My 3 Sons cast on cover. There is a photo of John and Robert leaning on a wagon wheel.

Movie Friends No. 2 Japanese Magazine is issued. He is on left half of cover.

Lolita Magazine No. 27 (Spain publication). Article has photos (with lots of girls, one with girls and bikes). He is also on the back cover.

Return of Seven was written by Larry Cohen (7/15/1936-3/23/2019). Robert plays Vin and gets second billing after Yul Brynner (7/11/1920-10/10/1985). It was filmed in Alicante and Madrid, Spain for about 3 months. The start delayed until Robert finished the Europe promotion of Incident at Phantom Hill. Steve McQueen (3/24/1930-11/7/1980 www.stevemcqueen.com[3]) who had been in first film did not get along with Yul and Steve was not offered the sequel part. *Yul was living in Switzerland. Robert spoke about his meeting via Yul's dressing room mirror, answering Yul's questions honestly and later drinking Johnny Walker Black whiskey together many times. See Bob Fuller interview about meeting Yul Brynner at https://www.youtube.com/watch?v=0BEPmW1VbUs or Wild West Toys at www.youtube.com/watch?v=DBEPmW1VbUs[4] or at https://www.youtube.com/watch?v=0BEPmW1VbUs&list=PLA7C220117614C6E9 and Robert Fuller recalls "How I replaced Steve McQueen" in "Return of the Magnificent Seven" at https://www.youtube.com/watch?v=8oBc0Liakf0 .*

Yul and Robert got along well. Robert told a story about Yul being the scotch maker and how he, Yul and other cast / crew played poker. One Saturday it was down to Robert and Yul. Robert had 2 pairs and Yul said he had 3 kings. Yul's cards were 2 kings and he pointed to himself as the 3rd king. *Yul was one of Robert's favorite actors and they remained friends with Yul's death in 1985.*

Cast also includes:
    Claude Akins (5/25/192501/27/1994)
    Julian Mateos (1/15/1938-12/27/1996)
    Warren Oats (7/5/1928-4/3/1982)

---

3. http://www.stevemcqueen.com

4. *http://www.youtube.com/watch?v=DBEPmW1VbUs*

Fans can view the move at Return of the Seven 1966 FULL MOVIE HD] Action, Western - Yul Brynner, Robert Fuller, Julián Mateos at *https://www.youtube.com/watch?v=-NT66AXaM_4* .

Via http://www.western-locations-spain.com/r7/robert-fuller/seite.htm . Robert Fuller with his stunt double. Robert said he was a Spaniard, but he looks more like an American. Publicity photos with the two of them are created.

The stunt crew had a few injuries during the shooting of "Return of the Seven". One stuntman was seriously injured during a jump out the window (Colmenar de Oreja).

Publicity photos are of Robert by himself. Another is chest up and several are waist up with rifle.

Lobby cards were created. One is a seven person action shot with all holding weapons (two variations) while another is all seven on horseback. Yet another is the six of them fighting around a fountain. Other lobby card images are Robert and Yul; Robert and Yul watching dancers; Robert with Yul over boy's dead body; Robert, Mexican girl and another with Robert with a bottle in his hand with Mexican woman and man.

One 14 x 22 lobby window cards has the popular image is the seven men in a giant 7.

Other publicity and poster are Robert and Yul on horseback talking with priest and Mexican man and woman. One is a 30 x 40 inch poster has all seven standing men near the top.

Foreign countries publicity includes a Danish Movie Program, German lobby card has the five of them in front of church and another with Robert, one alive and one dead man. A German program brochure and posters are a close up of all seven men in a 7.

Japanese publicity is created. Magazine articles show action and posed photos. Some of the photos are used in more than one magazine. In 1967 a 10 x 14 poster is released.

Spanish = Regresso delessiuse Magniffris E - dubbed aka Regreso de los siete magnificos, El (Spain). Spain and Italian filmmakers tend to do more close up shots than in U.S.

Return of 7 Spanish Cinema card is created with four photos from the movie.

Return of 7 Spanish cards each featured two different movie scenes. At least six different cards were made.

United Kingdom 30 x 40 poster variation is printed In England by Stafford & Co Ltd, Nottingham and London. The poster art was done by Richard Amsel (1947 - 1985) who painted many film posters including The Life and Times of Judge Roy Bean, McCabe & Mrs. Miller and The Shootist. Photo is above knee shots of 7 male leads.

United Artist soundtrack album is made in 1966. The cover is close up photos of all in a 7. A Tsunami Album cover has a drawing on the lower half.

Movie release ad. Date given is 2/3. Many ads appear in newspapers and in magazines like Photoplay magazine. A popular visual is all seven men (above knees) across the top.

Chicago, Illinois newspaper ads feature all seven men full length near the top. . This image is also released as a poster. Another variation is the close up of men version in the 7.

The movie was released to television. One Los Angeles, California TV Guide ad with Robert and Yul is about 2 ½ x 3 ½ inches.

VHS tapes with Yul on cover are produced.

DVD's are released with Yul in front of the six men.

French DVD is released with all seven men standing with weapons.

Bravo Otto Award Gold for best male TV actor in Germany. It's like U.S.'s Emmy Award.

Robert campaigned for Ronald Regan when he was running for governor of California.

All Stars TV Parade Japanese Magazine.

Television Age Japanese Magazine. The cover says 10 Tops Super Pin-Ups and has John and Robert on right side. It is 84 pages including cover. Robert has several pages dedicated to him.

Japanese Magazine Visual Book No. 8. He is on the left lower side of the cover.

1/16 - 1/22/1966

Black River Falls, Wisconsin TV Guide given out by druggists has Laramie ad with Robert and John. Ben Gazzara (8/28/1930-2/3/2012) is on the cover. It contains photo of an early Laramie ad (seen elsewhere in this book) to advertise show being broadcast.

2/27 OR 3/27/1966

American Sportsman TV program.

3/5/1966

Bravo German Magazine. He is on the cover.

3/14 - 3/20/1966

Bravo German Magazine No. 11. He is on cover.

4/18 - 4/24/1966

Bravo German Magazine No. 16. He is not on cover.

5/2 - 5/8/1966

Bravo German Magazine No. 18. He is not on cover but includes a longer fold out of him standing with his pistol.

10/26/1966

Bob Hope Presents The Chrysler Theater - The episode is titled Massacre at Fort Phil Kearney. He plays a real person, Captain William Judd Fetterman. He and all his men are killed in an Indian attack. Others starring include:

Carroll O'Connor (8/2/1924-6/21/2001)

Phyllis Avery (11/14/1922-5/19/2011)

Richard Egan (7/29/1921-7/20/1987)

Robert Pine (7/10/1942-)

To view this MASSACRE AT FT PHIL KEARNEY 1 at https://www.youtube.com/watch?v=ZD0BSm2nlK4 , MASSACRE AT FT PHIL KEARNEY 02 at https://www.youtube.com/watch?v=CMAAnRK6-rs and MASSACRE AT FT PHIL KEARNEY (03) at https://www.youtube.com/watch?v=W0MtuEQB6zI .

10/26/1966

Chicago, Illinois TV guide ad appears with phone of Robert in uniform along with mini description. Program will be broadcast at 8 p.m. on Channel 4.

11/16/1966

The Monroes - The episode is titled Court Martial. He plays Captain Geoffrey Stone, a soldier helping an Indian names Jim. Cast included Michael Anderson, Jr. (8/6/1943-) and Barbara Hershey (2/5/1948-).

1967

Hollywood Squares - Living near the studio Robert often was a last minute fill in. *See www.youtube.com/ watch?v=QSFEOayvA4A*[5] . The program host was Peter Marshall (3/30/1926-) was host of Hollywood Squares which ran from 1966 to 1981. He was in the Army in Italy as a disc jockey during WWII. Peter has appeared in over fifty Broadway, movies and television programs. He has done plays in U.S. and England and hosted several other game shows. He is an author and more currently Peter has been hosting a radio show for 15 years.

Midsummer Night - Mittsommernacht is a German language movie made in Germany, Austria and Norway. His character is named Tore. Cast includes Marianne Hoffmann (10/18/1941-) who will later teach Robert the German words to sing when his German language albums released in 1969. *See www.youtube.ocm*[6] *Turkish Movie Poster created by James Culpeper.* Robert was the only person speaking English and his part was later dubbed into German. Several posters do not include his photo. *See the movie ROBERT FULLER-MITTSOMMERNACHT W/ ENGLISH SUBTITLES, PT1 at https://www.youtube.com/watch?v=FwUOQGqemok and https://www.youtube.com/ watch?v=FwUOQGqemok&list=PL75F64C530849A71E and Robert Fuller-Mittsommernacht w/Eng subtitles Pt 2 at https://www.youtube.com/watch?v=MqudH-nWK7M and Robert Fuller - MITTSOMMERNACHT PT 3 w/English subtitles at https://www.youtube.com/watch?v=9cMS-OTIX-w and Robert Fuller MITTSOMMERNACHT pt 4 subtitles at https://www.youtube.com/watch?v=Kx0SzbtSw1w and Robert Fuller MITTSOMMERNACHT PT 5 SUBTITLES at https://www.youtube.com/watch?v=JFnhUSKczT0 and Robert Fuller MITTSOMMERNACHT PT 6 at https://www.youtube.com/watch?v=8hUz5X5B-Rk and Robert Fuller MITTSOMMERNACHT PT 7 the end W ENG SUBTITLES https://www.youtube.com/watch?v=BugVmTWJ_6c .*

---

5.   *http://www.youtube.com/watch?v=QSFEOayvA4A*

6. *http://www.youtube.ocm*

German movie program shows Robert on the cover along with a partially dressed girl.

German publicity movie photos show Robert and female cast in period costume.

Film-Echo German magazine features movie with Robert and two other cast members on the front cover.

Bravo Otto Award Bronze for best male TV actor in Germany. It's like U.S.'s Emmy Award. Robert is first one of three to win for five consecutive years. The two others are David Hasselhoff (7/17/1952-) www.davidhasselhoffonline.com[7] , 1988 to 1992 and David Duchovny (8/7/1960 -) from 1996 to 2000.

German Hummingbird No. 8891 D postcards are released with Robert as a cowboy.

1/30/1967

Bravo German Magazine No. 6. He is not on cover.

2/18 - 2/19/1967

NC Boy's Home Telethon in Wilmington, North Carolina.

3/22/1967

The Virginian - The episode is titled A Welcoming Town. He plays Clint Richards, a rapist. Doug McClure (5/11/1935-2/5/1995) is series regular with guest stars Linda Day (12/11/1944- www.lyndadaygeorge.co[8]) and Carole Wells (9/4/1928-2/20/1992).

4/1967

Bravo German Magazine. He is not on cover.

5/1967

Argentinean TV Guide.

7/1967

7. http://www.davidhasselhoffonline.com

8.   http://www.lyndadaygeorge.co

Two articles appear in Norway about Robert being in Oslo area filming Midsummer Night - Mittsommernacht Midsummer Night – Mittsommernacht. He has more scenes to film later in Austria.

9/11/ 1967

Bravo No. 38 German Magazine. He is on the cover.

9/25/1967

Big Valley - The episode is titled Flock of Trouble. He plays Carl Wheeler, a rancher against sheep being in the valley. Series cast included Peter Breck (3/13/1929-2/6/2012 www.peterbreck.ca[9]), Linda Evans (11/18/1942-www.lindaevansofficial.com[10]), Lee Majors (4/23/1939-), Richard Long (12/17/1927-12/21/1974) and Barbara Stanwyck (7/16/1907-1/20/1990). *See The Big Valley S03E03 - A Flock of Trouble at https://www.youtube.com/watch?v=WuO67K-jFqE* .

10/2/1967

Bravo German Magazine No. 41. He is not on cover.

11/6/1967

Bravo German Magazine. He is not on cover.

1968

Adam-12 - The episode is titled Lost and Found. Cast includes Martin Milner (12/28/1931-9/6/2015) and Kent McCord (9/26/1942-) www.kentmccord.com[11] .

Der Tod Im Roten Jacquar or aka Morte in Jaguar Rossa - Charlie. It is a cameo role in a German movie playing a gangster. Robert's voice is dubbed. The English version is titled Death in a Red Jaguar. George Nader (10/19/1921-2/4/2002) also stars. It was filmed in a Berlin, Germany studio and on location in San Francisco, California. It may have been released in Germany on 8/14/1968.

Publicity photo #2 for Death in the Red Jaguar in Germany and Italy has Robert with four policemen.

---

9.   http://www.peterbreck.ca

10.   http://www.lindaevansofficial.com

11.   http://www.kentmccord.com

Sinai Commandoes – Sinai aka Matarah Tiran, Ha (Israel Hebrew title) aka Schatte uber Tiran (West German title) aka Sech Tage Krieg (West German title) aka Sinai Commandos aka Sinai Commanodes. The Story of the Six Day War. Robert plays Captain Uri Littman. He was in Europe at the time so was available to do since it was filmed in Israel Kommaniust 15 days after the war ended. Robert and the cast did each scene twice, once with cast speaking English and once with cast speaking in the language of the country. Robert's part was later dubbed. Due to the film's political views, the film was not released in England until the 1980's. *See*
https://www.youtube.com/watch?v=pzPKRdL6G-I . See SINAI COMMANDOS at https://www.youtube.com/ watch?v=wk21t9ZvnSY&list=PL35Uqs0IWWEVU7Jf27O-Zq4OZafqEGJVU .

Sinai lobby card visual was also used as a foreign poster has Robert with machine gun on cover. Another lobby card cover is a drawing of running Robert and female.

Super 8 movie are created. German ones are also made.

VHS tapes were created. The French version front and back cover focus is on other actors rather than Robert.

The Sinai movie had different titles in different countries. In German and Israel Arcade releases 101 minute version of the movie on DVD. One had a front cover drawing and a multi photo back cover.

1/13/1968

TV Guide with Bob Hope (5/29/1903-7/27/003) cover has Wagon Train ad inside. *See www.tvguidemagazine.com/archive/*[12]

5/12 - 5/18/1968

TV Times Magazines in Arlington, Minnesota. Joey Bishop (2/3/1918-10/17/2007) is on cover. Soldiers Seek Hijacked Gold is title to mini description of telecast of Incident at Phantom Hill on Tuesday at the Movies from 8 to 10 p.m.

5/20/1968

Bravo German Magazine No. 21. He is not on cover. It contains some of the same photos 1966's Lolita Magazine No. 27 (Spain publication). *He may be in Germany at this time.*

1969

Bearcats. Although Robert had some interest, he turned down the role. It may have been the beginnings of the 1971 short lived series with the same name.

Japanese Magazine - 25 Favored on Foreign TV Shows. He is not on cover.

Praline Magazine No. 11.1 / 41/1969 in Germany. He is not on cover but article mentions Jess Harper.

Robert makes a German album in Munich. His German agent presented him a German language contract where he thought he would be doing a talking album. Instead it was seven German language songs and four in English. He had an orchestra and work was done in two weeks after many sections were spliced together. The title translates to The Foot of the Blue Mountains. Robert is on cover and it reads:
Fighting
Cover has Am Fub
Der blanen
Berge / Laramie

Some songs can be heard at www.robertfulller.com[13] . A CD was made by Bear Family Records in 1996 and contains 12 songs.

Songs include:
Riding - Fighting (Am Fuss der blauen Berge)
Uberall auf der Welt
Schone Madchen sind wie Blumen
My Old Friend
Margerita (Einmal ist die Reise aus)
Hang My Hat Out in the Prairie
My Blue Mountains
Adios Mexicana
Baby Come Home
Beide heissen Jenny
A Horse and No Saddle
Ein einsamer Cowboy

Dutch Gum Trading Card - Film Star Series T, #37 E5. This same card was also issued in 1974.

---

13. *http://www.robertfulller.com*

The Gatling Gun. It was originally titled King Gun and was not released until 1971. Robert's site has it listed in 1973. He plays Private Sneed, a bad guy. Cast includes Guy Stockwell (12/16/1933-2/6/2002), Barbara Luna (3/2/1930-) www.barbaunaluna.com[14] , Woody Strode (7/25/1914-12/31/1994) and Patrick Wayne (7/15/-1939-). *See Gatling Gun (1971) / Full Movie / Guy Stockwell / Wood Strode / Robert Fuller/ BarBara Luna at https://www.youtube.com/watch?v=XaeYF71bWuY or* Robert Fuller , Sneed ,The Gatling Gun https://www.youtube.com/watch?v=Tv4Rv90yTww or *https://www.youtube.com/watch?v=Ok7it42CNSw or https://www.youtube.com/watch?v=lC5pxlCEMOA or https://www.youtube.com/watch?v=lC5pxlCEMOA or The Gatling Gun (1973) Guy Stockwell, Robert Fuller and BarBara Luna at https://www.youtube.com/watch?v=kdZMWUeFABE . To se a foreign version see A METRALHADORA GATLLING 1973 – Faroeste complete dublado com Robert Fuller at https://www.youtube.com/watch?v=WPxzu6TNsA8 .*

Gatling Gun two sided theater program is created in Yugoslavia. Robert's photo is not included.

An early VHS version is titled "King Gun", runs 93 minutes and Robert is not on cover. Spanish VHS is also made but Robert is not on cover drawing.

Croatian and German movie theater double sided programs created were about 10 x 7 inches and used the words "Massacre" and "King Machine Gun". A photo of Robert' is not included. These were never sold to the public.

DVD's are released. One of at least two different German DVD covers has five main characters in top half and gun in lower half. The other cover has gun only. Another DVD cover has Robert and three other male and one female actress around a close up of gun firing. Yet another cover shows Robert in front of a wagon wheel and behind the Gatling gun.

Whatever Happened to Aunt Alice? He plays Mike Darrah, a relative of housekeeper next in line to be killed. The movie stared Ruther Gordon (10/30/1896-8/28/1965), Geraldine Page (11/22/1924-6/13/1987) and Rosemary Forsyth (7/6/1943). Robert Aldrich (8/9/1918-12/5/1983) was producer of this movie and had his own studio in Tucson, Arizona. *He was also a screenwriter and director. When directing after a rehearsal scene he made suggestions vs. other directions who told you how to do it first without letting the actor do it first. Robert Aldridge died on kidney failure).* While shooting this movie, an episode of The High Chaparral was filming nearby and in the evening he and cast would get together.

One Whatever Happened to Aunt Alice? publicity photo is a close up of Robert.

Robert does Water Pic/Teledyne commercials for at least six years. *See www.youTube.com[15] .*

---

14. http://www.barbaunaluna.com

15. *http://www.youTube.com*

Robert turned down roles in Run for Your Life and Rat Patrol.

4/21/1969

Bravo German Magazine No. 17. He is not on cover.

5/12/1969

Bravo #20 German Magazine. He is on cover as a cowboy holding a revolver.

9/1/1969

Bravo #36 German Magazine. Robert is on cover wearing a long sleeve blue shirt.

10/1969

Bravo German Magazine No. 42 of 1969. He is not on cover.

12/1969

Photoplay Magazine. He is not on cover.

1970'S

Robert is wearing longer side burns.

Robert performed in several plays during his career. They may have been during this time period.
Mr. Roberts

Wait Until Dark at the Burt Reynolds Dinner Theatre in Florida. Robert's wife Patty Fuller was also in the play.

Oklahoma National Quail Hunt www.gngh.rog[16] . Robert attended about 20 times, at least once with actor Richard Farnsworth (9/1/1920-10/6/2000).

Foreign Matchbox Label B 30 Robert Fuller at 1 3/8 inch x 2 inches in size. is made.

---

16. http://www.gngh.rog

Many publicity photos are released.

1970

Buffalo Bill Award for Outstanding Western Entertainment.

Possible John Wayne (5/26/1897-6/11/1979 www.johnwayne.com[17]) movie that did not happen.

Robert enjoys deer, elk and quail hunting in California, Nevada and Utah.

Traveler, Robert's horse from Laramie and Wagon Train, is 27 years old.

Japanese magazines feature Robert. A 72 page issue with Wayne Maunder (12/19/1937-11/11/2018) includes Robert. He appears as a cowboy including a popular Laramie photo of him leaning over a wood fence rail holding his revolver.

1 - 2/8/1970

Boeing, Boeing- Play at Pheasant Run, Illinois. He played a playboy pilot. Cast included Dan Conway (7/5/ 1942-10/22/2012), Vicki Raywood, Faith Quablus (2/5/1940-), Rebecca Phillips and Geraldine Power. At least six articles or ads promoting Robert in the play Boeing Boeing in Illinois appear. One is with a female co star. The stage bill program included some bio info like that Robert enjoyed fishing and hunting in California, Nevada and Utah and quail hunting in Northern California and the Rockies.

12/9/1970

Dan August - The episode is titled The Trouble with Women where Robert plays William Britain again. It is a 2 hour TV movie starring Burt Reynolds (2/11/1936-9/6/2018). Cast also includes Richard Anderson (8/8/ 1926-8/31/2017) and Norman Fell (3/24/1924-12/14/1998). *See Dan August "The Trouble With Women" part 1 Burt Reynolds, Robert Fuller at https://www.youtube.com/watch?v=tTshz5UWaAA and part 2 at https://www.youtube.com/ watch?v=o1LUyU9n_cg and Dan August "The Trouble With Women" part 3 Burt Reynolds, Robert Fuller at https://www.youtube.com/watch?v=WIamVf5L0LE and Dan August "The Trouble With Women" part 4 Burt Reynolds, Robert Fuller at https://www.youtube.com/watch?v=Hiok53mTDFQ .*

1971

Paramedic.

---

17. http://www.johnwayne.com

The Hard Ride. He plays Phil Duncan, a returning soldier who comes to bury a friend. Movie has a surprise ending. Cast includes Sherry Bain (5/26/1948-) and Tony Russell (1/25/1943- 3/18/2018). Hard Ride's motorcycle was a 1938 Harley worth about $5,000. It had been modified and was illegal to ride on real streets. It was dangerous to be riding at 70 to 80 miles per hour with girl on the back.

See Robert Fuller – The Hard Ride – a movie trailer at https://www.youtube.com/watch?v=hK2ww36bkgY . To view the movie see Robert Fuller - THE HARD RIDE 1 at https://www.youtube.com/watch?v=-tBWWVL0CUE and THE HAD RIDE 2 at https://www.youtube.com/watch?v=iM6HU4CU_ck and Robert Fuller THE HARD RIDE 3 athttps://www.youtube.com/watch?v=zaYV-DAyeaQ and THE HARD RIDE (4) at https://www.youtube.com/watch?v=6IHawgGp3RU and Robert Fuller THE HARD RIDE (5) at https://www.youtube.com/watch?v=s7VZOrfMx0c and The Hard Ride Pt 6 at https://www.youtube.com/watch?v=K2uEQ0e04Ws and Robert Fuller The Hard Ride (7) The finale at https://www.youtube.com/watch?v=5QuELNO-KIs .

Lobby cards are created. Popular ones include a sunglass wearing Robert with a girl on a motorcycle along with a drawing of a girl looking over her shoulder.

Hard Rider German Movie Program used in several countries including Germany. The cover has Robert wearing a jacket and sunglasses with a biker doing a wheelie in background.

The Hard Ride publicity often shows a girl looking over her shoulder on the left side and action shot on right side . Action shots can be Robert and girl on motorcycle or Robert on motorcycle by himself. There are at least three other fight scenes on the right side.

The Hard Ride Movie Soundtrack LP Record is released. It is red with drawing of Robert and girl on a motorcycle.

Twelve songs are on this movie soundtrack album. Side one includes Swing Low, Sweet Chariot; I Came A Long Way To Be With You; Fallin' In Love With Baby; Another Kind of War; Be Nobody's Fool and Let The Music Play. Side 2 includes Where Am I Going Today; Carry Me Home; The Hard Ride; Victorville Blues; Shannon's Hook Shop and Love Theme from "The Hard Ride.

Posters are created using the same red drawing as the movie album. One is 12 x 18 inches.

Another 12 x 18 poster created in U.S. and Britain and U.S. is a different design with the over the shoulder looking girl being larger with Robert on motorcycle smaller sized.

VHS tapes were released. Robert's face is focus of cover.

Robert did a commercial for United Airline's DC-10 airplane.

New reimbursement laws for reruns go into effort. Up until this time only the first seven showings were paid. However, most actors are still only getting checks totaling pennies.

1/7/1971

Dan August - The episode is titled The Titan where he plays Bill Britain. Series stars Burt Reynolds (2/11/1936-9/6/2018). Other cast is Richard Anderson (8/8/1926-8/31/2017) and Norman Fell (3/24/1924-12/14/1998). *See Robert Fuller The Titan at https://www.youtube.com/watch?v=D9rhSNTw55w or https://www.youtube.com/watch?v=D9rhSNTw55w&list=PLH2qbkcAOZv8U4Wg5—k7gRRGKJ1Eewls*[18] .

2/17/71

Virginian, Men from Shiloh - The episode is titled Flight from Memory. He plays Carl Ellis, a bad guy who gets shot. Cast includes Stewart Granger (5/6/1913-8/16/1993) and James Drury (4/18/1934-4/6/2020) www.thevirginian.net[19]).

FALL OF 1971

Movieland & TV Time Annual Magazine. He is not on cover.

1972

CD - Am FuB derblauen Berge/Laramie. It is CD version of Robert's German made, German language album. (Bear Family records created a 1996 CD version).

Hollywood Squares - as himself/guest often in top corner squares. Celebrities were never given the questions but had a variety of answers and Robert was an excellent bluffer. *See www.youtube.com/watch?v=QSFEOayvA4A*[20] .

---

18.   https://www.youtube.com/watch?v=D9rhSNTw55w&list=PLH2qbkcAOZv8U4Wg5--k7gRRGKJ1Eewls

19.   http://www.thevirginian.net

20. *http://www.youtube.com/watch?v=QSFEOayvA4A*

Robert with Jock Mahoney (2/7/1919-12/14/1989) and stuntman Rick Arnold appear at Kern County Fish & Game Protective Association for annual barbeque in Bakersfield, California.

Robert with Jock Mahoney (2/7/1919-12/14/1989) and stuntman Rick Arnold appear at a rodeo in Yuma, Arizona. These three men attend benefits that included for youth summer sports leagues. One included a softball game where they hit the ball sitting on a donkey and then rode to first base. Jock was so tall he could stand over back of donkeys.

Japanese Magazines continue to feature Robert. This one is 72 pages and has David McCallum 99/19/1`933-) on the cover. It shows Robert as a cowboy.

EMERGENCY YEARS 1972 - 1979

Three key people involved in creating the Emergency television program were Harold Jack Bloom (4/26/1924-8/27/1999), Robert A. Cinader (11/10/1924-11/16/1982) and Jack Webb (4/2/1920-12/23/1982).

Emergency publicity photos include Robert dressed as a doctor.

Hospital staff photos include Robert, Julie and Bobby. Some are waist up while others are full length shots. . Other photos include Robert, Julie and Bobby in front of Randy and Kevin on truck.

One photo shoot has Robert in a checked suit and tie. There are waist up shots and full length with various left and right poses. One of these poses became a poster in the United Kingdom.

Other posters are created that included Kevin and Raymond.

A 3x5 index chard with Robert as Dr. Brackett on half was also created.

1/1972

Studio releases publicity photo shows Kevin, Robert, Julie, Bobby and Raymond around a gurney.

1/9 - 1/15/1972

Sunday New TV Week in Philadelphia, Pennsylvania has Julie London and Bobby Troop on cover. Article focuses on Bobby Troop with Robert in photo with Bobby and Julie.

1/15/1972

Emergency series premier. Emergency One - Syndication Title and Emergencia was USA/Spanish title for Emergency. Emergency's world premier episode VHS tape is later released. He is not on the cover.

Robert plays Dr. Kelly Brackett, M.D./F.A.C.S. Emergency - Dr. Kelly Brackett. *After Paul Donnelly (2/14/1914-10/1/1990), Universal Studio Executive Producer (later Assistant Director on Emergency) had seen Robert in The Hard Ride he encouraged Jack Webb (4/2/1920-12/23/1982) to view him in the movie. Jack did and decided he wanted Robert for new medical TV drama Emergency.* Wearing a suit and tie Robert attended a 7 p.m. meeting just say no in person since he wants to be in westerns not a medical show. It was a huge room and he was told to make himself a drink. The program, 2 hour pilot and 13 episodes had been sold without a pilot. After 2 hours Robert signed 8 year contract. He was given a huge medical dictionary.

Robert's training was one day in a hospital, one day with the fire department. Robert's great memory skills and two paramedics were on the set for accuracy. Filming was to start in 3 days. (Robert has talked about many times. *See www.youtube.com/watch?v=JpDflDsOaP8*[1] *with James Drury. He was now working seven months instead of 11 months and although h*is contract allowed him to direct if he wanted. Directing would have involved two weeks to prep and a week to film each episode. Robert, Julie and Bobbie did tour the U.S., including Puerto Rico and a few other countries visiting paramedic departments. Some of Robert's remaining free time was spent shooting and fishing on Lake Okeechobee, Florida where he may have owned a home.

Robert appeared in about 125 of the episodes. Episode descriptions seem to show fewer story lines involving his character over time. The focus was taken away from the hospital and more on the paramedics. Robert may have voiced his disappointment in the direction the series was taking and he cut back his hours starting in the sixth year (1976). Robert appeared in only one 2 hour movie. Despite good ratings, the series was cancelled.

The show aired early on Saturday nights. Over the years its competition included Alias, Smith and Jones, All in the Family, Doc, Saturday Night Live w/Howard Cosell, The Jeffersons, The Bob Newhart Show, The Mary Tyler Moore Show and The Partridge Family.

Medical movies and television programs reflected the times they are made. For instance, from 1961 to 1966 both Ben Casey and Dr. Kildare television programs would have had stories showing doctors joining the ambulance crew. With the introduction of the concept of creating paramedic programs, writers recreated real situations to educate viewers on the paramedic program and current treatment options. When the show premiered, there were only 12 fire departments or ambulance services in North America fielding paramedics; the show is credited with introducing its audience to the concept of pre-hospital care, fire prevention and CPR. In 1971 about eighty seven percent of heart attack deaths occurred on the way to the hospital. There were only 13 real paramedics at the time and Emergency series helped develop the paramedic program. After Emergency these heart attack death statistics lowered to about 55 percent. Over time the rates lowered to about 23 percent.

Robert along with his other co-stars' convincing portrayal of their caring television characters helped inspire people to join the fire department or pursue medical careers. Emergency creators, writers, actors and crew all can be proud to have played a part in changing people's lives.

Robert enjoyed working with director Georg Fenady (7/29/1930-5/29/2008). He felt good directors let you know where to go vs. how to perform scenes.

Cast included:

Julie London as nurse Dixie McCall. She was born 9/26/1926. Julie was married to Jack Webb from m 1947 to 1954. Robert met her when he got out of Army in 1955 opening night in a club (Johnny Washes 98 Club) along with a guitarist. Robert often attended her performances. Jack Webb (4/2/1920-12/23/1982) was creator and producer of Emergency. Julie married Bobby Troup in 1959. Because her former husband Jack Webb preferred actors to use teleprompter she did all through the series. Starting in 1944 Julie was in more than fifty roles in film and television. In the mid 1950's she got a record contract creating 32 albums and received a star on the Hollywood Walk of Fame for her music. Julie enjoyed time with her family. Julie was a smoker and had a stroke in 1995 and died of a heart attack on 10/ 18/2000 at age 74. *See www.julielondon.org[2] .*

Bobby Troup as Dr. Joe Early. Bobby Troup (10/18/1918-2/7/1999). Bobby married Julie London in 1959. He was a jazz pianist and singer who wrote songs from 1944 to 1969. Bobby was a Marine stationed in the U.S. and did a little acting from 1957 to 1979. He died of a heart attack. The Emergency cast attended his funeral.

Raymond Mantooth as paramedic John Gage. (9/19/1945-). For training he sat in on paramedic classes and took rides with the Los Angeles Fire Department. In 1973-1974 he voiced the cartoon series Emergency+4 and narrated an episode about the work of paramedics in LA County with Mantooth on NBC's Go! Raymond thought the pay was low. Starting in 1968 he has appeared in about one hundred roles. Raymond is a speaker promoting EMT's, firefighters, paramedics and other emergency medical providers. He also shared stories about his days on Emergency. In 2001 (with 2013 additions) Raymond appeared with Kevin Tighe in the video *The Pioneers of Paramedicine Story*, a history. In 2012 he and Kevin became Honorary Fire Chiefs and given traditional white leather firefighter helmets by the Los Angeles County Fire Department.

Kevin Tighe as paramedic Roy DeSoto. (9/13/1944-). For training he sat in on paramedic classes and took rides with the Los Angeles Fire Department. In 1973-1974 he voiced his character on the cartoon series Emegency+4 and narrated an episode about the work of paramedics in LA County with Mantooth on NBC's Go! In 2001 (with 2013 additions) Kevin appeared with Raymond Mantooth in the video *The Pioneers of Paramedicine Story*, a history. Kevin was an honorary committee member on Project 51 and its efforts to honor Emergency. Kevin did interviews and compiled some history of American EMS for the project. In 5/2000 his uniform (along with other show items) were put in the Smithsonian Institution's National Museum of American History in the Public Services Division. In 2002 Kevin was best man at Raymond's second wedding. In 2012 he and Raymond became Honorary Fire Chiefs and given traditional white leather firefighter helmets by the Los Angeles County Fire Department. Starting in 1967 Kevin has been in over 100 roles. He teaches and has worked on stage in U.S. and Britain.

---

2.   *http://www.julielondon.org*

There were many other cast members at the firehouse and hospital. One special guests was John Smith (3/6/1931-1/25/1995). He played a fire captain on a few episodes filmed at Carson, CA, Station 127. John had an opportunity to join cast but John wanted equal billing and pay.

See EMERGENCY! THEN AND NOW 2020 at https://www.youtube.com/watch?v=7-hOHqYUIeg . See Emergency! Behind the Scenes Facts & Secrets at https://www.youtube.com/watch?v=nwNtTFjqw14 . See Robert Fuller Season 6 Emergency Disclaimer at https://www.youtube.com/watch?v=bkcL_PIixRY .

Only one person was hurt during the filming. He was am European stuntman trying to get his green card in U.S. Without consulting special effects he used airplane glue to put himself on fire and they couldn't get the fire out.

Robert and his wife Patty spent time with cast members at Jack Webb's home or Julie and Bobby Troup's home. One time while at Julie's home, a guest became ill and 911 was called. Young paramedics arrived shocked to see TV medical cast present and needed encouragement to do their job.

Robert's work schedule usually started at 7:30 or 8 a.m. and might end by six or 7:30 p.m. but go until 9 or 10 p.m. too. One time when Robert had a later call, about 10 a.m. both Kevin Tighe and Randy Rantooth drove the Emergency vehicle five or six blocks from the studio into his Toluca Lake home driveway at 6 a.m. making much noise to wake Robert up.

Publicity would have included press releases, photos. Emergency marketing included colouring books, comics, game, lunch box and flask/thermos, puzzles, toy paramedical kit and toy survival kit. NBC also creates two View Master reels with Robert's image included. Universal Studios created metal die cast fire trucks.

The show has fans around the world.

During one interview Robert did during Emergency he is smoking, working only two days a week vs. the 12 hour days five days a week during Laramie and Wagon Train. Robert enjoys hunting and fishing including in the Dallas, Texas area. He is anxious to make Westerns again. *See Robert Fuller "Emergency" - Bobbie Wygant Archive at https://www.youtube.com/watch?v=rxVo6VDEysU .*

See www.emergencyfans.com[3] .
   youtube.com with Emergency include:

---

3. *http://www.emergencyfans.com*

Emergency - Dr. Brackett: The Prize (www.youtube.com/watch?v=ZJNvMwsgSsg[4] .

Emergency episodes were often based on real incidents. The program, the acceptance of using paramedics, did save lives.

Episodes can be viewed on some websites.

Bloopers can be found although some are poor quality. Some include: *Emergency! Bloopers - You Tube (www.youtube.com/watch?v=lphLBSWUP9Q[5]).*

Emergency! Bloopers 1 - You Tube (www.youtube.com/watch?v=incWycpNocQ[6]).

Emergency! Bloopers 14 (www.youtube.com/watch?v=x0bfsSuJW0E[7]) and (https://www.youtube.com/watch?v=IphLBSWUP9Q&list=PLP9z9s4Zmh601Rm-OMOiAyVJEQb3obPG9&index=3).

Emergency! Bloopers 18 - You Tube(www.youtube.com/watch?v=8GsQljdBRQ0[8]).

Emergency? Bloopers 19 - You Tube(www.youtube.com/watch?v=saWEMFVg6vw[9]).

Emergency! Bloopers 20: The Final Cut - You Tube (www.youtube.com/watch?v=lphLBSWUP9Q[10] .

Emergency! Funny bloopers - You Tube(www.youtube.com/watch?v=UsJ3e8-ci0Q[11]).

Emergency! (1972) TV mistakes, goofs and bloopers - Movie mistakes (www.moviestakes.com/tv6889[12]).

---

4. *http://www.youtube.com/watch?v=ZJNvMwsgSsg*

5. *http://www.youtube.com/watch?v=lphLBSWUP9Q*

6. *http://www.youtube.com/watch?v=incWycpNocQ*

7. *http://www.youtube.com/watch?v=x0bfsSuJW0E*

8. *http://www.youtube.com/watch?v=8GsQljdBRQ0*

9. *http://www.youtube.com/watch?v=saWEMFVg6vw*

10. *http://www.youtube.com/watch?v=lphLBSWUP9Q*

11. *http://www.youtube.com/watch?v=UsJ3e8_ci0Q*

12. *http://www.moviestakes.com/tv6889*

The American Medical Association gave the show an award.

Robert did a public service commercial for FDA (Food Drug Administration) about Poison Control center. *See www.youtube.com/watch?v=8CMNnJTTNY*[13] .

Robert met and had breakfast with Dr. Heimlich (Heimich maneuver) while at a celebrity tennis tournament.

The 51 fire engine is now a part of the Los Angeles Fire Museum.

DVD's for Seasons 1 have Raymond and Kevin with hospital staff behind. Season 2 has cast of five on top but the fire engine, truck and station on bottom half. Season 3 cover has top half of staff split into two sections. Kevin and Raymond are larger on left than three shot of Robert, Julie and Bobby to the right with same fire station photo on bottom half. Season 4 DVD has similar top but only fire engine on bottom half There are at least two versions of all seasons. One has similar top but action shot of firemen on truck on bottom half. The other is a large photo of Kevin and Raymond in front of a fire engine on top half and larger photos of Robert, Jill and Bobby on lower half.

1/15/1972
Emergency Episode - The Wedsworth-Townsend Act[14]
Dr. Brackett opposes but then speaks for a pending state bill introducing extension paramedic programs.

1/22/1972
Emergency Episode - Mascot[15]
Doctors treat a girl with breathing problems and a drunken man.

1/29/1972
Emergency Episode - Botulism[16]
A student nurse is having trouble working with Dr. Brackett.

2/12/1972

13. *http://www.youtube.com/watch?v=8CMNnJTTNY*

14.   https://www.imdb.com/title/tt0067046/?ref_=ttep_ep1

15.   https://www.imdb.com/title/tt0570660/?ref_=ttep_ep2

16.   https://www.imdb.com/title/tt0570607/?ref_=ttep_ep3

Emergency Episode - Emergency Episode - Cook's Tour[17]
Focus is other hospital staff and paramedics.

2/19/1972

Emergency Episode - Brushfire[18]
Focus is other hospital staff and paramedics.

2/26/1972

Emergency Episode - Dealer's Wild[19]
Dr. Brackett spends off duty time with Dixie. Drs. Brackett, Early and Morton care for husband suffering from a severe hemorrhage.

3/4/1972

Emergency Episode - Nurse's Wild[20]
Dr. Brackett and Dixie work on a man with chest pains.

3/11/1972

Emergency Episode - Publicity Hound[21]
Important man unhappy about his son's treatment threatens to take Dr. Brackett to court. Dixie and Dr. Early help defuse the situation.

St. Louis Post TV Magazine. It has a photo of Robert and nurse Patricia Mickey (7/3/1950-).

3/18/1972

Emergency Episode - Weird Wednesday[22]
Focus is other hospital staff and paramedics.

3/25/1972

Emergency Episode - Emergency Episode - Dilemma[23]

17.   https://www.imdb.com/title/tt0570616/?ref_=ttep_ep4

18.   https://www.imdb.com/title/tt0570609/?ref_=ttep_ep5

19.   https://www.imdb.com/title/tt0570619/?ref_=ttep_ep6

20.   https://www.imdb.com/title/tt0570666/?ref_=ttep_ep7

21.   https://www.imdb.com/title/tt0570676/?ref_=ttep_ep8

22.   https://www.imdb.com/title/tt0570724/?ref_=ttep_ep9

23.   https://www.imdb.com/title/tt0570622/?ref_=ttep_ep10

Student nurse making mistakes around Dr. Brackett and Dixie helps her cope.

4/8/1972

Emergency Episode - Hang-Up[24]

Dr. Brackett treats a woman with a neurological disorder.

4/15/1972

Emergency Episode - Crash[25]

Focus is other hospital staff and paramedics.

9/16/1972

Emergency Episode - Decision[26]

Focus is other hospital staff and paramedics.

FALL OF 1972

Movieland Annual Magazine. He is not on cover.

9/23/1972

Emergency Episode - Emergency Episode - Kids[27]

Dr. Brackett follows up on case of possible child abuse abusive.

9/30/1972

Emergency Episode - Show Biz[28]

Focus is other hospital staff and paramedics.

10/4/1972

Adam-12 - The episode is titled Lost and Found. He plays is Emergency character, Dr. Kelly Brackett. Crossover episode. Cast includes Martin Milner (12/28/1931-9/6/2015) and Kent McCord (9/26/1942-) www.kentmccord.com[29] .

24.   https://www.imdb.com/title/tt0570641/?ref_=ttep_ep11

25.   https://www.imdb.com/title/tt0570617/?ref_=ttep_ep12

26.   https://www.imdb.com/title/tt0570620/?ref_=ttep_ep1

27.   https://www.imdb.com/title/tt0570657/?ref_=ttep_ep2

28.   https://www.imdb.com/title/tt0570684/?ref_=ttep_ep3

29.   http://www.kentmccord.com

10/7/1972

Emergency Episode - Virus[30]

Highly contagious disease started by a monkey puts Dr. Brackett and John Gage into the hospital.

10/14/1972

Emergency Episode - Peace Pipe[31]

Dr. Brackett explains treatment necessary to parents after a drunk injuries their child.

10/21/1972

Emergency Episode - Saddled[32]

Dr. Brackett and Dr. Early both keep Dixie from working after she injures her toe.

11/1972

Japanese Magazine. David McCallum (9/19/1933-) on cover titled The Metamorphosis History of 20 TV Faves. Robert is shown more in cowboy (in photos and drawing) than modern (suit).

11/4/1972

Emergency Episode - Fuzz Lady[33]

Dr. Brackett speaks to Dr. Morton about his attitude.

11/11/1972

Emergency Episode - Trainee[34]

Focus is other hospital staff and paramedics.

11/25/1972

Emergency Episode - Women[35]

Focus is other hospital staff and paramedics.

30.   https://www.imdb.com/title/tt0570723/?ref_=ttep_ep4

31.   https://www.imdb.com/title/tt0570671/?ref_=ttep_ep5

32.   https://www.imdb.com/title/tt0570681/?ref_=ttep_ep6

33.   https://www.imdb.com/title/tt0570637/?ref_=ttep_ep7

34.   https://www.imdb.com/title/tt0570719/?ref_=ttep_ep8

35.   https://www.imdb.com/title/tt0570727/?ref_=ttep_ep9

12/2/1972

Emergency Episode - Dinner Date[36]

Focus is other hospital staff and paramedics.

12/9/1972

Emergency Episode - Musical Mania[37]

Focus is other hospital staff and paramedics.

12/16/1972

Emergency Episode - Helpful[38]

When doctor is absent from duty both Drs. Brackett and Early follow up.

1972 - 1973

Who's Who in TV No. 22. He is not on cover and it costs 50 cents.

1973 - 1976

Milton Bradley is making an Emergency Board Game.

1973

Password - as himself (? also with his daughter Christine). Host is Allen Ludden (10/5/1917-6/9/1981).

Budweiser Malt Liquor. Budweiser - 1973 - The Malt Liquor Express takes place on a train and is over 23 minutes long where he presents statistics and marketing ideas. *See The Malt Liquor Express - Robert Fuller at https://www.youtube.com/watch?v=61ZnaRtQbNg*.

Robert wears a real person's M.I.A. bracelet. Some time after his release in 1973 Robert meets pilot James Robinson Risner. James spent more than three years in solitary confinement and overall seven years as a prisoner. General James Robinson Risner was born 1/16/1925 and died 10/22/2013. (Senator John McCain, born 8/29/1936, was also held in the same location and was born 8/29/1936 and shot down in 10/1967. He was in solitary confinement in 8/1968 for at least a year and released 3/14/1973 and died 8/25/2018).

Marketing items include:

---

36.   https://www.imdb.com/title/tt0570623/?ref_=ttep_ep10

37.   https://www.imdb.com/title/tt0570663/?ref_=ttep_ep11

38.   https://www.imdb.com/title/tt0570643/?ref_=ttep_ep12

Emergency coloring book #1840 by Saalfield.

Emergency lunch box by Aladdin Industries (Robert has lunch box as a souvenir of the program).

Emergency Squad Action Accessories.
Emergency trucks by LIN & Dinky Toys.

Japanese magazines include:
One with Richard Thomas (6/15/1951-) on cover. He is in both suit and tie and smaller as a cowboy.

1/9 - 1/15/1973
Philadelphia, Pennsylvania TV Guide with Julie London and Bobby Troop on cover. Article is titled Bobby Troop Will Star in a New Drama Series and includes a picture of Julie, Bobby and Robert.

2/18/1973
Hec Ramsey - The episode is titled Mystery of Chalk Hill playing Dixie Hollister in a cameo role. Richard Boone (6/18/1917-1/10/1981) stars. *See Hec Ramsey - Season 1, Episode 5 : The Mystery of Chalk Hill at https://www.youtube.com/watch?v=os3oolwT2yI* .

1/6/1973
Emergency Episode - Drivers[39]
Focus is other hospital staff and paramedics.

1/13/1973
Emergency Episode - School Days[40]
Doctors treat a baseball player hit by ball during game.

2/3/1973
Emergency Episode - The Professor[41]
Government interferes with Dr. Brackett's treatment of injured Secret Service agent.

39.	https://www.imdb.com/title/tt0570624/?ref_=ttep_ep13

40.	https://www.imdb.com/title/tt0570682/?ref_=ttep_ep14

41.	https://www.imdb.com/title/tt0570711/?ref_=ttep_ep15

2/10/1973

Emergency Episode - Syndrome[42]

Focus is other hospital staff and paramedics.

2/17/1973

Emergency Episode - Honest[43]

Focus is other hospital staff and paramedics.

2/24/1973

Emergency Episode - Séance[44]

Dr. Brackett and Dixie treat a young man after he took some one else's tranquilizers.

3/3/1973

Emergency Episode - Boot[45]

Hospital staff tries to diagnosis sick firemen's dog. Dr. Brackett and staff help rescue people and records from Rampart's lab after explosion.

3/10/1973

Emergency Episode - Rip-Off[46]

Focus is other hospital staff and paramedics.

4/7/1973

Emergency Episode - Audit[47]

Dr. Brackett and Dixie find a patient is missing. Dr. Brackett treats a pregnant hippie woman with breathing difficulty.

7/15/1973

Detroit Free Press TV Guide. Miss Universe is on the cover.

8/18 - 8/24/1973

42.   https://www.imdb.com/title/tt0570691/?ref_=ttep_ep16

43.   https://www.imdb.com/title/tt0570644/?ref_=ttep_ep17

44.   https://www.imdb.com/title/tt0570683/?ref_=ttep_ep18

45.   https://www.imdb.com/title/tt0570605/?ref_=ttep_ep19

46.   https://www.imdb.com/title/tt0570679/?ref_=ttep_ep20

47.   https://www.imdb.com/title/tt0570602/?ref_=ttep_ep21

TV Guide – Emergency. This one also features Robert's wife Patty and is titled Anybody Want to Buy 14 Pairs of Boots. Article talks about turning down Run For Your Life, Rat Patrol and the Rounders. Patty sells saddles and his children Robert is 9 and Christine is 7 1/2. His work in voice commercials earns him $65,000 of his earning of $250,000 per year. It says his movie The Hard Ride cost $113,000 to make and that Robert formed his own production company. *See www.tvguidemagazine.com*[48] . Cover is Robert as a doctor. Inside has a great photo of Patty behind / side of Robert.

Spanish Language TV Guide was also issued this year. Cover is Robert as Dr. Brackett.

9/1973

Boston, Massachusetts Sunday Herald TV Magazine with Dom DeLuise (8/1/1933-5/4/2009) on cover. Article is titled Robert Fuller Traded Saddle for a Scalpel. Photo is face only (no neck) drawing.

9/12/1973

Emergency Episode - Frequency[49]
Focus is on other hospital staff and paramedics.

9/29/1973

Emergency Episode - The Old Engine[50]
Focus is on other hospital staff and paramedics.

10/6/1973

Emergency Episode - Alley Cat[51]
Dr. Brackett cares for stage actress.

10/13/1973

Emergency Episode - An English Visitor[52]
Focus is on other hospital staff and paramedics.

10/20/1973

Emergency Episode - Heavyweight[53]

48. *http://www.tvguidemagazine.com*

49. https://www.imdb.com/title/tt0570636/?ref_=ttep_ep1

50. https://www.imdb.com/title/tt0570709/?ref_=ttep_ep2

51. https://www.imdb.com/title/tt0570599/?ref_=ttep_ep3

52. https://www.imdb.com/title/tt0570600/?ref_=ttep_ep4

53. https://www.imdb.com/title/tt0570642/?ref_=ttep_ep5

Dr. Brackett and Dixie talk to a new mother about her baby's cleft palate.

10/27/1973

Emergency Episode - Snakebite[54]

Focus is on other hospital staff and paramedics.

11/3/1973

Emergency Episode - Promotion[55]

Focus is on other hospital staff and paramedics.

11/101973

Emergency Episode - Insomnia[56]

Drs. Brackett and Early with Dixie treat boy with skull fracture and a marijuana smoker.

11/17/1973

Emergency Episode - Inheritance Tax[57]

Focus is on other hospital staff and paramedics.

11/24/1973

Emergency Episode - Zero[58]

Drs. Brackett and Early suspect child abuse.

12/1/1973

Emergency Episode - The Promise[59]

Focus is on other hospital staff and paramedics.

12/8/1973

Emergency Episode - Body Language[60]

Drs. Brackett, Early and Morton agree a patient doesn't need hospitalization.

54.   https://www.imdb.com/title/tt0570687/?ref_=ttep_ep6

55.   https://www.imdb.com/title/tt0570674/?ref_=ttep_ep7

56.   https://www.imdb.com/title/tt0570651/?ref_=ttep_ep8

57.   https://www.imdb.com/title/tt0570649/?ref_=ttep_ep9

58.   https://www.imdb.com/title/tt0570728/?ref_=ttep_ep10

59.   https://www.imdb.com/title/tt0570712/?ref_=ttep_ep11

60.   https://www.imdb.com/title/tt0570604/?ref_=ttep_ep12

12/15/1973

Emergency Episode - Understanding[61]

Dr. Brackett and Dixie lecture on the importance of insulin shots to a male patient.

12/22/1973

Emergency Episode - Computer Error[62]

Focus is on other hospital staff and paramedics.

1973-1974

Emergency board game by Milton Bradley is being made.

When Kevin Tighe and Raymond Mantooth were doing the voices for the cartoon series Emergency+4 Robert was fishing in the Bahamas.

1974 - 1980

Hollywood Squares - as himself. He is a great liar and often in top corner squares. Robert's home was very near the studio in Hollywood. His appearances gave him more opportunity to meet people in the entertainment field.

1974

Hollywood Squares - as himself.

Japanese fans magazines. A variety of photos as a cowboy, his visits to Japan are included. Article is tied into 25 Favorites.

Television Age, Japanese Magazine. He is not on cover but there is a photo of him sitting behind the wheel of a car. The magazine is 48 pages.

TV Star Directory Magazine. He is not on cover and sells for 50 cents.

1/5/1974

Emergency Episode - Inferno[63]

Focus is on other hospital staff and paramedics.

61.   https://www.imdb.com/title/tt0570721/?ref_=ttep_ep13

62.   https://www.imdb.com/title/tt0570614/?ref_=ttep_ep14

63.   https://www.imdb.com/title/tt0570648/?ref_=ttep_ep15

1/12/1974

Emergency Episode - Messin' Around[64]

Drs. Brackett and Early and Dixie suspect man may be a hypochondriac.

1/19/1974

Emergency Episode - Fools[65]

Dr. Brackett orders intern to ride with paramedics.

1/26/1974

Emergency Episode - How Green Was My Thumb?[66]

Dr. Brackett's patient religious parents prevent treatment.

2/2/1974

Emergency Episode - The Hard Hours[67]

Focus is on other hospital staff and paramedics.

2/3/1974

Carlos the Sierra Coyote - He is narrator and voice of coyote in Walt Disney TV episode. *See Walt Disney's Wonderful World of Color" Carlo, the Sierra Coyote at https://www.youtube.com/watch?v=A-VGw5bnuM4* .

2/9/1974

Emergency Episode - Floor Brigade[68]

Focus is on other hospital staff and paramedics.

2/16/1974

Emergency Episode - Propinquity[69]

Focus is on other hospital staff and paramedics.

---

64.   https://www.imdb.com/title/tt0570662/?ref_=ttep_ep16

65.   https://www.imdb.com/title/tt0570634/?ref_=ttep_ep17

66.   https://www.imdb.com/title/tt0570645/?ref_=ttep_ep18

67.   https://www.imdb.com/title/tt0570702/?ref_=ttep_ep19

68.   https://www.imdb.com/title/tt0570633/?ref_=ttep_ep20

69.   https://www.imdb.com/title/tt0570675/?ref_=ttep_ep21

3/1974

Movieland Magazine. He is not on cover.

TV and Movie Screen Magazine. He is not on cover.

SPRING OF 1974

Movieland and TV Time Annual Magazine. He is in the Big Mates section with a photo of Robert and Patty and another couple. Magazine sells for 75 cents.

3/23/1974

Emergency Episode - Inventions[70]
Focus is on other hospital staff and paramedics.

6/2/1974

Lancaster, Pennsylvania TV Guide with Barbara Feldon (3/12/1933-) cover. Article is titled Emergency! Answer the Bell for Next Season and has a photo of Robert as Dr. Brackett.

8/10/1974

Huntsville Fire Department presents Robert Outstanding Service Award for bring recognition to the firefighting profession and his support for emergency assistance personnel throughout U.S.

9/14/1974

Emergency Episode - The Screenwriter[71]
Focus is on other hospital staff and paramedics.

9/21/1974

Emergency Episode - I'll Fix It
Drs. Brackett and Morton treat a boy knowing much medical terminology.

9/28/1974

Emergency Episode - Gossip[72]
Focus is on other hospital staff and paramedics.

70. https://www.imdb.com/title/tt0570652/?ref_=ttep_ep22

71. https://www.imdb.com/title/tt0570713/?ref_=ttep_ep1

72. https://www.imdb.com/title/tt0570638/?ref_=ttep_ep3

10/5/1974

Emergency Episode - Nagging Suspicion[73]

Dr. Brackett and Dixie treat a dancer with mono.

10/12/1974

Emergency Episode - Communication Gaffe[74]

Dr. Brackett treats an abused child.

10/19/1974

Emergency Episode - Surprise[75]

Focus is on other hospital staff and paramedics.

11/1974

Movie Mirror Magazine. He is not on cover.

11/2/1974

Emergency Episode - Daisy's Pick Blind Date[76]

Focus is on other hospital staff and paramedics.

11/9/1974

Emergency Episode - Quicker Than the Eye[77]

Dr. Brackett seeks information from husband about his wife's pregnancy after she is shot.

11/16/1974

Emergency Episode - Foreign Trade[78]

Focus is on other hospital staff and paramedics.

11/23/1974

73.   https://www.imdb.com/title/tt0570664/?ref_=ttep_ep4

74.   https://www.imdb.com/title/tt0570612/?ref_=ttep_ep5

75.   https://www.imdb.com/title/tt0570688/?ref_=ttep_ep6

76.   https://www.imdb.com/title/tt0570618/?ref_=ttep_ep7

77.   https://www.imdb.com/title/tt0570677/?ref_=ttep_ep8

78.   https://www.imdb.com/title/tt0570635/?ref_=ttep_ep9

Emergency Episode - Camera Bug[79]
Dr. Brackett attacked by violent teenager and he and Dixie delivery a baby at a restaurant during lunch.

11/30/1974

Emergency Episode - The Firehouse Four[80]
Focus is on other hospital staff and paramedics.

12/7/1974

Emergency Episode - Details[81]
Focus is on other hospital staff and paramedics.

12/21/1974

Emergency Episode - Parade[82]
Focus is on other hospital staff and paramedics. *See John Gage's (Randy Mantooth) Accident on the Set of the 70's TV Show "Emergency!" at https://www.youtube.com/watch?v=CDOWUZL1Bs8 .*

The Tonight Show with guest host Burt Reynolds (2/11/1936-9/6/2018). Other guests that evening were Bert Convy (7/23/1933=2/15/1991), Jack Warden (9/18/1920-7/19/2016) and Jonathan Winters (11/1/1925-4/11/2013 www.jonathanwinters.com[83] . He appears as himself.

12/28/1974

Emergency Episode - The Bash[84]
Dr. Brackett treats a man suffering from trichinosis (parasite / worms).

1975

Emergency Squad 51 eight inch action figures are being made by LTN toys.

Fleetwood Toys is making an Emergency Stamp set for $1.00.

---

79.   https://www.imdb.com/title/tt0570610/?ref_=ttep_ep10

80.   https://www.imdb.com/title/tt0570698/?ref_=ttep_ep11

81.   https://www.imdb.com/title/tt0570621/?ref_=ttep_ep12

82.   https://www.imdb.com/title/tt0570670/?ref_=ttep_ep13

83. http://www.jonathanwinters.com

84.   https://www.imdb.com/title/tt0570694/?ref_=ttep_ep14

Universal Studio's Placo Emergency Fireman's Hat is being made.

Minnesota State TV Guide - All Emergency Cast is on cover.

Japanese Magazines include photos of Robert with first year Laramie cast.:

Japanese Magazines include this one where some sources show this one as Television Age in 1977. Robert is on cover wearing a suit and tie. It includes photos from all three of his TV series.

The Oregon Trail. The episode is titled Suffer the Children and Robert plays Hancock, a religious fanatic.

1/1975
Screen & TV Album magazine. He is not on cover.

1/4/1975
Emergency Episode - Transition[85]
Focus is on other hospital staff and paramedics.

1/11/1975
Emergency Episode - Smoke Eater[86]
Focus is on other hospital staff and paramedics.

1/14/1975
Robert's third child a son, Patrick D., is born. (Prior to Patrick's birth they were refurnishing the house and Patty was working too much and went into labor 2 months early. At 9:20 with a C-section, Patrick was born. The first 5 days it was unknown whether he would live or die. Robert was on Hollywood Squares at this time and shared some details when asked. (Some time afterward, Robert brought baby Patrick on to Hollywood Squares. Patrick's godfather is Patrick Wayne (7/15/1939-) and in 1999 his son Patrick is working in Los Angels at a bronco bull place. He is also a good shot).

85.   https://www.imdb.com/title/tt0570720/?ref_=ttep_ep15

86.   https://www.imdb.com/title/tt0570686/?ref_=ttep_ep16

Publicity Introducing Patrick Fuller - Robert's new son is later released including a family shot with Robert, wife Patty, daughter Christine and oldest son Robert hold younger baby Patrick.

1/18/1975

Emergency Episode - Kidding[87]
Focus is on other hospital staff and paramedics.

1/25/1975

Emergency Episode - Prestidigitation[88]
Dr. Brackett's father is in the hospital.

2/1/1975

Emergency Episode - It's How You Play the Game[89]
Focus is on other hospital staff and paramedics.

2/8/1975

Emergency Episode - The Mouse[90]
Focus is on other hospital staff and paramedics.

2/15/1975

Emergency Episode - Back-Up[91]
Focus is on other hospital staff and paramedics.

3/1/1975

Emergency Episode - 905-Wild[92]
Focus is on other hospital staff and paramedics. This episode was a pilot that failed to sell, for a new series about animal control staff.

3/6/1975

The Dinah Shore (2/29/1916-2/24/1994) Show. He appears as himself.

87.   https://www.imdb.com/title/tt0570656/?ref_=ttep_ep17

88.   https://www.imdb.com/title/tt0570673/?ref_=ttep_ep18

89.   https://www.imdb.com/title/tt0570655/?ref_=ttep_ep19

90.   https://www.imdb.com/title/tt0570707/?ref_=ttep_ep20

91.   https://www.imdb.com/title/tt0570603/?ref_=ttep_ep21

92.   https://www.imdb.com/title/tt0570596/?ref_=ttep_ep22

4/16/1975

Robert receives a star on Hollywood's Walk of Fame at 6608 Hollywood Boulevard in Hollywood, California. At the time it was near Frederick's of Hollywood but the business is no longer there. The author's photo is below.

ROBERT'S STAR IN HOLLYWOOD

4/21/1975

The Dinah Shore (2/29/1916-2/24/1994) Show. He appears as himself.

5/4/1975

Lancaster, Pennsylvania TV Guide. Robert is not on cover but article title is "Emergency's Robert Fuller Advises Would-Be Doctors". Robert is wearing a suit and tie.

6/18/1975

The Dinah Shore (2/29/1916-2/24/1994) Show. He appears as himself.

6/22 - 6/28/1975

Washington Post TV Guide. It is titled The surprise of 'Emergency!" is its stars. The cover is the five member cast. Article mentions that Robert, Jr. is 11 and Christine is 10 years old.

7/15/1975

Detroit Free Press Weekly Magazine (TV Guide). He is not on cover. He photo is in the Q & A section mentioning the usual background info and that on his first job interview he was told he looked too much like Tony Curtis.

8/3/1975

St. Louis Post-Dispatch TV Guide. Robert is not on cover. Article title is "Emergency" Emerges a Winner. Photo is a close up as Dr. Brackett.

8/4/1975

Magnificent Marble Machine - Game Show teams a celebrity with contestant playing a giant pinball machine. He appears as himself.

8/6/1975

The Dinah Shore (2/29/1916-2/24/1994) Show. He appears as himself.

8/16 - 8/22/1975

Minnesota TV Guide. The cast of five is on the cover.

9/1975

Movie World Magazine. He is not on cover.

Rona Barrett's Gossip Television Magazine. He is not on cover.

9/13/1975

Emergency Episode - The Stewardess[93]
Focus is other hospital staff and paramedics.

9/20/1975

Emergency Episode - The Old Engine Cram[94]
Focus is other hospital staff and paramedics.

FALL OF 1975

Robert appeared on Hollywood Squares. *See Hollywood Squares- Fall 1975 (Martha vs. Charles) at https://www.youtube.com/watch?v=1gWh4YcSzng&list=PLEfV88OMgZ2pItO4wyfBj5VEiPkSEAshE* .

---

93.   https://www.imdb.com/title/tt0570715/?ref_=ttep_ep1

94.   https://www.imdb.com/title/tt0570710/?ref_=ttep_ep2

Movie Land and TV Time Annual Magazine. He is not on cover.

Movie World Magazine. He is not on cover.

9/27/1975

Emergency Episode - Election[95]

Dr. Brackett asks parents to make treatment decision for their son.

10/4/1975

Emergency Episode - Equipment[96]

Focus is other hospital staff and paramedics.

10/6/1975

The Dinah Shore (2/29/1916-2/24/1994) Show. He appears as himself.

10/11/1975

Emergency Episode - The Inspection[97]

Dr. Brackett and Dixon treat a veterinarian bit by a dog and a traffic accident victim.

10/18/1975

Emergency Episode - The Indirect Method[98]

Focus is other hospital staff and paramedics.

10/25/1975

Emergency Episode - Pressure 165[99]

Drs. Brackett and Early deal with very angry shot young person who may not be able to dance again.

11/1/1975

Emergency Episode - One of Those Days[100]

95.   https://www.imdb.com/title/tt0570625/?ref_=ttep_ep3

96.   https://www.imdb.com/title/tt0570629/?ref_=ttep_ep4

97.   https://www.imdb.com/title/tt0570704/?ref_=ttep_ep5

98.   https://www.imdb.com/title/tt0570703/?ref_=ttep_ep6

99.   https://www.imdb.com/title/tt0570672/?ref_=ttep_ep7

100.   https://www.imdb.com/title/tt0570668/?ref_=ttep_ep8

Focus is other hospital staff and paramedics. Scripts, including this one, can sometimes be bought.

11/15/1975

Emergency Episode - The Lighter-Than-Air Man[101]
Focus is other hospital staff and paramedics.

11/21/1975

Cleveland Press TV Showtime TV magazine. The title is A fuller life for Bob and mentions he made $600 a week on Laramie, is 42 years old, loves his wife of 12 years and is working 2 ½ days a week leaving Wednesday for a 'long weekend'.

11/22/1975

Emergency Episode - Simple Adjustment[102]
Focus is other hospital staff and paramedics.

11/29/1975

Emergency Episode - Tee Vee[103]
Dr. Brackett is trying to take care of an aquarium that appears without his knowledge in his office.

12/1975

Photoplay Magazine introduces Robert's son Patrick Daniel. Patrick's godfather is Patrick Wayne.

12/6/1975

Emergency Episode - On Camera[104]
Focus is other hospital staff and paramedics.

12/13/1975

Emergency Episode - Communications[105]
Focus is other hospital staff and paramedics.

101.   https://www.imdb.com/title/tt0570705/?ref_=ttep_ep9

102.   https://www.imdb.com/title/tt0570685/?ref_=ttep_ep10

103.   https://www.imdb.com/title/tt0570692/?ref_=ttep_ep11

104.   https://www.imdb.com/title/tt0570667/?ref_=ttep_ep12

105.   https://www.imdb.com/title/tt0570613/?ref_=ttep_ep13

12/20/1975

Emergency Episode - To Buy or Not to Buy[106]
Focus is other hospital staff and paramedics.

12/26/1975

The Dinah Shore (2/29/1916-2/24/1994) Show with Robert and the cast of Emergency. *See Dinah Shore with Emergency! Cast* *https://video.search.yahoo.com/search/ video?fr=yfp-t&p=robert+fuller+interviews#id=65&vid=0e5c345a0ff2e04d077f4472d1d20b27&action=view[107]*.

1976

Charlton Comics releases Emergency TV Show Vol. 1, Number 1. Robert is not on cover drawing.

Charlton Comics releases Emergency TV Show Vol. 1, Number 2. Robert is not on cover drawing. His character is in the comic and he is pictured in the Official "Emergency" Cast Photo Gallery in Vol. 1, # 2.

Hollywood Squares - Game show where Robert appears as himself trying to stump contestants.

Mustang Country. Robert plays Griff in a cameo and doubled for Joel McCrea (11/5/1905-10/20/1990). It was written by Laramie creator John C. Champion (10/13/1923-10/3/1994) who got Joel to come out of retirement to take the role. John wrote, directed and produced this movie. It took one month to film in Banff, Canada. Australia and U.S. used the same marketing poster of Robert and Patrick both dressed warmly in front of snow capped mountains. Mustang Country film wins a Western Heritage Trustees Award for outstanding family entertainment in a western motion picture.

Mustang Country's primary publicity photo is Joel McCrea, an Indian boy (first and only film) with wilderness animals in front of a mountain scene. This design was also used as for Australian lobby cards and a 27 x 40 inch poster. VHS and DVD's with the same drawing are also released.

Emergency decides to change the focus of the show. There are fewer and fewer hospital scenes and more and more rescues.

106.	https://www.imdb.com/title/tt0570718/?ref_=ttep_ep14

107.	*https://video.search.yahoo.com/search/*

video?fr=yfp-t&p=robert+fuller+interviews#id_43ec3e5dee6e706af7766fffea512721_65_6cff047854f19ac2aa52aac51bf3af4a_vid_43ec3e5dee6e706af7766fffea5127

21_0e5c345a0ff2e04d077f4472d1d20b27_6cff047854f19ac2aa52aac51bf3af4a_action_43ec3e5dee6e706af7766fffea512721_view

Who's Who in Movies and TV - Giant Gossip Issue. He is not on cover.

1/10/1976

Emergency Episode - Right at Home[108]

Dr. Brackett is with a helicopter rescuing a father and son.

1/17/1976

Emergency Episode - The Girl on the Balance Beam[109]

Focus is other hospital staff and paramedics.

1/24/1976

Emergency Episode - Involvement[110]

Focus is other hospital staff and paramedics.

1/31/1976

Emergency Episode - Above and Beyond. Nearly[111]

Drs. Bracket and Early and Dixie treat a man who passed out while at the dentist.

2/7/1976

Emergency Episode - Grateful[112]

Focus is other hospital staff and paramedics.

2/21/1976

Emergency Episode - The Great Crash Diet[113]

Focus is other hospital staff and paramedics.

2/28/1976

Emergency Episode - The Tycoons[114]

Focus is other hospital staff and paramedics.

108.   https://www.imdb.com/title/tt0570678/?ref_=ttep_ep15

109.   https://www.imdb.com/title/tt0570700/?ref_=ttep_ep16

110.   https://www.imdb.com/title/tt0570653/?ref_=ttep_ep17

111.   https://www.imdb.com/title/tt0570597/?ref_=ttep_ep18

112.   https://www.imdb.com/title/tt0570639/?ref_=ttep_ep19

113.   https://www.imdb.com/title/tt0570701/?ref_=ttep_ep20

114.   https://www.imdb.com/title/tt0570716/?ref_=ttep_ep21

3/6/1976

Emergency Episode - The Nuisance[115]

Focus is other hospital staff and paramedics.

7/1976

Emergency Comic Book Vol. 1, No. 1 by Chalton Publications, is printed.

9/1976

Emergency Comic Book Vol. 2 by Chalton Publications is printed.

9/25/1976

Emergency Episode - The Game[116]

Focus is other hospital staff and paramedics. In the sixth season changes in the hospital staff included both Robert Fuller and Booby Troup's characters having another certification and Julie London with new outfit and no nurse's cap. The beginning credits changed for a third time this year showing Robert talking with dispatcher.

10/2/1976

Emergency Episode - Not Available[117]

Focus is other hospital staff and paramedics.

10/9/1976

Emergency Episode - The Unlikely Heirs[118]

Focus is other hospital staff and paramedics.

10/23/1976

Emergency Episode - That Time of Year[119]

Focus is other hospital staff and paramedics.

10/30/1976

---

115. https://www.imdb.com/title/tt0570708/?ref_=ttep_ep22

116. https://www.imdb.com/title/tt0570699/?ref_=ttep_ep1

117. https://www.imdb.com/title/tt0570665/?ref_=ttep_ep2

118. https://www.imdb.com/title/tt0570717/?ref_=ttep_ep3

119. https://www.imdb.com/title/tt0570693/?ref_=ttep_ep4

Emergency Episode - Fair Fight[120]
Focus is other hospital staff and paramedics.

11/1976

Emergency Comic Book Vol. 3 by Chalton Publications is printed.

11/6/1976

Emergency Episode - Rules of Order[121]
Focus is other hospital staff and paramedics.

11/[122]13/1976

Emergency Episode - The Exam[123]
Focus is other hospital staff and paramedics.

11/20/1976

Emergency Episode - Captain Hook[124]
Focus is other hospital staff and paramedics.

12/1976

Emergency Comic Book Vol. 4 by Chalton Publications is printed.

12/4/1976

Emergency Episode - Computer Terror[125]
Focus is other hospital staff and paramedics.

12/25/1976

Emergency Episode - Welcome to Santa Rosa County[126]
Focus is other hospital staff and paramedics.

120.	https://www.imdb.com/title/tt0570630/?ref_=ttep_ep5

121.	https://www.imdb.com/title/tt0570680/?ref_=ttep_ep6

122. https://www.imdb.com/title/tt0570697/?ref_=ttep_ep7

123.	https://www.imdb.com/title/tt0570697/?ref_=ttep_ep7

124.	https://www.imdb.com/title/tt0570611/?ref_=ttep_ep8

125.	https://www.imdb.com/title/tt0570615/?ref_=ttep_ep9

126.	https://www.imdb.com/title/tt0570725/?ref_=ttep_ep10

1977

Studio Press Emergency photos are released. One is an almost full length of Bobby and Robert as their doctor characters.

The Oregon Trail. The episode is titled Suffer the Children and Robert plays Hancock, a religious fanatic.

Japanese Magazine - Television Age. *See 1975 where one source has this magazine instead of 1977.*

1/8/1977

Emergency Episode - Paper Work[127]
Focus is other hospital staff and paramedics.

1/15/1977

Emergency Episode - Loose Ends[128]
Dr. Brackett is in a car accident and blames himself when a death occurs.

1/22/1977

Emergency Episode - An Ounce of Prevention[129]
Focus is other hospital staff and paramedics.

2/5/1977

Emergency Episode - Insanity Epidemic[130]
Dr. Brackett comes into conflict with new hospital administrator.

2/12/1977

Emergency Episode - Breakdown[131]
Focus is other hospital staff and paramedics.

---

127.   https://www.imdb.com/title/tt0570669/?ref_=ttep_ep11

128.   https://www.imdb.com/title/tt0570659/?ref_=ttep_ep12

129.   https://www.imdb.com/title/tt0570601/?ref_=ttep_ep13

130.   https://www.imdb.com/title/tt0570650/?ref_=ttep_ep14

131.   https://www.imdb.com/title/tt0570608/?ref_=ttep_ep15

2/19/1977

Emergency Episode - Family Ties[132]

Dr. Brackett doesn't want to go to a convention in Acapulco and Dr. Early and Dixie try to convince him to go.

2/26/1977

Emergency Episode - Bottom Line[133]

Focus is other hospital staff and paramedics.

3/5/1977

Emergency Episode - Firehouse Quintet[134]

Focus is other hospital staff and paramedics.

3/[135]12/1977

Emergency Episode - The Boat[136]

Focus is other hospital staff and paramedics.

3/19/1977

Emergency Episode - Isolation[137]

Focus is other hospital staff and paramedics.

3/26/1977

Emergency Episode - Limelight[138]

Drs. Brackett and Morton treat a boy who accidentally shot himself with a BB gun.

4/2/1977

Emergency Episode - Upward and Onward[139]

Dr. Brackett confronts soap opera doctor with mono and his studio after producer is filming ill patient at hospital.

132.   https://www.imdb.com/title/tt0570631/?ref_=ttep_ep16

133.   https://www.imdb.com/title/tt0570606/?ref_=ttep_ep17

134.   https://www.imdb.com/title/tt0570632/?ref_=ttep_ep18

135. https://www.imdb.com/title/tt0570695/?ref_=ttep_ep19

136.   https://www.imdb.com/title/tt0570695/?ref_=ttep_ep19

137.   https://www.imdb.com/title/tt0570654/?ref_=ttep_ep20

138.   https://www.imdb.com/title/tt0570658/?ref_=ttep_ep21

139.   https://www.imdb.com/title/tt0570722/?ref_=ttep_ep22

4/16/1977

Emergency Episode - Hypochondri-Cap[140]

Dr. Brackett gives info to Roy about his Captain's arthritis. Drs. Bracket and Early and Dixie treat a woman's botched plastic surgery.

5/15/1977

Robert attended the NBC TV Affiliate Dinner with his wife Patty. *(NBC shows from the 1976-1977 season include Columbo, Emergency, Gemini Man, Gibbsville, Kingston: Confidential, Lanigan's Rabbi, McCloud, McMillian & Wife, Quinn, Serpico, Sirota's Court, Tales of the Unexplained, The Fantastic Journey, The Kallikaks, The McLean Stevenson Show, The Quest, The Practice, The Runaways and Van Dyke and Company. Returning NBC shows in the 1977-1978 season include Chico and the Man, C.P.O. Sharkey, Headlines With David Frost, Little House on the Prairie, Police Woman, Quark, Quincy, M.E., The Black Sheep Squadron, The Life and Times of Grizzly Adams, The Rockford Files and The Wonderful World of Disney).*

5/28/1977

Emergency Episode - All Night Long[141]
Focus is other hospital staff and paramedics.

10/3/1977

To Say the Least - Game Show. One of his partners is actor Jamie Farr (7/1/1934 -) - *See www.youtube.com*[142] .

12/21/1977

The Dinah Shore (2/29/1916-2/24/1994) Show. He appears as himself.

1978

Hollywood Squares - as himself/guest in top corner square. He is a great liar.

Robert is made up as a monster for Universal Studios Tour . The author's photo is below.

---

140.   https://www.imdb.com/title/tt0570646/?ref_=ttep_ep23

141.   https://www.imdb.com/title/tt0570598/?ref_=ttep_ep24

142.   *http://www.youtube.com*

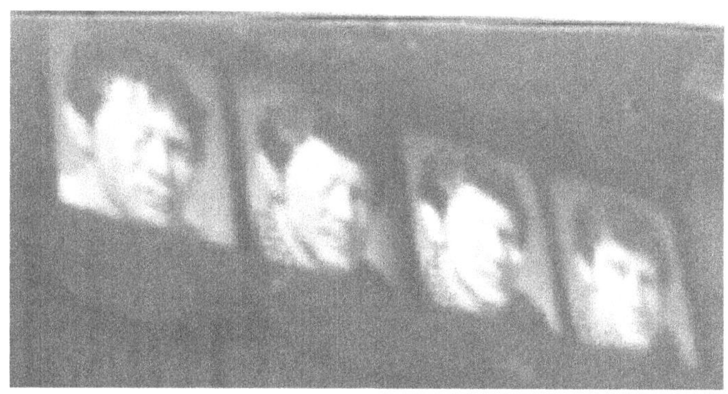

MONSTER MAKE-UP FOR UNIVERSAL STUDIO TOUR

You Don't Say - Game Show

Cincinnati, Ohio TV Guide - The WIZ is on the cover.

Wisconsin TV Guide. Emergency One! ad is drawings of cast saying it is on Monday through Friday at 4 p.m. on WEAD-TV, Eau Claire.

1/1978

Guns Magazine. He is not on cover.

1/7/1978

Emergency Made for TV Movie – The Steel Inferno
Dr. Brackett's last appearance on series.

3/28//1978

Emergency Made for TV Movie - Survival on Charter #220[143]
Robert Fuller is not in and focus is on other hospital staff and paramedics.

4/4/1978

Emergency Made for TV Movie - Most Deadly Passage[144]
Robert Fuller is not in and focus is on paramedics.

---

143.   https://www.imdb.com/title/tt9167816/?ref_=ttep_ep4

144.   https://www.imdb.com/title/tt9167844/?ref_=ttep_ep5

5/1978

Rona Barrett's Gossip Magazine. He is not on cover.

10/1978

Robert worked with Karen Black (7/1/1930-8/8/2013) in Valentine.

10/21/1978

TV Guide for the week of 10/21 to 10/27 with WKRP cover but inside has Donner Pass: The Road to Survival promo world premier ad.

10/24/1978

Donner Pass: The Road to Survival - TV movie. Robert plays James Reed and narrator. It is based on a true story of the Donner Party wagon train. It was filmed in Knab, Utah in the winter, in the cold and snow. See *Robert Fuller as James Reed - See https://www.youtube.com/watch?v=qAC5kXuZqGI and* Donner Pass (1978) Robert Fuller | John Doucette - True Adventure HD at https://www.youtube.com/watch?v=VPZ4mxx-cWY *and Robert Fuller telling a little about filming The Donner Party Movie at https://www.youtube.com/watch?v=jWhyAR79-hs when he attended the 2010 Western Toy Show.*

Other cast members include:
    Andrew Prine (2/14/1936-)
    Diane McBain (5/18/1941-)
    John Anderson (10/20/1922-8/7/1992)
    John Doucette (1/21/1921-8/16/1994)
    Lance LeGault (5/2/1936-9/10/2012)
    Michael Callan (11/22/1936-)
    Royal Dano (11/16/0122-5/15/1994)

VHS tapes were created. One version has Robert is wearing a hat with scarf over his ears. Another version is mountain scene with wagons.

12/31/1978

Emergency Made for TV Movie - Greatest Rescues of Emergency![145]
Flashbacks of series and focus is on paramedics.

---

145.   https://www.imdb.com/title/tt0295287/?ref_=ttep_ep7

1979

Chapter Two by Neil Simon was after his performance in Wait Until Dark at the Windmill Dinner Theatre in Scottsdale, Arizona. Robert is wearing a suit and tie on program cover. He is playing George Schneider. Program includes career summary and quote "I'm tired of us putting down our country. We should start looking at the positive values of our society and crease being critical and destructive. Let's try and keep the traditions we have unless we can substitute them without better ones".

Patty Fuller, Robert's wife plays Jennie Malone. The play program also shares her career info. At this time Robert and Patty have been married 17 years and their children Robert John is 15 ½, Christine Ann is 14 and Patrick Daniel is 4 (born 1/14/1975). Patty has also been an interior designer for several years and recently played a nurse in Harvey at the Burt Reynolds Dinner Theater and the Coconut Grove in Miami, Florida.

Television Age Japanese Magazine. He is not on cover. It is 48 pages.

TV Guide ad for the showing of A Return of Seven movie on TV station KCOP13 at 4 p.m. is titled A Western in the Tradition of The Greats. The ad with pistol drawn Robert and Yul is about 2 ½ inches x 3 ½ inches.

1/16/1979

The Dinah Shore (2/29/1916-2/24/1994) Show. He appears as himself.

6/26/1979

Emergency Made for TV Movie - What's a Nice Girl Like You Doing.?[146]
Robert Fuller is not in and focus is on paramedics.

7/3/1979

Emergency Made for TV Movie - The Convention[147]
Robert Fuller is not in and focus is on paramedics.

10/28/1979

Disaster on a Coastliner. It is a TV movie starring Lloyd Bridges (1/5/1913-3/10/1998) and William Shatner (3/22/1931-). He has a small part playing Matt Leigh, a womanizer. *See LSTV presents: DISASTER ON THE COASTLINER (1979) at https://www.youtube.com/watch?v=byiXyDtK98w* .

---

146.   https://www.imdb.com/title/tt0570726/?ref_=ttep_ep8

147.   https://www.imdb.com/title/tt0570696/?ref_=ttep_ep6

OUTDOOR YEARS 1980 - 1996

1980

Superior, Wisconsin TV Guide - Channel 6 one half page ad for Emergency cast drawing for shows airing Monday through Friday at 3 p.m.

Hollywood Square - as himself, a celebrity guest often in corner square.

Robert campaigned for Ronald Reagan (2/6/1911-6/5/2004) when he was running for U.S. presidency.

4/15/1980

Jake's Way. Robert plays a former rodeo rider now a modern sheriff named Jake Rudd who searches for his friend's killer. One of the actors on the show is Slim Pickens (6/29/1919-12/8/1983) playing a retired law enforcement officer. It contained helicopter, motorcycle and horseback riding action. Robert appeared on Hollywood Squares during this time talking about this pilot. (It never sold). *See jakes way.mp4 at https://www.youtube.com/watch?v=6Oq3J6dXVoM* .

6/15/1980

St. Louis Post-Dispatch TV Magazine with Debbie Boone on the cover. Robert and Ben Lemon and Steve McNaughton are pictured.

6/22 – 6/28/1980

Chicago Tribune TV Guide. He is not on cover. Photo shows Robert with Slim Pickens.

1981

Separate Ways. He plays Woody, a friend of actor Tony Lo Bianco (10/19/1936-)'s character with marriage difficulties. Cast also includes Karen Black (7/1/1936-8/8/2013).

Variety Clubs Dinner - Robert attended with wife Patty. Tawny Little (Miss America 1976) was also there.

1/1 - 1/18/1981

Wait until Dark play at the Coventry Dinner Playhouse in Albuquerque, New Mexico.

MARCH 1981

Guns Magazine. Robert in on cover in hunting attire (vest) with a rifle.

1981 - 1983

Fishing Fever - 26 episodes filmed in the Bahamas fishing for mahi-mahi, tuna and wahoo. The Bahamas was Robert's favorite place to see underwater life. *See https://www.youtube.com/watch?v=SER7vLUZ_lI to see clip from show.* Guests include:

Bo Hopkins (2/2/1942-)

Christopher George (2/25/1931-11/28/1983)

Dan Hagerty (11/19/1941-1/15/2016)

Doug McClure (5/11/1935-2/5/1995)

Foster Brooks (5/11/1812-12/20/2001)

James Caan (3/26/1940-)

James MacArthur (12/8/1937-10/28/2010 www.jamesmacarthur.com[1]).

Lee Meriwether (5/27/1935- www.leemeriwether.com[2]).

Lynda Day George (12/11/1944-).

Martin Milner (12/28/1931-9/6/2015)

Patrick Wayne 97/15/1939-)

Red West (3/8/1936-7/18/2017)

Richard Anderson (8/8/1926-8/31/2017)

Richard Jaeckel (10/10/1925-6/14/1997)

Ron Ely (6/2/1938-)

Slim Pickens (6/29/1919-12/8/1983)

Tom Kennedy (2/26/1927-)

1982

Megaforce. It is an unsold pilot about soldiers saving the world from evil but in reality its audience was children more than adults. Robert may have indicated it was worse than critics stated.

1/2/1982

The Love Boat. The episode is titled A Business Affair (other segments are/ Doc Takes the 5th/ Safety Last) . He plays- Ralph Kirby, a business executive trying to get a former female staff member back. Guest cast includes Judy Norton (1/29/1958-) www.judynorton.com[3] . Regular cast include Gavin MacLeod (2/28/1931-5/30/2021), Bernie Kopell (6/21/1933-) www.berniekopell.com[4] , Fred Grandy (6/29/1948-), and Ted Lange (1/5/1948-).

5/8/1982

---

1. http://www.jamesmacarthur.com

2. http://www.leemeriwether.com

3. http://www.judynorton.com

4. http://www.berniekobell.com

Fantasy Island. The episode is titled The Ghost Story / The Spoilers. He plays Nick Tanner, a bank robber, who is caught by a bounty hunter. Cast includes Bo Hopkins (2/2/1942-) and Joann Pflug (5/2/1940-) www.joannpflug.com[5] . *See Fantasy Island- S05E22- The Ghost's Story/The Spoilers at https://www.youtube.com/watch?v=hAL9MJy2xDg* .

10/31/1983

Scott's World Article - Robert Fuller Gone fishin' - *See https://www.upi.com/Archives/1983/10/31/Scotts-WorldNEWLNRobert-Fuller-Gone-fishin/1919436424400/* .

11/30/1983

The Fall Guy - The episode is titled Hollywood Shorties. He plays Lt. Ryan, a crooked cop. The series starred Lee Major (4/23/1939-). Other cast include Heather Thomas (9/8/1957-) and Douglas Barr (5/1/1949-). *See The Fall Guy 3x10 Hollywood Shorties [Full Episode] at https://www.youtube.com/watch?v=pBi6h06IAYw* .

1984

Mord ist ihr Hobby. It might be a subbed German retitle of Murder She Wrote as Murder is Her Hobby.

Patricia Lee Lyon and Robert divorced after 22 years with three children (Robert - Robin /Rob, Christine and Patrick). (In 1984 she is diagnosed with cancer and Robert decides to quit smoking).

1/26/1985

The Love Boat - The episode is titled Her Honor the Mayor. He plays Phil Haines, a male political candidate running against a woman played by Shelley Fabares (1/19/1944-). Regular cast includes: Gavin MacLeod (2/28/1931-5/30/2021), Bernie Kopell (6/21/1933-) www.berniekopell.com[6] , Fred Gandy (6/29/1948-) and Ted Lange (1/5/1948-).

2/8/1985

Matt Houston - The episode is titled A New Orleans Nightmare. He plays Phil Caudler. Shari Belafonte (9/22/1954-) also guests. Series regular cast includes Lee Horsley (5/15/1944-) and Pamela Hensley (10//1950-).

2/23/1985

Finder of Lost Lives - The episode is titled Tricks and he plays Matt Dayton. Cast includes Anthony Franciosa (10/25/1928-1/19/2006).

5.	http://www.joannpflug.com

6.	http://www.berniekobell.com

1986 OR 1987

Robert was a judge in a beauty contest in Okeechobee, Florida, an area where he fished.

1986

Adam 12 title Lost and Found combines storyline with Emergency television program. Cast includes Martin Milner (12/28/1931-9/6/2015) and Kent McCord (9/26/1942-) www.kentmccord.com[7] .

Cast of Emergency, minus ill Julie London, appears on Good Morning America. *See www.youtube.com title Good Morning America! Emergency! Cast Interview at https://www.youtube.com/watch?v=v2Mj3hRx-Ag* .

2/7/1986

The Fall Guy - The episode is titled Lucky Stiff. He plays Mr. Watson. Emergency co star Randy Mantooth (9/19/ 1945-) also appears. The series starred Lee Majors (4/23/1939-). Other cast include Heather Thomas (9/8/1957-) and Douglas Barr (5/1/1949-).

2/12/1986

Blacke's Magic - The episode is titled Vanishing Act. He plays Chief Rocky Datchery, a small town sheriff. Cast includes Harry Morgan (4/10/1915-12/7/2011 and Hal Linden (3/20/1931-).

5/27/1986

TV Special - The Wildest West Show of the Stars. Robert, as himself, presents the quick draw award to Dirk Benedict and Joey for slingshot. It also stars Dennis Weaver (6/4/1924-2/24/2006) www.dennisweaver.com[8] .

1987

Robert had planned to stay single but is with Jennifer Savidge (7/6/1952-). *(They met at a Celebrity Tennis Tournament in Tucson, Arizona at a western party at a western bar. He was with Richard Anderson and Jennifer asked him to dance). Jennifer was previously married to Timothy Burns. She was an actress who had started her career in 1982 and from 1982 to 1988 she played a nurse named Lucy Papandrao on NBC's St. Elsewhere. Jennifer appeared in several TV movies, L.A. Law, Lois & Clark: The New Adventures of Superman, Sisters, Star Trek: DeepSpace Nine and Beverly Hills, 90210 and from 2000 to 2005 appeared as Commander Amy Helfman on CBS's JAG. Her movie credits include Clifford and Magic King both in 1994, True Crime in 1996 and Evolution in 2001. When working Jennifer had had long hours often starting before 6 a.m.).*

2/18/1988

7.   http://www.kentmccord.com

8.   http://www.dennisweaver.com

Tour of Duty - The episode is titled Soldiers. He plays Jake Purcell, father of a solider. Cast includes Terence Knox (12/16/1946-), Stephen Caffrey (9/27/1959-) and Tony Becker (9/14/1963-).

3/23/1988

Bonanza: The Next Generation - TV movie. He plays Charlie Poke, a ranch foreman for Ponderosa. Although it goes on to become a series, Robert is only hired for this one episode. Cast includes John Ireland (1/30/1914-3/21/1992), Peter Mark Richman (4/16/1927-) www.petermarkrichman.com[9] , John Amos (12/27/1939-) and Michael Landon, Jr. (6/20/1964-). *See Bonanza The Next Generation (1988) Western Robert Fuller at https://www.youtube.com/watch?v=shM2jEmUdmE .*

David Dortort's 1987 TV Press material includes information on main characters. Robert's role is included along with a photo of him and his hours.

DVD cover created has Robert's image the largest.

5/8/1988

Murder She Wrote - The episode is titled Body Politic. He plays Arthur Drelinger, a politician. The series starred Angela Landsbury (10/16/1925-). Guest cast also includes Eddie Albert (4/22/1906-5/26/2005) and Peter Fox.

7/1988

UK Photoplay Magazine.

8/19/1988

Robert attended the 6th Annual Golden Boot Wards at Marriott Hotel in Woodland Hills, California.

1989

All Dogs Go to Heaven - He is the voice of Harold in a Disney cartoon.

20th Anniversary Reunion for Emergency with stars and fans around the world.

1989 OR 1990

9.   http://www.petermarkrichman.com

The Comeback - Japan. It was filmed in Tokyo and Kamakura, Japan. He plays a boxing manager. Cast includes world champion boxer Guts Ishimatus (6/5/1949-).

4/22/1989

The Second Academy Awards for the Handicapped at the Westin Hotel in Boston, Massachusetts.

8/5/1989

Golden Boot Award. The award, a plaque, is given by the Motion Picture and Television Fund to someone for the best personification and lifestyle of a cowboy. Event consists of a casual party night before award ceremony and then a huge dinner affair for ticket holders only. Fund money is used to assist actors, unemployed or indigent with medical expenses, food, treatment and clothing. They also fund a hospital, clinic and assisted care housing and nursing home. Pictures of Robert holding his award show he is wearing a white short sleeve shirt and blue jeans.

9/16/1989

Guns of Paradise - The episode is titled Home Again. He plays Sam Clanton, a gunman after Wyatt Earp (played by Hugh O'Brien (4/19/1925-9/5/2016). Cast includes Lee Horsley (5/15/1955-) and Jenny Beck (8/3/1974-).

1980'S

Robert father retires.

1990 OR 1991

Robert and Jennifer both attended a Salute to Chuck Norris's "Kick Drugs Out of America" event (founded 8/10/1990).

1990

Repossessed. It is a cameo role as Dr. Hackett, a take off of his Emergency character of Dr. Bracket. Movie stars Linda Blair (1/22/1959-) www.reallindablair.com[10] . *See Robert Fuller as Dr. Hackett in Repossessed 1990 at https://www.youtube.com/watch?v=7es9IhOwvOQ or A Robert Fuller Cameo for Halloween at https://www.youtube.com/watch?v=vK95uMPgpGM* .

He may have turned down the role of Holling Vincoeur (bar and restaurant owner) in Northern Exposure. The role was played by John Cullum (3/2/1930-).

3/18/1990

Festival of the West in Scottsdale, Arizona. James Drury (4/18/1934-4/6/2020 www.thevirginian.net[11]) also attends.

1991

Goldrush - One part mini series filmed in Russia. His role is Jim Bowie.

Under Western Skies #41 Magazine features Robert Fuller in Texas Rangers Series. Robert is on the cover in an often used photo of him at the fence rails holding his pistol.

1/4/1991

Guns of Paradise - The episode is titled Out of Ashes. He plays Marshall Blake, a crooked marshal who gets killed. Cast includes Lee Horsley (5/15/1955-) and Jenny Beck (8/3/1974-). Behind the scenes photo has Robert sitting on the western town set chair taking a cigarette break.

4/1991 - 4/2016

Encore pay cable station operates showing some of Robert's westerns.

1992

Emergency Reunion attended by most of stars and fans from all over world.

1993

Colorado River Adventure - series host and presenter. Guests include Alex Hyde-White (1/30/1959-), Andrew Prine (2/14/1936-), Buck Taylor (5/13/1938-), Dan Haggerty (11/19/1941-1/15/2016), Dennis Cole (6/19/1941-11/15/2009), Doug McClure (5/11/1935-2/5/1995), Frank Bonner (2/28/1942-), Jennifer Savidge (7/6/1952-), Morgan Woodward (9/16/1925-2/22/2019) www.morganwoodward.com[12] , Richard Anderson (8/8/1926-8/31/2017) and Patrick Wayne (7/15/1939-).

Colorado River Adventure series that Robert hosted releases a DVD over six hours. The cover includes four travel photos with a fifth of Robert Fuller near the top right corner.

6/6/1993

After their divorce, Patty had been diagnosed with cancer. Patricia Lyon Lee Fuller, dies with Robert and her children present in Palm Beach, Florida at age 49.

11.   http://www.thevirginian.net

12.   http://www.morganwoodward.com

12/16 AND 12/23/1993

Alaska Kid, a German-Russian-Polish TV series. Robert plays Oberst Bowie in two episodes, the 10th Das grobe Rennen and 11th Todliches Poker. It starred English born actor Mark Pillow (4/14/1959-).

8/1993

Robert attended the Golden Boot Awards to honor and speak at Chuck Courtney's induction. *(Chuck played a key role in Robert's life. Born 7/23/1930 he was the son and step-son of stuntmen. From 1950 to 1992 Chuck acted, was a stunt man and stunt coordinator in many movies and television programs. He became first known in 1950 to 1955 and later in his role as the Lone Ranger's nephew. Chuck also wrote his autobiography. He honored his mother and was married to Geraldine for 25 years. Chuck had a series of strokes and committed suicide on 1/20/2000 at age 69).*

8/23/1993

The Adventures of Briscoe County Jr. His cameo role in this pilot is Kenyon Drummond. Cast includes Bruce Campbell (6/22/1958-) www.bruce-campbell.com[13] , Christian Clemenson (3/17/1958-) and Julius Carry (3/12/1952-8/19/2008). A pilot cast photo of seven men is taken.

9/17/1993

The Adventures of Briscoe County Jr. - Briscoe in Jalisco. He plays Kenyon Drummond in a cameo role. Cast includes Bruce Campbell (6/22/1958-) www.bruce-campbell.com[14] , Christian Clemenson (3/17/1958-) and Julius Carry (3/12/1952-8/19/2008).

9/24/1993

The Program - He played Tim Waymen and cast includes James Caan (3/26/1940-) and Halle Berry (8/14/1966-).

1994 - 2005

Encore pay cable station now has an entire channel, Westerns, showing some of Robert's work. *(Robert was happy fans and a new audience could be exposed to great westerns).*

1994

Maverick. He plays a cameo role of a riverboat poker player. Filming took about ten days. Cast includes Mel Gibson (1/3/1956-), Jody Foster (11/19/1962-), James Gardner (4/7/1928-7/19/2014) and Doug McClure (5/11/1935-2/5/1995). A cast photo of eight men is taken.

---

13.   http://www.bruce-campbell.com

14.   http://www.bruce-campbell.com

Robert helps get Doug McClure (5/11/1935-2/5/1995) a star on the Hollywood Walk of Fame before he dies. *(Starting in 1956 Doug had 65 roles over his acting career including appearing in five television series (1962-1973's The Virginian /Man From Shiloh, 1972-1973's Search, 1975's Barbary Coast and 1988's Out of This World). Doug, like many celebrities, donated his time to charities like Ben Johnson's Annual Children's Benefit. Knowing he was ill, Robert helped get him a star on its Walk of Fame on 12/16/1994. This gave Doug more incentive to get well and Robert thought he was getting better. Doug was more worried about his family than himself. On 1/8/1994 he collapsed while working and doctors discovered he had lung cancer that had spread to his bones and liver).*

1994 - 1995

Blue Water Challenge - co-host. It is 13 episodes shot around the world. Marlin, sailfish and swordfish fishing locations include Australia, Bahamas, Mexico and Venezuela. His co-host is Marsha Bierman a championship fisherwoman and one of the founding members of Florida's Bonefish and Tarpon Trust at (www.bonefishtarpontrust.org[15]) . Also see www.marshalbierman.com[16] and www.dto.com/Swfishing/article/559[17] .

See Robert Fuller Holds a Koala at https://www.youtube.com/watch?v=9hnMuCicsAk .

2/27/1995

Kung Fu" The Legend Continues. The episode is titled The Gunfighters and he plays McBride. Clint Walker (5/30/1927-5/21/2018 www.clintwalker.com[18]) as Cheyenne Bodie also appears. Other cast includes David Carradine (12/8/1936-6/3/2009), Chris Potter (8/23/1960-), Kim Chan (12/28/1917-10/5/2008) and Robert Lansing (6/5/1928-19/23/1994). A cast photo of five standing men is taken.

9/25/1995

Betty M. Simpson, Robert's mom, dies. She had been living in Studio City, California with zip 91604.

10/1995

Robert's Grape Fed Quail recipe appears in the All American Cowboy Cookbook by Ken Beck and Jim Clark.

10/23/1995

---

15.   http://www.bonefishtarpontrust.org

16.   http://www.marshalbierman.com

17.   http://www.dto.com/Swfishing/article/559

18.   http://www.clintwalker.com

Renegade - The episode is titled Dead Heat. He plays Sam Crow, a racehorse trainer whose horses are being killed. Cast includes Lorenzo Lamos (1/20/1958-) and Branscombe Richmond (8/8/1955-). *See Renegade - Season 4, Episode 6 - Dead Heat - Full Episode at ttps://www.youtube.com/watch?v=i6DUNppfEqA* .

THE LATER YEARS 1997 - 2021

1/30/1997

Seinfeld - The episode is titled The Comeback. It is a cameo and uncredited of a doctor's voice. Cast includes Jerry Seinfeld (4/29/1954-). A card is created.

8/30/1997

Email interview with Robert. *See www.emergencyfans.com/people/robert-fuller.htm*[1] .

10/2/1997

Diagnosis Murder - The episode is titled Malibu Fire. He plays Chris Newman whose house is in way of fire. The series stared Dick Van Dyke (12/13/1925-), Victoria Lynn Rowell (5/10/1959-) and Barry Van Dyke (7/31/1951-). *See Diagnosis Murder S5E3 MALIBU FIRE, Robert Fuller & Randolph Mantooth (Emergency!) at https://www.youtube.com/watch?v=yiTnX8zL1Go* .

11/8/1997

Walker Texas Ranger - The episode is titled Last of a Breed - Part 2. (He is not in Part 1). Cabe Wallace is a Texas Ranger who dies. The series starred Chuck Norris (3/10/1940-). *Walker Texas Ranger was filmed in Dallas about 75 miles from Robert's home.* A cast photo of five men is created.

1998

Info Commercial - Hidden Hooker. It is a fishing lure.

McDonalds commercial.

Radio - West Coast commercial.

Robeck's Juices - East Coast commercial.

4/20/1998

Viper - 2 Part story. The episode is titled The Homecoming. He plays Ethan Cole, a father of one of main characters. It was suppose to be recurring role but this character left series. Cast includes Jeff Kaake (1/10/1959-) and Joe Nipote (5/19/1956-). Robert filmed in Vancouver, Canada for two weeks.

---

1.   *http://www.emergencyfans.com/people/robert_fuller.htm*

6/1998

Memphis Film Festival in Tennessee.

7/2 - 7/4/1998

Western Film Fair in Charlotte, North Carolina. There is a DVD with Robert, Peter Brown and William Smith on a panel together. A brief summary of Robert's topic areas are a poker game with Yul Brynner, how he got started in Hollywood (move from Florida, 2 jobs, extra and stunt work, Korea, studying with Richard Boone and in New York City up to Teenage Thunder), motorcycle in Hard Ride movie, Laramie directors, playing the heavy / bad guy, his role on Wagon Train twice as guest and as regular, not taking over from Robert Horton (7/29/1924-3/9/2016), New York City arrest, cowboys / western stars he admired, the Rhonda Fleming Story, knowing Peter Brown and working with him in Lawman, working with William Smith in Wagon Train, long time friendships, his fear of spiders and other practical jokes.

10/9 - 10/11/1998

Emergency Convention at the he Burbank Airport Hilton in Burbank, California. Robert attends along with many others from the program. *See www.emergencyfans.com* .

1999

Robert is a good pool player.

Robert competes in many shooting competitions and wins awards including one International event this year,

30th anniversary of Emergency celebrations and tours.

2/22/1999

Robert spoke at Bobby Troup's funeral (5/11/1935-2/5/1995).

4/19/1999

True Hollywood Story - himself in author's James Stacy (12/23/1936-9/8/2016) biography.

6/1999

Memphis Film Festival.

12/1999 - 1/2000

Western Celebrity Hollywood Party with many movie and television stars is held in Laughlin, Nevada Jennifer Savidge attends with him. The author's photo is below.

PLAYING SPOONS IN LAUGHLIN, NEVADA

2000

Wildest Westerns Magazine. Robert Fuller - Collectors Issue No. 2. He is not on cover.

1/2000

Hollywood Collectors Show in Hollywood, California.

1/13/2000

Diagnosis Murder - The episode is titled Frontier Dad. He plays Bob McLane, a stunt co-coordinator thought to be a murderer. The series starred Dick Van Dyke (12/13/1925-), Victoria Lynn Rowell (5/10/1959- and Barry Van Dyke (7/31/1951-).

1/15/2000

Walker Texas Ranger - The episode is titled A Matter of Principle. He plays Wade Harper, a former Texas Ranger who is descendent of Jess Harper and after jewel thieves who shot his daughter. The series starred Chuck Norris (3/10/1940-). *Walker Texas Ranger was filmed in Dallas about 75 miles from Robert's home.*

See Robert fuller as Wade Harper on Walker Texas Ranger part 1at https://www.youtube.com/watch?v=1cAf925sFPM and part 2 at https://www.youtube.com/watch?v=gtvTZalxtoc and part 3 at https://www.youtube.com/watch?v=O0WN57h4_pg .

MAY 2000

Emergency truck and Station 51 set items (coats, defibrillator, hats, shirts, uniforms) are accepted by the National Museum of American History, part of the Smithsonian, to celebrate beginning of paramedic program.

5/14/2000

White House private tour for Emergency cast members.

2001

Drive-In Movie Memories. He shares his thoughts as he remembers drive-in movies in this documentary. See Drive In Movie Memories at https://www.youtube.com/watch?v=GfnTStV-gcQ . One of things Robert talked about in about 38 minutes is his movie The Brain from Planet from Arous.

Wildest Westerns - Collector's Issue No. 3 (Robert Fuller - Cowboy King of Cool). He is not on cover and is 97 pages.

2/27/2001

JAG - The episode is titled Retreat Hell and he plays a cameo role of a Marine Corps General. Cast includes David James Elliott (9/21/1960-), Catherine Bell (8/14/1968-) and Tracey Needham (3/28/1967-).

3/13/2001

JAG - The episode is titled Vallo and he plays a Marine Corps General. Cast includes David James Elliott (9/21/1960-), Catherine Bell (8/14/1968-) and Tracey Needham (3/28/1967-).

5/19/2001

Actress Jennifer Savidge and Robert marry at the Little Brown Church in Studio City, California. It is a second marriage for each of them. Robert's dad arrives too early, at 9 a.m. and sits through four weddings while waiting. *(Robert had proposed to Jennifer in Bernie Kopell's living room. He went down on one knee had a hard time getting up).* Alex Cord is best man. *(Later when Alex married Susannah Miller Robert was his best man).* The 25 minute ceremony is followed by a poolside reception at Diane McClure's (widow of Doug). Doug McClure's daughter, Tane McClure (6/8/1958-), an actress and singer and daughter Valarie McClure, also attended.

Others invited guests were Ed Ames *(7/9/1927- Ed sang with his brothers from1947 to early 1960's. Ed had singes from 1965-1970 and created albums from 1963 to 2001. His acting career started on Broadway and then into television;* Bo Hopkins *(2/2/1942- has had over 100 roles in movies and television starting in 1967 into 2020. Bo has been married to Sian Eleanor Green for over 30 years)* and Andrew Prine (2/14/1936- *From 1959 to 2008 he has had almost 200 roles in movies and television. He has been married to Heather Lowe for 35 years).*

(Jennifer continues to work in the television series Jag and in 2011 appears in Searching for Sonny, in 2014 in Rudderless in 2014 and in 2015 as Ruth Taylor in American Crime).

Walker, Texas Ranger - The Final Showdown. He plays Wade Harper in this 2 hour end of series. The part was written for him and he plays former episode character who dies. It is Robert's last role. The series starred Chuck Norris (3/10/19490-). *Walker Texas Ranger was filmed in Dallas about 75 miles from Robert's home.*

JULY - AUGUST 2001
Western Clippings Magazine has wedding details and photo.

2002
Calico Ghost Town.

Robert is included in Neil Summers book The Official TV Western Round-up.

Western Legends Round-Up.

1/9/2002
Robert and Jennifer attended NBC's 75th Anniversary All Star Reception in Los Angeles, California.

4/19 - 4/21/2002
Charity Tennis Tournament.

8/21 - 8/24/2002

Robert is honored at Kanab Western Legends Round Up and receives key to the town of Kanab and a sidewalk plaque in their Walk of Fame. Robert had filmed in Kanab, Utah during Death Valley Days, Donner Pass, Rin Tin Tin and Wagon Train.

12/6/2002

Southern California Motion Picture Council, Golden Star Halo Award of Special Merit for Outstanding Contribution to the Entertainment Industry.

2003

When Cowboys were King via History channel. Robert shares his thoughts in this documentary.

Kanab Western Legends Roundup Festival in Kanab, Utah.

3/2003

Festival of the West in Phoenix, Arizona.

5/6/2003

Robert's dad, Robert C. Simpson. (stage name Robert Cole), dies. He had been in Studio City, California with zip code 91604.

2004

Robert retires after being in the business 52 years. Over the course of his career Robert had about 95 different roles and made films in 17 countries. He was nominated for Germany's Bravo Magazine's 'Best Male TV Star' five times (winning three times). His wife Jennifer is still working.

Robert and Jennifer had previously visited an area in Texas near where friend actor Alex Cord (5/3/1933-) had recently purchased a ranch called Valley View. They found a property with two ponds just eight miles from the Cords. They decide to leave the noise, traffic and people in Los Angeles and move to a ranch in Northern Texas (south of the Red River in Oklahoma) in Cooke County (same as Gainesville). Ranch house has valley view with water. After retirement at the ranch Bob got himself a bass boat. They stock two ponds with bass and catfish. Fish that Robert doesn't clean and eat are caught and released. They grow hay harvesting 65 to 200 bales each cutting for their horses. They sell remaining Bermuda hay to nearby ranchers. Rain always affect cutting and the first cut usually goes to cattle. They may have a tornado shelter. Another fish Robert enjoys is blackjack.

Alex Cord's wife Susanne shows quarter horses so Jennifer enjoys doing dressage with her. They have a 9 year old Welsch cob that is 15' 2 inches high.

Wildest Westerns Magazine. Robert Fuller - Collectors Issue No. 6.

3/2004

Festival of the West in Phoenix, Arizona.

3/11 - 3/13/2004

Williamsburg Nostalgia Film Festival in Virginia.

3/20/2004

Robert receives the Cowboy Spirit Award at National Festival of the West in Phoenix, Arizona. The award design includes a saddle.

4/12/2004

Robert and his wife Jennifer attend Paramount / CBS party after 200th JAG episode at the Mondrian / Asia de Cuba in West Hollywood, California. *(Jennifer had worked on JAG as Amy Helfman its last six seasons. She had long work hours often 5:30 or 6 a.m. to 11 p.m. or midnight).*

7/1 - 7/4/2004

Tombstone Western Film and Book Exposition. Robert is one of several celebrity attendees who signs his name in cement. On 7/4 Robert created his 30 x 30 cement handprints for its Walk of Fame. The brochure cover includes quest photos. Robert is in the lower left corner.

3/2005

Festival of the West in Phoenix, Arizona. Wagon Train series is featured.

7/1 - 7/4/2005

Western Film and Book Expo. On 7/4 Robert created his 30 x 30 cement handprints for its Walk of Fame.

3/2006

Festival of the West in Phoenix, Arizona.

3/18/2006

The Robert Fuller Fandom and the National Festival of the West in Phoenix, Arizona give Robert a bronze sculpture of Jess Harper on Traveler in recognition of his years of work in the entertainment industry. (The event was last held in 2013).

2/10/2007

Nostalgia Convention in Baltimore, Maryland interview. *See www.youtube.com/watch?v=qMB3welaDIY*[2] .

3/2007

Festival of the West in Phoenix, Arizona. *See Festival of the West 2008 at https://www.youtube.com/watch?v=EGRmScvPB30* .

6/2007

Memphis Film Festival. Dennis Holmes (10/3/1950-), Robert Crawford, Jr. (5/31/1944-) and James Drury (4/18/1934-4/6/2020 www.thevirginian.net[3]) also attend.

10/12/2007

Silver Spur Award for lifetime achievement held in Studio City, California. Peter Brown (10/5/1935-3/21/2016. www.peterbrown.tv[4], Olympic gold medal winner and stunt double Dean Smith (1/32/1932-) and Stuart Whitman (2/1/1928-3/16/2020) also receive the award. *See www.reelcowboy.org*[5] *and https://silverspurawards.com/pasthonorees.php* .

3/2008

Festival of the West in Phoenix, Arizona.

4/12/2008

National Cowboy & Western Heritage Museum in Oklahoma City, Oklahoma. Robert is inducted into the Hall of Great Western Performers. He receives a bronze statue of a cowboy on a horse. In addition to actual Wrangler Award a plaque hangs in the museum. His wife Jennifer and son Robert also attend. This is Robert's most treasured award. See www.nationalcowboymuseum.org[6] .

---

2. *http://www.youtube.com/watch?v=qMB3welaDIY*

3. http://www.thevirginian.net

4. http://www.peterbrown.tv

5. *http://www.reelcowboy.org*

6. http://www.nationalcowboymuseum.org

Robert considers this award his best. *He said "something I never dreamt would happen...I've got a big plaque up on the wall next to Gary Cooper (5/7/1901-5/13/1961) and John Wayne (5/26/1907-6/11/1979) and all the big guys. Next to all the great Western performers...".*

11/6/2008

The Palm Beach Post 's Entertainment section contains an article titled "The Florida childhood of actor Robert Fuller". It shares Robert's joy of fishing in Key West along with insight into Whiskey Row dressing rooms area during Laramie and Wagon Train and life on his ranch.

11/28/2008

Will Harris wrote an article, A Chat with Robert Fuller. The conversation focuses on the release of the Wagon Train DVDs and Robert's career. *See www.premiumhollywood.com/2008/11/28/a-chat-with-robert-fuller-laramie-wagon-train-emergency*[7] .

2009

Robert appears as himself in Red Steagal's series. This episode is titled In the Bunkhouse.

Laramie Robert Fuller FOTW 2009 Q&A , PAUL SAVAGE AND BRUCE DERN – *See https://www.youtube.com/watch?v=FI0tzxg1n6s&list=PLF683D699AC8A04E4&index=8* and https://www.youtube.com/watch?v=FI0tzxg1n6s Also see Robert Fuller, Paul Savage and Bruce Dern swap stories at FOTW 2009 Q&Q at *https://www.youtube.com/watch?v=9wORWvX43LI&list=PLF683D699AC8A04E4&index=7* .

Robert's father, Robert Simpson, Sr. dies.

3/2009

Festival of the West in Phoenix, Arizona.

3/1/2009

True West Magazine - The Adventures of Wagon Train with cast photo - *See https://truewestmagazine.com/article/the-adventures-of-a-wagon-train/* .

3/12/2009

7.   *http://www.premiumhollywood.com/2008/11/28/a-chat-with-robert-fuller-laramie-wagon-train-emergency/*

Article titled The Adventures of A Wagon Train - Robert Fuller is Still Foolin' em by Henry Cabot Beck appears in www.truewestmagine.com[8] . Article states Robert now owns about 27 pairs of boots, 40 pairs of Levi jeans and 20 cowboy hats.

6/4 - 6/6/2009

Memphis Film Festival: A Gathering of Guns: A TV Western reunion at Olive Branch, Mississippi.

8/17/2009

Interview with Robert about Wagon Train. *See www.popflock.com/learn?s=Robert-Fuller-(actor[9]) .*

8/17/2009

Article in On Screen and Beyond.

9/18 - 9/20/2009

Spirit of the West Festival - Sioux Falls, South Dakota.

3/2010

Festival of the West in Phoenix, Arizona.

3/10/2010

Robert gave James Drury (4/18/1934-4/6/2020 www.thevirginian.net[10]) the Cowboy Spirit Award at the Festival of the West in Phoenix, Arizona. James Drury is living in Houston, Texas. Robert also gave a tribute to John Smith (3/6/1931-1/25/1995).

5/24/2010

Robert talks to his fan club, Fandom, about Laramie. *See www.youtube.com,/watch?v=HkGCQcpJC8M* .

6/3 - 6/5/2010

Memphis Film Festival at Whispering Wood Hotel & Convention Center in Olive Branch, Mississippi.

---

8.   http://www.truewestmagine.com

9.   *http://www.popflock.com/learn?s=Robert_Fuller_(actor*

10.   http://www.thevirginian.net

7/23 - 25/2010

Hollywood Collector Show in Burbank, California.

9/17 - 19/2010

Spirit of the West Festival in Sioux Falls, South Dakota.

10/9/2010

Robert attended the Wild West Toy Show in Azle near Fort Worth, Texas. James Drury (4/18/1934-4/6/2020 www.thevirginian.net[11]) also attends. The show's focus is riding horses and western merchandise. *Also see www.youtube[12] to find Robert Fuller Telling a Little About Filming - Wild West Toy.*

10/16/2010

Robert talks about how he got Laramie part. *See www.youtube.com/watch?v=nINSEUfHlml/*[13] .

2011

Hal Needham's book Stuntman! My Car Crashing, Plane-Jumping, Bone-Breaking, Death-Defying Hollywood Life mentions Robert and Laramie time.

3/2011

Festival of the West in Phoenix, Arizona.

5/2011

Robert was in Italy.

6/2 - 6/6/2011

Memphis Film Festival.

JULY - AUGUST 2011

Western Clippings No. 102 Magazine. It covers Robert's attendance at A Gathering of the Guns 3 - a TV Western Reunion and is 36 pages.

---

11.   http://www.thevirginian.net

12.   *http://www.youtube*

13.   *http://www.youtube.com/watch?v=nINSEUfHlml/*

7/8/2011

Crossroads Festival of Western Legends. James Drury (4/18/1934-4/6/2020 www.thevirginian.net[14]) also attends. *See Western Legends – Crossroads Festival – James Drury & Robert Fuller – at https://www.youtube.com/ watch?v=NNaa1fs6G1w .*

7/16/2011

Robert talks about Laramie and Emergency. *See www.youtube.com/watch?v=JpDflDsOaP8[15] .*

6/2012

Robert has right rotator cuff shoulder surgery and then surgery for arm blood clots.

8/24/2012

Western Legends Round Up in Kanab, Utah. Honored in the Little Hollywood Walk of Fame. See Western Legends Round up 2012 at https://www.youtube.com/watch?v=QcrHoejJFw0 to see Robert visually and overview of whole festival.

9/2012

The First Annual Spirit of the Cowboy Western Festival occurs in Chestnut Square in McKinney, Texas. It is about a 30 minute truck drive from their home. Attendees include Alex Cord, (10 miles away and 5/3/1933-), Anne Lockhart (9/6/1953-) www.galactica.tv/battlestar-galactica-1978-news/official-site-for-anne-lockhart.html[16], Denny Miller (4/ 25/1944-9/9/2014) and Paul Peterson (9/23/1945-). www.paulpeterson.com[17] .

6/13 - 6/15/2013

Memphis Film Festival / The Gathering of the Guns. It's the first time it is held at Sam's Town in Mississippi.

Interview with Tom Blixa of TWVN.

7/29/2013

Robert celebrates his 80th birthday with his wife Jennifer and fans while on vacation on a ranch in Libby, Montana.

14.   http://www.thevirginian.net

15.   *http://www.youtube.com/watch?v=JpDflDsOaP8*

16.   http://www.galactica.tv/battlestar-galactica-1978-news/official-site-for-anne-lockhart.html

17.   http://www.paulpeterson.com

9/2013

Spirit of the Cowboy Western Festival.

10/12/2013

Robert is very first recipient of a new award, Spirit of the Cowboy Lonestar Legacy Award, that recognizes his western hero status in the entertainment industry.

2014

Robert is mentioned in Jock Mahoney (2/7/1919-12/14/1989)'s - The Life and Films of a Hollywood Stuntman by Gene Freese and is 224 pages.

Western TV Heroes creates mini booklet with twenty images each about 2 ¾ x 3 ½ inches in size. It features photos from Laramie of Robert, John, Bobby and guest Ruta Lee.,

3/5 - 3/8 2014

Williamsburg Nostalgia Film Festival in Virginia. See Alex Cord's (5/3/1933-) Tribute to Robert Fuller at _https://www.youtube.com/watch?v=4nzEjPUp4qs_[18] .

6/2014

Memphis Film Festival. *See partial panel titled The Celebrity Panel discussion Memphis Film Festival 2014 at https://www.youtube.com/watch?v=j985FTtnzmc and a full another panel titled The Celebrity Panel discussion Memphis Film Festival 2014 at https://www.youtube.com/watch?v=WE477M2V3Xw. Also see Bob Fuller&Tony Gill stunt fight demonstration MemphisFilmFestival 2014 at https://www.youtube.com/watch?v=afLbAvM_M90 and one titled Robert Fuller at the banquet Memphis Film Festival 2014 at https://www.youtube.com/watch?v=WQgGjpYfk5I.*

7/29/2014

Robert, Jennifer and Ken Stormer host a fun day for fifteen Wounded Warriors and their wives and children. The Warriors enjoy shooting and wives and kids visit the Gainesville Zoo. An evening banquet is held in Warrior's honor.

8/2014

Nick Thomas from the Daily Press interviews Robert.

8/21 - 8/23/2014

18.　　https://www.youtube.com/watch?v=4nzEjPUp4qs

Western Legends Roundup in Kanab, Utah. *See Robert fuller Fandom Party - Doug and Bob at https://www.youtube.com/watch?v=C19sswTERCk which took place in Utah.*

8/28/2014

Tinseltown Talks About Robert Fuller. See https://www.morganton.com/news/local/tinseltown-talks-about-robert-fuller/article_21162cc0-2ec7-11e4-a7e3-0017a43b2370.html .

8/29/2014

Article about Robert and his honor in Oklahoma. The article also his thoughts on Marilyn Monroe and the end of television westerns caused by the PTA and Senator Teddy Kennedy. *See www.mesquitelocalnews.com/2014/08/29/robert-fuller-keeps-tv-cowboys-spotlight*[19] .

9/12 - 9/14/2014

Spirit of the Cowboy in McKinney, Texas. *See www.spiritofthecowboy.net*[20] *and interview with Robert at Show 62 – laramie - robert fuller part 1 at https://www.youtube.com/watch?v=_fUrjPn_erc .*

11/9/2014

Robert and Jennifer attend actor, producer and director Norman Lloyd's (11/8/1914-) 100th birthday party in Los Angeles, California. Norman's career in radio, theater, movies and television started in 1923 and continued until 2015. He is an actor with over sixty movie and TV credits plus was a director and producer. Robert's wife Jennifer Savidge (as nurse Lucy Papandrao) worked with Lloyd (as Dr. Daniel Auschlander) on St. Elsewhere from 1982 to 1988. Actor James Best (7/26/1926-4/6/2015) was one of the others attending.

2015

Robert is briefly mentioned in section 3 / Pro Wrestling and Crying Cowboys in Modernization, Nation-Building and Television History by S. Anderson and Melissa Chakars. It is 218 pages.

Robert's wife Jennifer's last television series, American Crime ends. She has appeared in at least 13 movies and television programs besides series she had reoccurring roles in.

4/2015

Twenty-two inches of rain falls in two days along with 70 miles per hour winds causing damage to Robert's ranch. Robert and Jennifer are kept busy retrieving fish no longer in their ponds.

19.　　http://www.mesquitelocalnews.com/2014/08/29/robert-fuller-keeps-tv-cowboys-spotlight/

20.　　http://www.spiritofthecowboy.net

4/24 - 4/26/2015

Cowboy Up for Vets in Swanton, Ohio. This was the sixth time this event has occurred. *See 2015 Cowboy Up for Vets Q&A at https://www.youtube.com/watch?v=hwdJ80z00Nc . Robert is on a short time before and during a phone call to James Drury (4/18/1934-4/6/2020 www.thevirginian.net[21]) .*

6/2015

Memphis Film Festival.

JULY - AUGUST 2015

Western Clippings Magazine No. 126. It is 32 pages.

9/2015

Western Heritage Festival in Old Tucson, Arizona.

9/14/2015

Examiner article titled TV Doctors and Nurses - Where Are They Now?

9/15 - 9/17/2015

Mid-Atlantic Nostalgia Convention.

11/25/2015

Bob Terry interview with Robert. *See Robert Fuller and Bob Terry Discuss LARAMIE and SUNDOWN western TV shows at https://www.youtube.com/watch?v=nNSc1xUHY9g .*

2/14/2016

Robert talks about Laramie and Emergency. *See www.youtube.com/watch?v=lhdn45L9PXM[22] .* James Drury (4/18/1934-4/6/2020 www.thevirginian.net[23]) is also present.

3/2016

---

21.   *http://www.thevirginian.net*

22.   *http://www.youtube.com/watch?v=lhdn45L9PXM*

23.   http://www.thevirginian.net

The High Chaparral Reunion at Casino Del Son in Tucson, Arizona. Some others that attended are Don Collier (10/17/1928-) and Roberta Shore (4/7/1943-) and Arizona's Film Historian Charles Thomas LeSueur (1/22/1951-11/10/2019). *See High Chaparrel Reunion Don Collier and Robert Fuller, Boise at https://www.youtube.com/watch?v=A5MLuOgMtkgandThe High Chaparral Reunion: Saddle Up With The Stars Part 2 Barbara Luna at https://www.youtube.com/watch?v=MY1Rr-JbpTc* and *https://www.broadwayworld.com/phoenix/article/Photo-Coverage-Inside-the-High-Chaparral-Reunion-2016-20160401.* The event was held in two different states.

5/1/2016

Robert talks about his western career with Jeremy Roberts from www.examiner.com[24].

6/2016

Memphis Film Festival. Robert appeared on several panels including this one. *See Memphis Film Festival10June 2016 at https://www.youtube.com/watch?v=s_wpa6hwf5I* .

9/15 - 9/17/2016

Mid Atlantic Nostalgia Convention in Hunt Valley, Maryland. Huge crowds and Robert's lines are long. *See Robert talking with Bernie Kopell (6/21/1933-) at* https://video.search.yahoo.com/search/video?fr=yfp-t&p=robert+fuller+interviews#id=20&vid=c7fd59b656590c82024a066e0b3d6b74&action=view[25] .

Mark J. Gross has interviewed Robert several times over the years. *See www.youtube.come/watch?v=hZKbFLaU7O0*[26] *titled Robert Fuller Interview: Still Alive and Charming ! Laramie. Also see https://video.search.yahoo.com/search/video?fr=yfp-t&p=robert+fuller+interviews#id=3&vid=9513d7397856e28809224655303fc627&action=view*[27] *and* https://video.search.yahoo.com/search/video?fr=yfp-t&p=robert+fuller+interviews#id=4&vid=84be61d351bf24dac18a82225272a5bf&action=view[28] and Robert Fuller Interviewed at www.youtube.com/watch?v=qMB3welaDIY[29] .

---

24.   http://www.examiner.com

25.   https://video.search.yahoo.com/search/
        video?fr=yfp-t&p=robert+fuller+interviews#id_43ec3e5dee6e706af7766fffea512721_20_6cff047854f19ac2aa52aac51bf3af4a_vid_43ec3e5dee6e706af7766fffea5
        12721_c7fd59b656590c82024a066e0b3d6b74_6cff047854f19ac2aa52aac51bf3af4a_action_43ec3e5dee6e706af7766fffea512721_view

26. *http://www.youtube.come/watch?v=hZKbFLaU7O0*

27. *https://video.search.yahoo.com/search/*
        video?fr=yfp-t&p=robert+fuller+interviews#id_43ec3e5dee6e706af7766fffea512721_3_6cff047854f19ac2aa52aac51bf3af4a_vid_43ec3e5dee6e706af7766fffea51272
        1_9513d7397856e28809224655303fc627_6cff047854f19ac2aa52aac51bf3af4a_action_43ec3e5dee6e706af7766fffea512721_view

28. https://video.search.yahoo.com/search/
        video?fr=yfp-t&p=robert+fuller+interviews#id_43ec3e5dee6e706af7766fffea512721_4_6cff047854f19ac2aa52aac51bf3af4a_vid_43ec3e5dee6e706af7766fffea51
        2721_84be61d351bf24dac18a82225272a5bf_6cff047854f19ac2aa52aac51bf3af4a_action_43ec3e5dee6e706af7766fffea512721_view

29. http://www.youtube.com/watch?v=qMB3welaDIY

10/21/2016

Article Chewin' the Fat With Iron-willed 'Laramie' Cowboy star Robert Fuller. *See* https://medium.com/@jeremylr/chewin-the-fat-with-iron-willed-laramie-cowboy-star-robert-fuller-89c473fe9cd9 .

Although retired by this time Robert has been offered at least three Western but nothing at the caliber of work he's already done. He still gets fan mail and is popular at any celebrity shows he attends.

2017

Argentina 54 different poker playing cards are made by F & D. *See 2018.*

3/15/2017

Robert Fuller says "I wanna fight like Jock Mahoney" – A Word on Westerns – Williamsburg – at https://video.search.yahoo.com/search/ video?fr=yfp-t&p=robert+fuller+interviews#id=40&vid=80fc25bf449e0bdd9a06967ba412f66b&action=view[30] or Robert Fuller says "I wanna fight like Jock Mahoney" - A WORD ON WESTERNS at https://www.youtube.com/ watch?v=fDYUEpYxt-k .

6/2017

Memphis Film Festival. *See Memphis Film Festival 2017 - Robert Fuller Highlights at https://www.youtube.com/watch?v=vhj9dbboh18 which shows his airport arrival and Robert with fans although he isn't talking and author is seen dancing). Also see Turkish Movie Poster Surprises Robert Fuller at Memphis Film Fest at https://www.youtube.com/watch?v=Xf19qTk6B6E .*

7/25/2017

Laramie Jubilee Days in Laramie, Wyoming. Robert Fuller on the Streets of Laramie! *See www.youtube.com/ watch?v=1P3ydwQOHcc[31] and* Robert Fuller in Laramie- Laramie Jubilee Days 2017 https://www.youtube.com/ watch?v=b0pCFg0CWNs .

Robert makes a Laramie, Wyoming tourism commercial. See www.visitlaramie.org/vendors/laramie-tv-show[32] .

9/2017

---

30. https://video.search.yahoo.com/search/
video?fr=yfp-t&p=robert+fuller+interviews#id_43ec3e5dee6e706af7766fffea512721_40_6cff047854f19ac2aa52aac51bf3af4a_vid_43ec3e5dee6e706af7766fffea512721_80fc25bf449e0bdd9a06967ba412f66b_6cff047854f19ac2aa52aac51bf3af4a_action_43ec3e5dee6e706af7766fffea512721_view

31. *http://www.youtube.com/watch?v=1P3ydwQOHcc*

32. http://www.visitlaramie.org/vendors/laramie-tv-show

Interview with Joe Collurn of Quad-City Times. See https://qctimes.com/robert-fuller/article_f0868906-8eb8-11e7-bf8a-13ebef303ce9.html .

10/27 - 10/29/2017

Chiller Theatre Expo Winter at the Parsippany Hilton in Parsippany, New Jersey. Raymond Mantooth (9/19/1945-) also attended.

2018

Argentina two box set made by F& D. Each box has 34 individual cards along with one explanation card. Each one is different and are from Laramie to Emergency.

Argentina 2 box set made by F& D. Each box has 50 individual cards with photos from Robert's career. They are in Spanish.

Robert's ranch in Texas has two horses, two donkeys (Jennifer would keep in house if could), two cats, one dog and skunks.

Jennifer is enjoying dressage riding.

1/22/2018

The Absolute Best Historically Accurate Westerns When Hollywood Got it Right - Starts with movies in the 1920's to more current ones - See https://truewestmagazine.com/historically-accurate-westerns/ .

3/2018

Williamsburg Nostalgia Film Festival in Virginia. *See Robert Fuller - Williamsburg Nostalgia Fest 2018 www.youtube.com/watch?v=Af95JDw9KA8*[33] *. Also see Robert Fuller – Williamsburg at https://www.youtube.com/ watch?v=Af95JDw9KA8&list=PL2YYPNORBEDaIuUEOpYIQxjYsldrjwxU2&index=3&t=0s .*

4/5/2018

Cheryl Rogers (daughter of Roy Rogers, 6/6/1940-) interviews Robert at his ranch. *See www.cherylrogers.com/my-interview-with-robert-fuller/*[34] *for her Western Stars Theater - Along the Trail.*

---

33.   *http://www.youtube.com/watch?v=Af95JDw9KA8*

34.   *http://www.cherylrogers.com/my-interview-with-robert-fuller/*

4/10/2018

Robert Fuller Interview - Still Alive and Charming - talks about Laramie, Emergency and Walker Texas Ranger (YouTube).

6/2018

Memphis Film Festival. Robert's 10th time appearing. *See Robert Fuller - Memphis Film Fest 2018 at https://www.youtube.com/watch?v=EC9z2lDweaQ* .

See Robert with stuntman Diamond Farnsworth (10/7/1949-) www.watch?v=3-8w8peo21Y[35] and Diamond Farnsworth – Memphis 2018 at https://video.search.yahoo.com/search/video?fr=yfp-t&p=robert+fuller+interviews#id=24&vid=1ea89d013c86167c0a51d0ff45ee6303&action=view[36]

See Robert Fuller & Diamond Farnsworth Antics At MFF 2018 at https://www.youtube.com/watch?v=3_8W8peo21Y .

Also see Fandom Presentation to Robert Fuller at Memphis Film Fest 2018at https://www.youtube.com/watch?v=KWUiMcbKtUg or Memphis Film Festival - Fandom gift at https://video.search.yahoo.com/search/video?fr=yfp- t&p=robert+fuller+interviews#id=23&vid=44c05151078f4b644124d1686c055b43&action=view .

Western Heritage Hall of Fame in Texas.

7/7 - 7/15/2018

Laramie Jubilee in Laramie, Wyoming.

10/27/2018

Texas Trail of Fame Award for a lifetime helping protect the western way of life. His star is on the sidewalk in Fort Worth, Texas. See www.texastrailoffame.org/inductees/robert-fuller[37] and *Induction in "Texas Trail of Fame" and a Day in the Stockyard www.youtube.com/watch?v=NMMS7zkrVwo[38]* .

---

35. http://www.watch?v=3_8w8peo21Y

36. https://video.search.yahoo.com/search/
   video?fr=yfp-t&p=robert+fuller+interviews#id_43ec3e5dee6e706af7766fffea512721_24_6cff047854f19ac2aa52aac51bf3af4a_vid_43ec3e5dee6e706af7766fffea5
   12721_1ea89d013c86167c0a51d0ff45ee6303_6cff047854f19ac2aa52aac51bf3af4a_action_43ec3e5dee6e706af7766fffea512721_view

37. http://www.texastrailoffame.org/inductees/robert-fuller

38. *http://www.youtube.com/watch?v=NMMS7zkrVwo*

2/19/2019

True West Magazine - The Adventures of Wagon Train - See https://truewestmagazine.com/the-adventures-of-a-wagon-train/ .

4/11/2019

Patrick Fuller, Robert's son, accepts the Newhall Walk of Fame of Western Stars award in Santa Clarita, California on his behalf. A bronze saddle appears on terrazzo titles on Main Street in Old Town Newhall. This event is part of the Santa Clarita Cowboy Festival. The award has Robert's name and a saddle.

For his recognition Robert wrote "I am deeply honored to receive this award and proud to be joining the many great Western stars who have already been honored with a place on the Walk Of Western Stars — Western stars who dedicated their lives to promoting great Western entertainment. Names like Charles Bronson, Steve McQueen, Lee Marvin, Glenn Ford, Gary Cooper, James Stewart, William Boyd, Roy Rogers and John Wayne, just to name a few".

"In fact, my hero Joel McCrea was honored in 2009, and I am very proud to be alongside him in what is one of the most famous of Western locations".

"I am proud to be considered among the elite of the Western genre, a genre I loved to work in and a genre which gave me the chance to play the best part I could ever have wished for when I got the part of Jess Harper in "Laramie."

"I have a lot to be thankful for in my life. I have had a great career, and still today I am reaping the rewards of that career with awards like this and support from fans from all around the world. Thank you very much for this great honor".

5/2 - 5/5/2019

Cowboy Way Jubilee in Ardmore, Oklahoma. *See Crossroads Live Show 98 at https://www.youtube.com/watch?v=7XbwHX-mexE . Robert's voice is in first few minutes taking about John Smith (3/6/1931-1/25/1995).*

6/6 - 6/8/2019

Memphis Film Festival in Tunica, Mississippi. *See www.youtube.com/watch?v=7nxk-in3_E8*[39] *(fan with Robert, Randy Mantooth and Bruce Bump).*

7/2019

Voice interview with Connor Corner. *See https://video.search.yahoo.com/search/video?fr=yfp-t&p=robert+fuller+interviews#id=1&vid=8ae6ace61c6abb40fd4c8927f23f0467&action=click*[40] *and*

---

39.   http://www.youtube.com/watch?v=7nxk-in3_E8

https://www.youtube.com/watch?v=p6JuEjnxwIc .

7/12 - 7/14/2019

60th Laramie Reunion in Laramie, Wyoming. Robert Crawford (5/13/1944-) and Dennis Holmes (10/3/1950-) also appear. *See Our Photo Shoot w/the Cast of Laramie - Laramie 2019 at https://www.youtube.com/ watch?v=ipQx-iQhH5E* .

9/29/2019

Robert, although not present, is one of the stars honored at the Comic Book Nostalgia Convention held at the Watson Hotel in New York City, New York.

9/30/2019

Robert spoke via video and his letter is read by his son Patrick at the Silver Spur Awards (hosted by the Reel Cowboys) given for Lifetime Achievement to Dennis Holmes and Robert Crawford, Jr. (5/13/1944-). See ww.silverspsurawards.com and Robert Fuller's Lifetime Achievement Award from the "Silver Spur Awards." at https://www.youtube.com/watch?v=QKZs484l4Ag and Robert Fuller, Bobby Crawford & Dennis Holmes - Silver Spur Awards 2019 at https://www.youtube.com/watch?v=R0eyrQGOMbw .

10/28/2019

Interview - https://www.promipool.com/celebrities/laramie-this-is-why-robert-fuller-decided-to-retire-from-acting - site includes many ads.

5/20/2020

Survey of top 50 Western TV Shows. Ratings of shows Robert was in are Wagon Train at #48, Death Valley Days at #42, Virginian at #35, Big Valley at #34, Laramie at #32, Kung Fu at #29 and Lawman at #21. Find your other favorites at https://rivercountry.newschannelnebraska.com/story/42222927/50-best-western-tv-shows-of-all-time .

6/4 - 6/6/2020

MidSouth Nostalgia Festival in Tunica, Mississippi was cancelled because of COVID-19. (It was formerly Memphis Film Festival).

11/5 - 11/7/2020

40.   *https://video.search.yahoo.com/search/*

video?fr=yfp-t&p=robert+fuller+interviews#id_43ec3e5dee6e706af7766fffea512721_1_6cff047854f19ac2aa52aac51bf3af4a_vid_43ec3e5dee6e706af7766fffea51272

1_8ae6ace61c6abb40fd4c8927f23f0467_6cff047854f19ac2aa52aac51bf3af4a_action_43ec3e5dee6e706af7766fffea512721_click

Larry Floyd's Williamsburg Nostalgia Festival in Virginia was cancelled due to COVID-19.

6/10 - 6/12/2021

MidSouth Nostalgia Festival in Tunica, Mississippi was cancelled because of COVID-19.

DATES UNKNOWN

While in Arizona Robert was at Ralph Gaines Steak House and signed a menu for a fan.

Robert was in Yakima, Washington for a fundraiser.

LATE 1980's - ?

Robert and Jennifer attend the Wildlife 8th Annual Safari Brunch at a private home in Pasadena, California. *(The organization was founded in 1973 and incorporated in 1984. The facility had fires in 2009 and 2017 and in 2020 is closed).*

??

Prior to Patty's death in 1984 Robert attended Local L L Celebrity event with a hand injury.

Robert visited 1800 Town in Midland, South Dakota.

Robert visited Germany while doing or after Emergency and signed autographs.

Robert visited Mori Teppan's restaurant in Glendale, California with Julie London and signed a photo which may be from Jake's Way (1980) that still hangs in the restaurant in May of 2020. *See SHAW CELEB STORIES ROBERT FULLER EMERGENCY TV SHOW DR BRACKET JULIE LONDON MORI TEPPAN JUNE 27 2020 at https://www.youtube.com/watch?v=d33i89OuCdE .*

Robert visited Rawah Guest Ranch in Northern Colorado. During the summer they have fly fishing, horseback riding, hiking, etc. *See https://rawahranch.com .*

ARTICLES / MAGAZINES

These listed below are not included with others where exact dates are known.

Back at the Ranch (Wagon Train time).

Burglar (House burglar at back door in San Fernando Valley home. (Robert may have talked about at Great Western Performers at the National Cowboy and Western Heritage Museum in Oklahoma City, Oklahoma). Hollywood, California newspaper article is titled TV Gunslinger Bags Burglar, Real-life One.

Do You Remember...Laramie by Boyd Magers. See www.westernclippings.com[1] .

Full-Time Dare-Devil. He is playing piano in photo.

Let's Get Married Again.

Screen Spotlight.

Trail Dust Magazine - Fall and Winter. Robert is on the lower right corner of the cover.

True West Magazine - April – See www.truewestmagazine.com/past-issues[2] .

Western Clippings - March - April 19?? Issue talks about the Memphis Film Festival.

Other magazines he appeared in include:
    TV Movie Males Album Magazine.

Foreign publications not included elsewhere are:

---

1. http://www.westernclippings.com

2. http://www.truewestmagazine.com/past-issues

Japan - All TV Star Parade Magazine and many other magazines

BOOKS MENTIONING ROBERT

A few books where Robert is mentioned include:
   Collectible Television Memorabilia by Dian Zillner
   1996. 181 pages

How Sweet is Was – Television: A Pictorial by Arthur Shulman
   1966, 446 pages

Prime Time Television by Fred and Stan Goldstein
   1983, 384 pages

Television's Cowboys, Gunfighters and Cap Pistols by Rudy A. D'Angelo
   1999, 288 pages

The Complete Directory to Prime Time Network TV Shows 1946 - Present by Tom Blanks and Earle Marsh
   1979/1981, 1205 pages

The First Official TV Western Book by Neil Summers
   1987, 122 pages

The Golden Age of Television by Arthur Shulman and Roger Youman
   1966, 448 pages

The Hollywood Walk of Fame by Marianne Morino
   1987, 396 pages

TV Book – The Ultimate Television Book by Judy Fireman
   1977, 408 pages

TV Land Legends
   2006, no page numbers

Wagon Train - The Television Series by James Rosin
    2008, 269 pages

Who's Who in Hollywood 1900-1976 by David Ragan
    1976, 864 pages

OTHER INTERNET SITES MENTIONING ROBERT

A few more interesting Internet sites that pop up when you type in Robert's name are listed below.

<u>Robert Fuller - Google</u>[1]

https://www.google.com/search/static/gs/m07ws2p.html .

Robert Fuller (actor) facts for kids

<u>Kids Encyclopedia Facts</u>[2]

<u>https://kids.kiddle.co/Robert_Fuller_(actor)</u>

<u>Robert Fuller (actor) | Project Gutenberg Self-Publishing - eBooks ..</u>[3]

http://self.gutenberg.org/articles/eng/robert_fuller_(actor) .

<u>Robert Fuller - Rotten Tomatoes</u>[4]

https://www.rottentomatoes.com/celebrity/robert_fuller .

---

1.   https://www.google.com/search/static/gs/m07ws2p.html

2.   https://kids.kiddle.co/

3.   http://self.gutenberg.org/articles/eng/robert_fuller_(actor)

4. https://www.rottentomatoes.com/celebrity/robert_fuller

ROBERT ON YOUTUBE.COM

Some links to Robert are listed earlier in this timeline. When a fan types in Robert Fuller - actor on the website www.youtube.com[1] you can find many choices or just type in the title if you know it. Availability can change and some I find one time, I can't find another. The titles listed below and their website links are ones Robert is really in. He is being interviewed vs. ones created showing movie or television clips or sites created by his fans (musical tributes, birthday greetings, etc). Those are listed in the next chapter titled youtube.com Sites About Robert.

Accidents on western TV show sets Virginian and Laramie (with James Drury)
https://www.youtube.com/ watch?v=69gRh00UBW4&list=PL2YYPNORBEDZZxJothnpuAyCoz4ctmQcI&index=5 and Accidents on western TV show sets Virginian and Laramie at https://www.youtube.com/watch?v=C19sswTERCk .

Bob Fuller about Television show Laramie
https://www.youtube.com/watch?v=UHYnLojmyBc .

Face of America 12/24/2019
www.youtube.com.RFCowboy/Robert Fuller . Part 2 continues. See www.youtube.comm.RFCowboy2Robert Fuller2 .

Faded Love, Ben Alexander with Robert Fuller on spoons
https://www.youtube.com/watch?v=X9fTgmP4tMQ .

James Drury interview and acting advice – with Robert *https://www.youtube.com/ watch?v=LoH0HycaYys&list=PLF683D699AC8A04E4&index=1 .*

Laramie - Jubilee Days
Robert Fuller at Laramie Jubilee Days- Day 3- Parade, Q/A and Dinner. https://www.youtube.com/ watch?v=Nd0vJSHiX68 .

LARAMIE JUBILEE DAYS
https://www.youtube.com/watch?v=jeS6eg0MYZs .

Laramie - Robert Fuller - Part 1 (Show 62) Crossroads Live
https://www.youtube.com/watch?v=_fUrjPn_erc .

MEETING ROBERT FULLER - Laramie Jubilee Days- Day 2 Vlog https://www.youtube.com/watch?v=4H3K3xPo-ok .

RFCowboy1
https://www.youtube.com/watch?v=elAR2aM9Iq0 .

RFcowboy2 Robert Fuller 2
https://www.youtube.com/watch?v=lt30r_P-3Lc .

RFCowboy1-Robert Fuller
https://video.search.yahoo.com/search/
video?fr=yfp-t&p=robert+fuller+interviews#id=25&vid=d838da93271ca9736a43370338a1501f&action=view[2] .

RFCowboy2Rolbert Fuller2 *(Robert tells Burt Reynolds / Fabian story)* https://video.search.yahoo.com/search/
video?fr=yfp-t&p=robert+fuller+interviews#id=21&vid=a24c5d248daff7301c40b31fb9fba2a3&action=view[3]

Robert Fuller talks about Emergency & Laramie days
https://www.youtube.com/watch?v=JpDfIDsOaP8 .

Robert Fuller talks about his days on Emergency & Laramie – With James Drury *https://www.youtube.com/watch?v=lhdn45L9PXM* .

Robert Fuller & James Drury *https://www.youtube.com/watch?v=0Ip0f_vMfa0&list=PLF683D699AC8A04E4&index=9* .

---

2. https://video.search.yahoo.com/search/
    video?fr=yfp-t&p=robert+fuller+interviews#id_43ec3e5dee6e706af7766fffea512721_25_6cff047854f19ac2aa52aac51bf3af4a_vid_43ec3e5dee6e706af7766fffea5
    12721_d838da93271ca9736a43370338a1501f_6cff047854f19ac2aa52aac51bf3af4a_action_43ec3e5dee6e706af7766fffea512721_view

3. https://video.search.yahoo.com/search/
    video?fr=yfp-t&p=robert+fuller+interviews#id_43ec3e5dee6e706af7766fffea512721_21_6cff047854f19ac2aa52aac51bf3af4a_vid_43ec3e5dee6e706af7766fffea5
    12721_a24c5d248daff7301c40b31fb9fba2a3_6cff047854f19ac2aa52aac51bf3af4a_action_43ec3e5dee6e706af7766fffea512721_view

Robert Fuller & James Drury – The Dancer – Lunch at MGM
https://www.youtube.com/watch?v=kGHwjgyPvLQ .

Robert Fuller on The Streets Of Laramie! Laramie Jubilee
www.youtube.com/watch?v=IP3ydwQOHcc[4] ,

Robert Fuller Signing Two of My Art Photos
https://www.youtube.com/watch?v=2Bb75fRXcnc .

Robert Fuller talks about his many names https://www.youtube.com/watch?v=DAGSrHK62hA&list=PL8LEkfRT_R93oV7DJ5RZnZhOtKSx57vmv .

SOIO Question and Answers - 4 parts. Guests include Paul Petersen (9/23/1945-)
www.paulpetersen.com[5]).

The Robert Fuller Story. It is a portion of Memphis Film /festival panel
www.youtube.com/watch?v=nkzuTZz7z0[6] .

When the West Was Fun - A Reunion
https://www.youtube.com/watch?v=7cDfth_ql4A .

4.   *http://www.youtube.com/watch?v=IP3ydwQOHcc*

5.   *http://www.paulpetersen.com*

6.   *http://www.youtube.com/watch?v=nkzuTZz7z0*

YOUTUBE.COM SITES ABOUT ROBERT

Like all YouTube websites, some might be more easily found and viewed than others that seem to disappear.

A Few Words of Wisdom from Jess Harper
    https://www.youtube.com/watch?v=okvpNx9A5LM .

All I want for christmas
    https://www.youtube.com/watch?v=pkEMak75Cto&list=PLPV36wN5O62H9qTqvZWH5EhDAqbGGNatX .

An Innocent Man Jess
    https://www.youtube.com/watch?v=y3Su6FQ2ttY .

Another One Bites the Dust Harper Style
    https://www.youtube.com/watch?v=oxOjZOin18E .

Bad Company. Bad, Bad Bob Fuller.
    https://www.youtube.com/watch?v=oQx_i8wgWQQ .

Ballad of Jess Harper
    https://www.youtube.com/watch?v=9HXLTGOnwcI .

Bob Fuller 85th Birthday Part 1
    https://www.youtube.com/watch?v=E8LSgnHYHw8 .

Bob Fuller 85th Birthday Part 2
    https://www.youtube.com/watch?v=mycwXrZ7230 .

Bob Fuller 85th Birthday Part 3 (Simply The Best)
    https://www.youtube.com/watch?v=wnGkGqGrck8   or   https://www.youtube.com/watch?v=wnGkGqGrck8&list=PLnll6GXwv4sPNiK6ZVlRuS4gcqeYs1QeX .

Bob Fuller 85th Part 4
https://www.youtube.com/watch?v=HGQqYVrA_Zk .

Happy 85th Birthday Robert Fuller part one
https://www.youtube.com/watch?v=MpVP_p6vic8 .

Bob Fuller Birthday, My Way, Happy 85th
https://www.youtube.com/watch?v=uUGGr6F6alM .

Bobby's Girl Song-Marcie Blane - Robert"Bob"Fuller - Actor - Laramie Western TV
https://www.youtube.com/watch?v=vHB3cS1nXgs&list=RDvHB3cS1nXgs&start_radio=1&t=50 .

Brave
https://www.youtube.com/watch?v=JuMC9b-Pslw .

"Brave " Coop Smith Wagon Train
https://www.youtube.com/watch?v=BraVQi8l6DI .

Broke Record Chaperitis
https://www.youtube.com/watch?v=HV2MeRB-nSc .

Bullets in My Gun
https://www.youtube.com/watch?v=T9QjcyR0ZEY .

Christmas for Cowboys
https://www.youtube.com/watch?v=rZb_AVb0Vnw .

Christmas Wish
https://www.youtube.com/watch?v=HyFlhBjnQM4 .

Coop A Hero Within
https://www.youtube.com/watch?v=Of0Fl7K2ZN0 .

Coop Smith .When I Was Your Man (Should Have Brought You Flowers)
https://www.youtube.com/watch?v=fXGNVZMN3co .

Cooper Smith Wind Beneath My Wings
https://www.youtube.com/watch?v=X6wqvvwrnco&list=RDX6wqvvwrnco&start_radio=1&t=48 .

Cowboy Christmas 2015 On the Line
https://www.youtube.com/watch?v=SRMWXpSdoDg .

Cowboy Dreams
https://www.youtube.com/watch?v=ix0vPbFpYkI .

"Cowboys Like Us" lyrics - Slim and Jess (Laramie)
https://www.youtube.com/watch?v=hFbAFYyHip4 .

Cute and Sweet Robert Fuller
https://www.youtube.com/watch?v=NU8tOGf0QPs .

Dirty Shirt Sweaty O-Cowboy
https://www.youtube.com/watch?v=_WgY-zkMAik .

Don't Mess With Jess Already a Dead Man
https://www.youtube.com/watch?v=774HaCkIHC4 .

Dr Brackett
https://www.youtube.com/watch?v=NaoST7xz-24 .

Dreaming
https://www.youtube.com/watch?v=fP1f80j5Yic .

E!~Dr. Brackett: The Price

https://www.youtube.com/watch?v=ZJNvMwsgSsg .

E!~Happy Birthday, Robert Fuller: July 29, 2013
https://www.youtube.com/watch?v=0Wq5Z8cZAj8 .

Fabulous Robert Fuller
https://www.youtube.com/watch?v=6JSMR7Fny7M .

Far From Home
www.youtube.com/watch?v=UpCON6R4aUQ[1] .

First Love
https://www.youtube.com/watch?v=HSKLOjvIUhQ .

Foot Loose and Free
https://www.youtube.com/watch?v=D99QxOleoac .

For The Love Of Ginny, Jess Harper The Lawless Seven
https://www.youtube.com/watch?v=3xTqFuBHwls .

Happy 83rd Birthday Robert Fuller tribute (part 2)
https://www.youtube.com/watch?v=1zMTWPOdgYk .

Happy 84th Birthday Robert Fuller!
https://www.youtube.com/watch?v=ONfdVpiF2Ug .

Happy 84th Birthday Robert Fuller! #2
https://www.youtube.com/watch?v=jeajg68cc-Q .

Happy 85th Birthday Robert Fuller Part 1

---

1.   http://www.youtube.com/watch?v=UpCON6R4aUQ

https://video.search.yahoo.com/search/
video?fr=yfp-t&p=robert+fuller+interviews#id=55&vid=e006e8a5407547abbfd319bf598b0280&action=view[2].

Happy 85th Birthday Robert Fuller part one
https://www.youtube.com/watch?v=MpVP_p6vic8 .

Happy 85th Birthday Robert Fuller part two
https://www.youtube.com/watch?v=O0K5pO88fGI .

Happy 86th Birthday Robert Fuller!!!
https://www.youtube.com/watch?v=7q5NktSoDME .

Happy 86th Birthday Robert Fuller!!! (part two)
https://www.youtube.com/watch?v=CrRYUOUSDWY .

Happy 86th Birthday to my favorite (as Dr. Brackett)
https://video.search.yahoo.com/search/
video?fr=yfp-t&p=robert+fuller+interviews#id=30&vid=6a3e3480a88d639822350aa450e2b7a3&action=view[3] .

Happy Birthday, Robert Fuller!
https://www.youtube.com/watch?v=PRbJGcPQwtY .

Happy Birthday Robert Fuller (as Dr. Brackett)
https://www.youtube.com/watch?v=x1qvHLaLPb8 .

happy birthday robert fuller (is low caps)
https://www.youtube.com/watch?v=C40-RRySZOI .

2. https://video.search.yahoo.com/search/
video?fr=yfp-t&p=robert+fuller+interviews#id_43ec3e5dee6e706af7766fffea512721_55_6cff047854f19ac2aa52aac51bf3af4a_vid_43ec3e5dee6e706af7766fffea5
12721_e006e8a5407547abbfd319bf598b0280_6cff047854f19ac2aa52aac51bf3af4a_action_43ec3e5dee6e706af7766fffea512721_view

3. https://video.search.yahoo.com/search/
video?fr=yfp-t&p=robert+fuller+interviews#id_43ec3e5dee6e706af7766fffea512721_30_6cff047854f19ac2aa52aac51bf3af4a_vid_43ec3e5dee6e706af7766fffea5
12721_6a3e3480a88d639822350aa450e2b7a3_6cff047854f19ac2aa52aac51bf3af4a_action_43ec3e5dee6e706af7766fffea512721_view

Happy Birthday Robert Fuller
https://www.youtube.com/watch?v=2EbOfT-oC_s .

Happy Birthday Robert Fuller 2016
www.youtube.com/watch?v=2EbOfT-oC_s&list=PL2YYPNORBEDacHOOhmmdXp4e3389FKLf_ [4] .

Harper and Sherman—Cowboy Detectives
https://www.youtube.com/watch?v=-REZ-m5VeT8 .

♫ He Was My Friend (Laramie, 1959–1963)
https://www.youtube.com/watch?v=PqKfdvX872Y .

I Feel Good(So Good)
https://www.youtube.com/watch?v=HuxPYoQkOeI .

I love you Baby
https://www.youtube.com/watch?v=fkYMF532rAg .

I Try To Be Humble
https://www.youtube.com/watch?v=0aMoGZRu8ew .

I'll Be Your Man
https://www.youtube.com/watch?v=fI3r5ajVFfk .

I'm Beginning to Care
https://www.youtube.com/watch?v=b-st59LPxS4 .

I'm Only Human
https://www.youtube.com/watch?v=NW8c9FQ8IKg .

Jess Harper/Slim Sherman ~ "Easy Rider"

4.	http://www.youtube.com/watch?v=2EbOfT-oC_s&list=PL2YYPNORBEDacHOOhmmdXp4e3389FKLf_

https://www.youtube.com/watch?v=XdBWvydpGUA .

Jess and Slim. Patience . (Sorry Jess)
https://www.youtube.com/watch?v=S5jgr3jDm20 .

Jess Harper and Slim Sherman - A Friend to Carry You
https://www.youtube.com/watch?v=RStCyp2jkQM .

Jess Harper and Slim Sherman - Along the Road
https://www.youtube.com/watch?v=cXDcXNBS-S8 .

Jess Harper and Slim Sherman - Blazing on a Summer's Night
https://www.youtube.com/watch?v=udcVn6O8CVo .

Jess Harper and Slim Sherman - There When You Need Me
https://www.youtube.com/watch?v=koirjjq5hgA .

Jess Harper and Slim Sherman - We'll Work It Out
https://www.youtube.com/watch?v=XtDVsqPMLIE .

Jess Harper, a Cowboy with Backbone
https://www.youtube.com/watch?v=0pmzyJoM1PU .

Jess Harper – A Good Old Boy
https://www.youtube.com/watch?v=DbXQSFK5Bqo .

Jess Harper ~ "A gun on the run.."
https://www.youtube.com/watch?v=IC8cD0b7Nzs .

Jess Harper - Always a Riser
https://www.youtube.com/watch?v=1Ptup7rxwU8 .

Jess Harper – Always on the Run
    https://www.youtube.com/watch?v=PVagG90N8IU .

Jess Harper Blue Bandana
    https://www.youtube.com/watch?v=eyBmSHtgZPA .

Jess Harper "Boots On"
    https://www.youtube.com/watch?v=8xfmVr3M114 .

Jess Harper ~ "Can't Get It Right"
    https://www.youtube.com/watch?v=qGIKsvb3cgs .

Jess Harper - Carry On Through the Storm
    https://www.youtube.com/watch?v=IrWzg0bVY_w .

Jess Harper - Catch Me If You Can
    https://www.youtube.com/watch?v=bAqOmnHPJuM .

Jess Harper - Chains and Broken Bones
    https://www.youtube.com/watch?v=Nyzzb4UoQ1o .

Jess Harper Cowboy Holiday
    https://www.youtube.com/watch?v=w62kJf6IQaY .

Jess Harper – Don't Give Up On Me
    https://www.youtube.com/watch?v=RfUQCtDMpss .

Jess Harper – Down a Long Road
    https://www.youtube.com/watch?v=usMP4o62K1c .

Jess Harper ......Every Move You Make
    https://www.youtube.com/watch?v=Y_foJcrWjaM .

Jess Harper ("Flyboys")
    https://www.youtube.com/watch?v=mlThbzViDKk .

Jess Harper ~ HARDLOVE
    https://www.youtube.com/watch?v=ErVvlpo5V8Q .

Jess Harper "Hay"
    https://www.youtube.com/watch?v=PxGk9q0Hls8 .

Jess Harper (He Rides Like The Wind)
    https://www.youtube.com/watch?v=iE40h6yfz5k .

Jess Harper, He's Already Home
    https://www.youtube.com/watch?v=tmj1zqlMGIE .

Jess Harper - Head 'em Straight
    https://www.youtube.com/watch?v=ezH2zmZaqRM&list=RDezH2zmZaqRM&start_radio=1&t=51 .

Jess Harper - Here Comes Trouble
    https://www.youtube.com/watch?v=Xob3qzoiEM4 .

Jess Harper ("Home")
    https://www.youtube.com/watch?v=62Kpn7WyC4c .

Jess Harper - Hope in the Darkest Hour
    https://www.youtube.com/watch?v=W5H_HNZpn_c

Jess Harper . "I Can Be Your Hero ".
    https://www.youtube.com/watch?v=7PEbSugTBeo .

Jess Harper: I Want You (HD)

https://www.youtube.com/watch?v=oPRZX5RJzH0 .

Jess Harper – In the Shadows
https://www.youtube.com/watch?v=CoMjDbGsrWo .

Jess Harper - In the Silence
https://www.youtube.com/watch?v=VHpKDA5rhqY .

Jess Harper - Just Ride with the Wind
https://www.youtube.com/watch?v=sqRBIlzlO68 .

♫ Jess Harper (Laramie, 1959–1963)
https://www.youtube.com/watch?v=0p5COMEldq4 .

Jess Harper - Legend
https://www.youtube.com/watch?v=79qHV1Zchp4 .

Jess Harper - Life is a Gun
https://www.youtube.com/watch?v=KQ1VJVstrnk .

Jess Harper - Like a Warrior
https://www.youtube.com/watch?v=Z-uKPSU6-qU .

Jess Harper – Looking for Shelter
https://www.youtube.com/watch?v=-RIJCP3IEvc .

Jess Harper – Meant for This
https://www.youtube.com/watch?v=8f6f0z4kH2U .

Jess Harper Mr Velvet Himself
https://www.youtube.com/watch?v=d1MheIlrbeM .

Jess Harper - Never Gonna Break Me
https://www.youtube.com/watch?v=7Q5tkEsK8B4 .

Jess Harper - Ready for Battle
https://www.youtube.com/watch?v=GbfeaKg1Xlw .

Jess Harper ~ RED
https://www.youtube.com/watch?v=jghKZDnbapc .

Jess Harper "Renegade"
https://www.youtube.com/watch?v=e08t6WgyHF0 .

Jess Harper Rides Like the Wind
https://www.youtube.com/watch?v=ylP6tozz-fY .

Jess Harper Riding Shotgun.
https://www.youtube.com/watch?v=OxUJbEEN9gI .

Jess Harper Room to Room
https://www.youtube.com/watch?v=_PX—qF9IyI[5] .

Jess Harper Shine
https://www.youtube.com/watch?v=ACcyTIvwlkM .

Jess Harper - So Far Away
https://www.youtube.com/watch?v=W9udyoeY-xE .

Jess Harper - Soldier's Eyes
https://www.youtube.com/watch?v=F6z4OqN4148 .

Jess Harper – Tearing Me Up

---

5.   https://www.youtube.com/watch?v=_PX--qF9IyI

https://www.youtube.com/watch?v=eHTrUuvth1A .

Jess Harper, that's the way it is
https://www.youtube.com/watch?v=nN8mBJatsd8&list=RDezH2zmZaqRM&index=3 .

Jess Harper - The Best There Is
https://www.youtube.com/watch?v=m9N59uGQ0Ys .

Jess Harper The cowboy in me
https://www.youtube.com/watch?v=rufz9EFAGdI .

Jess Harper - The Road Goes On
https://www.youtube.com/watch?v=8-9QJs54qDM .

Jess Harper - The Stranger
https://www.youtube.com/watch?v=zn4-AJ4Bn0g .

Jess Harper - The Way is Rough and Steep
https://www.youtube.com/watch?v=xKVfaTrZy04 .

Jess Harper - This Fire Never Stops
https://www.youtube.com/watch?v=F2WzlFznsA0 .

Jess Harper - This Fire Will Burn
https://www.youtube.com/watch?v=moPVJYOgvGg .

Jess Harper to Charlie Poke - Men of Mystery
https://www.youtube.com/watch?v=ry48Dhthtig .

Jess Harper – To Know a Man
https://www.youtube.com/watch?v=ZG9PDKCMGdE .

Jess Harper - Travelled So Far

https://www.youtube.com/watch?v=qwrymxQGCvk .

Jess Harper – Wandering Ghost

https://www.youtube.com/watch?v=WJhN4z4uSW8 .

Jess Harper Wanted Dead or Alive

https://www.youtube.com/watch?v=V4JQWgEtLhQ .

Jess Harper – We Just Disagree

https://www.youtube.com/watch?v=DmQWPFrjpEY .

Jess Harper Won't Back Down

https://www.youtube.com/watch?v=fuGhUmNXMS8 .

Jess Harper Won't Be Broken

https://www.youtube.com/watch?v=7zHCxvw8hsw .

Jess Love Wins

https://www.youtube.com/watch?v=NUgvch5-vXs .

Jess, the Man from Laramie

https://www.youtube.com/watch?v=OgfVo_ZQiGM .

Jess, Trampas, Little Joe, Chad, Nick= Cowboy Casanova

https://www.youtube.com/watch?v=IAoGzUx63Rs .

John Smith & Robert Fuller - Laramie & Wagon Train

https://www.youtube.com/
watch?v=0bizY20UIDg&list=PL2YYPNORBEDaIuUEOpYIQxjYsldrjwxU2&index=6&t=0s   and
https://www.youtube.com/watch?v=0bizY20UIDg&list=RD0bizY20UIDg&start_radio=1&t=40 .

John Smith & Robert Fuller - Laramie & Wagon Train
    https://www.youtube.com/watch?v=0bizY20UIDg&list=RD0bizY20UIDg&start_radio=1&t=74 .

JS&RF
    https://www.youtube.com/watch?v=_SDzCNf0CAo .

just the way you are ~ robert fuller ~ fan video by ashley n.
    https://www.youtube.com/watch?v=kQE6SSTVVmo&list=TLPQMjMwNjIwMjDcc3y_ZxUisQ&index=60 .

Kel - Jesus, Take The Wheel
    https://www.youtube.com/watch?v=E8x14DgtwZQ

Laramie (1959-1963)
    https://www.youtube.com/watch?v=cxHkVDu9xxo .

Laramie- A Cowboy's Born With a Broken Heart
    https://www.youtube.com/watch?v=e6Hr3l7M-gk .

Laramie - A Friend to Me
    https://www.youtube.com/watch?v=2KalziCKcLE .

Laramie, "Ballad of Jess Harper"
    https://www.youtube.com/watch?v=Q323cPH13yk .

Laramie "Breakheart Pass"
    https://www.youtube.com/watch?v=tyce3URRdyM .

Laramie Christmas - Robert Fuller, John Smith
    https://www.youtube.com/watch?v=QaVgOvTkWSM .

Laramie - Cowboys are my Weakness
    https://www.youtube.com/watch?v=QxWm496Rsng .

Laramie - Cowboys Forever

    https://www.youtube.com/watch?v=DhChdnHQEE8 .

Laramie- For Good

    https://www.youtube.com/watch?v=4g5H17a0t54&list=RDhXapkim7bx4&index=2 .

Laramie- Here In the Real World

    https://www.youtube.com/watch?v=m39vBh-Ua5I .

Laramie - Hold on Partner!

    https://www.youtube.com/watch?v=RXo6BtVzvfc .

Laramie I Will Always Love You

    https://www.youtube.com/watch?v=EwmAYbKhUX8 .

Laramie I'll Be There

    https://www.youtube.com/watch?v=SxvFd4ODVzI .

Laramie- If I Can't Love Her

    https://www.youtube.com/watch?v=QI0FUw1Tgvk .

Laramie in a Cowboy's Dream

    ttps://www.youtube.com/watch?v=yIOEUNNrr7w .

Laramie ~ Jess & Holly

    https://www.youtube.com/watch?v=LRrXARk7DUw .

Laramie - °*°Jess and Slim°*°

    https://www.youtube.com/watch?v=aGlpMMBT_Qc .

Laramie Jess and Slim - Cowboys on my weakness

https://www.youtube.com/watch?v=v4LQpbTURlc .

Laramie ~ Jess & Slim - Traveller
https://www.youtube.com/watch?v=xe_ejD5D_zI .

Laramie: Jess being bossy
https://www.youtube.com/watch?v=IDRcE-2wKRs .

Laramie - Jess Harper & Lottie "You're strong inside and you're not afraid.."
https://www.youtube.com/watch?v=DT681v_Sgyg .

Laramie - Jess Harper ~ Carry My Body Down
https://www.youtube.com/watch?v=Jxx3hl5FjKU .

Laramie~Jess Harper***Here in my Heart***
https://www.youtube.com/watch?v=5nquNUTUD_c

Laramie - Just One Look w/Robert Fuller and John Smith
https://www.youtube.com/watch?v=_RFzhRjigMo .

Laramie- Life's a Dance
https://www.youtube.com/watch?v=z-W-qrWwXOw .

Laramie ~ Mountain Song
https://www.youtube.com/watch?v=U57XSn0_eNQ .

Laramie Pards - Slim & Jess
https://www.youtube.com/watch?v=KZdI4YVM5l4 .

Laramie - Pards III - Robert Fuller, John Smith
https://www.youtube.com/watch?v=S7VacWe1C_E .

Laramie - Pards revisited
    https://www.youtube.com/watch?v=3LyB3EbeRsk .

Laramie- Riding Fences
    https://www.youtube.com/watch?v=WqOfYCGRBLw .

Laramie°*°*Robert Fuller°*°* part 2
    www.youtube.com/watch?v=59cSnUyLLQ[6] .

LARAMIE-ROBERT FULLER°*°A PICTURE OF YOU°*°
    https://www.youtube.com/watch?v=MbF2AHxbdX4 .

Laramie - Robert Fuller as Jess Harper - Won't Back Down.
    www.youtube.com/watch?v=ab8zTpPhKl[7] .

Laramie - Robert Fuller – Small Man
    www.youtube.com/watch?v+10K6qo86wQ0[8] .

Laramie, Running To The Future / Laramie ,Running To The Future
    https://www.youtube.com/watch?v=HbsArwnLvc4 .

Laramie .. Slim and Jess ♥ ♥
    https://www.youtube.com/watch?v=QEgUkpN-2Bk .

Laramie ♥ ♥ Slim and Jess ♥ ♥
    https://www.youtube.com/watch?v=kLeCuyyH1j8 .

Laramie .. Slim and Jess ♥ ♥ 360 Degrees of You ♥ ♥
    https://www.youtube.com/watch?v=dRxvxd2ZAR0 .

6.   http://www.youtube.com/watch?v=59cSnUyLLQ

7.   http://www.youtube.com/watch?v=ab8zTpPhKl

8.   http://www.youtube.com/watch?v+10K6qo86wQ0

Laramie ... Slim and Jess ♥ ♥ All I Want For Christmas ♥ ♥
https://www.youtube.com/watch?v=sy0NB9lTqgw .

Laramie ... Slim and Jess ♥ ♥ Always There ♥ ♥
https://www.youtube.com/watch?v=IzLne7RfGj8 .

Laramie .. Slim and Jess ♥ ♥ At Your Side ♥ ♥
https://www.youtube.com/watch?v=h5y0Zb9v9SI .

Laramie ... Slim and Jess ♥ ♥ Couldn't Ask For A Better Friend ♥ ♥
https://www.youtube.com/watch?v=HtOq3Llb3n8 .

Laramie .. Slim and Jess ♥ ♥ Cowboys Are My Weakness ♥ ♥
https://www.youtube.com/watch?v=vZFxfx7unSs .

Laramie ... Slim and Jess ♥ ♥ Heroes and Friends ♥ ♥
https://www.youtube.com/watch?v=62biD0lveBo .

Laramie ~ Slim & Jess "...I gotta go somewhere..."
https://www.youtube.com/watch?v=25LNYyucKWo .

Laramie ... Slim and Jess ♥ ♥ I Will Be There For You ♥ ♥
https://www.youtube.com/watch?v=5fc-YQ9vY1k .

Laramie .. Slim and Jess ♥ ♥ If There Hadn't Been You ♥ ♥
https://www.youtube.com/watch?v=S6rLX0I4EPg .

Laramie ... Slim and Jess ♥ ♥ Kiss a Girl ♥ ♥
https://www.youtube.com/watch?v=bqdlY7I8T54 .

Laramie ... Slim and Jess ♥ ♥ Once in Awhile ♥ ♥
https://www.youtube.com/watch?v=y8JhozjK110 .

Laramie ... Slim and Jess ♥ ♥ One Friend ♥ ♥
https://www.youtube.com/watch?v=qIpHhlsgIRE .

Laramie Slim and Jess Pards Forever
https://www.youtube.com/watch?v=hXapkim7bx4&list=RD0bizY20UIDg&index=4 .

Laramie ~ Slim & Jess - Renegades
https://www.youtube.com/watch?v=Xw4WXqN5t5w .

Laramie ... Slim and Jess ♥ ♥ What Would I Do Without You ♥ ♥
https://www.youtube.com/watch?v=ISqU9W7WRQA .

Laramie ... Slim and Jess ♥ ♥ You Raise Me Up ♥ ♥
https://www.youtube.com/watch?v=e-FXq75i7do .

Laramie ... Slim and Jess ♥ ♥ You've Got A Friend In Me ♥ ♥
https://www.youtube.com/watch?v=8CKnTUE7VjU&list=TLPQMjMwNjIwMjDcc3y_ZxUisQ&index=2 .

Laramie- Standing Outsde the Fire
https://www.youtube.com/watch?v=UxezX0OabAY .

Laramie Thank you For Being A Friend Jess and Slim
https://www.youtube.com/watch?v=fk3Qa8WG5dM .

Laramie – The Ones Who Love You
https://www.youtube.com/watch?v=fgcUgmgelbc .

Laramie Valentine 2012.wmv
https://www.youtube.com/watch?v=zHPS49_iPrc .

Laramie Valentines, Robert Fuller & John Smith.wmv

https://www.youtube.com/watch?v=Ff5E0Fuy4Gw .

Laramie Wallpaper - Last Hero
    https://www.youtube.com/watch?v=bL763c-xxik .

Laramie's Finest
    https://www.youtube.com/watch?v=CXItObqZDW0&list=RD0bizY20UIDg&index=5 .

Laramie's Island
    https://www.youtube.com/watch?v=E1gvOElpE9M .

Lawman / Johnny and Jess
    www.youtube.com/watch?v=kUClVEGQ0Ro[9] .

Lean On Me Pard
    https://www.youtube.com/watch?v=HBF6DM9GSco .

Life Comes At you Fast
    https://www.youtube.com/watch?v=qVU862eWNL0 .

♫ Life is... Good? (Laramie, 1959–1963)
    https://www.youtube.com/watch?v=p8mG8SRwqKw .

Like a Hurricane
    https://www.youtube.com/watch?v=oJP4i9gAT-w .

Like a Moth To Her Flame(Coop and Sandra)
    https://www.youtube.com/watch?v=hyMMffOqS9Q .

Live Like This Forever (Robert Fuller , The Hard Ride).
    https://www.youtube.com/watch?v=o2WUMVtvaAs .

9.   http://www.youtube.com/watch?v=kUClVEGQ0Ro

look for Robert Fuller.mpg
    https://www.youtube.com/watch?v=TZ82Rtf3mzM

Lovin Dr Brackett
    https://www.youtube.com/watch?v=wQW9Uzv34Uc .

Loving You
    https://www.youtube.com/watch?v=j1QTWej5sBU .

Man Of Action Holding out for a Hero
    https://www.youtube.com/watch?v=_jvyoA5WayE .

Mercy Mr. Harper
    https://www.youtube.com/watch?v=lat0_KF9XTE .

Mort and Jess. The Harper/Cory Story Beer For My Horses
    https://www.youtube.com/watch?v=herqehuMqts .

My Hero (Dr. Bracket)
    https://www.youtube.com/watch?v=eD0UThdATrk .

My Rife, My Pony And Me
    https://www.youtube.com/watch?v=3EEHvc__4L4 .

My yesterdays
    https://www.youtube.com/watch?v=1GbnrdcV3Us&list=RDQc_CcUREBO8&index=3 .

My yesterdays
    https://www.youtube.com/watch?v=1GbnrdcV3Us&list=RD1GbnrdcV3Us&start_radio=1&t=47 .

Nothing Breaks Like A Heart

https://www.youtube.com/watch?v=Z4IoKpsOc6M .

Pumped Up Kicks

https://www.youtube.com/watch?v=bs1J_3chDqE&list=RDezH2zmZaqRM&index=5 .

Push for the stride hop up and ride

https://www.youtube.com/watch?v=bB5pGI4gxCc .

Push My Button Jess

https://www.youtube.com/watch?v=0t2aoLJQ9rE .

Remember me

https://www.youtube.com/watch?v=aZWxWg9FyyQ&list=RDQc_CcUREBO8&index=2 .

Rescue Me

https://www.youtube.com/watch?v=KLLdNm7B25s .

Return of 7 – Vin

https://www.youtube.com/watch?v=J4cFZCMMRJc .

Ride On

www.youtube.com/watch?v=qckPinqM4k[10] .

Riding Fighting

https://www.youtube.com/watch?v=kIecpLQNo4g&list=RD0bizY20UIDg&index=3 .

Robert Fuller

www.youtube.com/watch?v=G5KELP6icrO[11] .

Robert Fuller

---

10.   http://www.youtube.com/watch?v=qckPinqM4k

11.   http://www.youtube.com/watch?v=G5KELP6icrO

www.youtube.com/xZyz36CWVhI[12] .

Robert Fuller After Dark - Robert Fuller & E! pics
www.youtube.com/watch?v=Kw6E6Ro-Z04[13] .

Robert Fuller and E! pics
https://www.youtube.com/watch?v=SStqoQCsgJw .

Robert Fuller - ("Archangel") Happy Birthday, JUDYCRAM
https://www.youtube.com/watch?v=1dzw1XRnCJk .

Robert Fuller as Cooper Smith[14]
www.youtube.com/watch?v=fGiDwtHQh1o[15] .

Robert Fuller as Cooper Smith – Dust on my Boots
https://www.youtube.com/watch?v=sLsq25v8KlM and https://www.youtube.com/watch?v=sLsq25v8KlM&list=RDsLsq25v8KlM&start_radio=1&t=4 .

Robert Fuller As Dr Bracket in Emergency
https://www.youtube.com/watch?v=YZ8x47EMGYQ

Robert Fuller as Dr. Kelly Brackett
https://www.youtube.com/watch?v=-crR_32p9k0 .

Robert Fuller as Dr Kelly Brackett in emergency
https://www.youtube.com/watch?v=KXFfdKxjBcQ .

Robert Fuller as Jess Harper - Won't Back Down
www.youtube.com/watch?v=ab8zTpPphKl[16] .

---

12.   http://www.youtube.com/xZyz36CWVhI

13.   http://www.youtube.com/watch?v=Kw6E6Ro-Z04

14. https://www.youtube.com/watch?v=fGiDwtHQh1o

15.   http://www.youtube.com/watch?v=fGiDwtHQh1o

Robert Fuller BABY COME HOME
   https://www.youtube.com/watch?v=8B8Fve9-IrQ .

Robert Fuller - Behind Those Eyes [17]
   https://www.youtube.com/watch?v=hknbf-nwp48[18] .

Robert Fuller - Blue Eyes
   https://www.youtube.com/watch?v=g1fzvqiYfIM .

Robert Fuller - Century
   www.youtube.com/watch?v=vdWkZgLvJ5c[19] .

Robert Fuller - Chains
   https://www.youtube.com/watch?v=POG8RQa8gDw .

Robert Fuller – Christmas for Cowboys
   https://www.youtube.com/watch?v=y9gWRH4q6eY .

Robert Fuller - Cool, cool, blue [20]
   https://www.youtube.com/watch?v=uPRwmY601U .

Robert Fuller (actor) - Early life [21]
   https://www.youtube.com/watch?v=PVRcaFyG4sQ .

Robert Fuller-Ein einsamer Cowboy (A Lonesome Cowboy) – Robert singing in German
   https://www.youtube.com/watch?v=sAr5kOzE1_I&list=PLTsQzB68gNOHZFSOeP173Fdf-b6Mps0zV .

---

16.   http://www.youtube.com/watch?v=ab8zTpPphKl

17. https://www.youtube.com/watch?v=hknbf_nwp48

18.   https://www.youtube.com/watch?v=hknbf_nwp48

19.   http://www.youtube.com/watch?v=vdWkZgLvJ5c

20. https://www.youtube.com/watch?v=uPRwmY601U0

21. https://www.youtube.com/watch?v=PVRcaFyG4sQ

Robert Fuller/Emergency!-The coolest Doc in the West! [22]
  https://www.youtube.com/watch?v=6UQ82OVP4jg .

<u>Robert Fuller Family Video With Wife Jennifer Savidge</u> [23]
  https://www.youtube.com/watch?v=Io-giDo8BPg . India - it contains errors.

robert fuller fan video By: ashley n.
  https://www.youtube.com/watch?v=NBdCR-7aYrU .

robert fuller fan video made by fuller fan
  https://www.youtube.com/watch?v=yo9rRk4Y21M .

Robert Fuller ... For Your Love ♥ ♥
  https://www.youtube.com/watch?v=IVG2bL7JFE4 .

Robert Fuller Forever
  https://www.youtube.com/watch?v=EIggWvCGU9k&list=PLTmoReNb2hE4eP4Q1TOO1-I4U13-QVmNi .

ROBERT FULLER: FOREVER A COWBOY [24] (song written by Hoagy Carmichael)
  https://www.youtube.com/watch?v=3r8IkOkLBwY .

Robert Fuller – "Get Started Then"
  www.youtube.com/watch?v=zghOOluOh91 [25].

Robert Fuller Hang My Hat Out In the Prairie
  https://www.youtube.com/watch?v=JqtHB3z9SDo .

Robert Fuller- Happy Birthday

22. https://www.youtube.com/watch?v=6UQ82OVP4jg

23. https://www.youtube.com/watch?v=Io-giDo8BPg

24. https://www.youtube.com/watch?v=3r8Ik0kLBwY

25.   http://www.youtube.com/watch?v=zghOOluOh91

https://www.youtube.com/watch?v=-oa5ep1m4Fo .

Robert Fuller-Happy Birthday—"Hero is in Town"
    https://www.youtube.com/watch?v=53eUAQBM5vM .

Robert Fuller Happy Birthday Tribute (part 1)
    https://www.youtube.com/watch?v=x4T9C9Yp7nY .

Robert Fuller ("Hero´s Theme")
    https://www.youtube.com/watch?v=1hQAg1PqMws .

Robert Fuller - Hey Bobby
    https://www.youtube.com/watch?v=N5P8wRYyb1M .

Robert Fuller - Holy cow, I love your eyes! [26]
    https://www.youtube.com/watch?v=AJ54EdQ9ctQ .

Robert Fuller, I Hang My Hat Out In The Prairie
    https://www.youtube.com/watch?v=d2Hre_rcqww .

Robert Fuller - I saw the light (is low caps)
    www.youtube.com/watch?v=4j7yNeaLYt4[27] .

Robert Fuller .. I've Grown Accustomed To His Face ♥ ♥
    https://www.youtube.com/watch?v=1gEZYY4Q5YI .

Robert Fuller in "Incident at Phantom Hill" slideshow
    www.youtube.com/watch?v=mdlzm96sLjU[28] .

26. https://www.youtube.com/watch?v=AJ54EdQ9ctQ

27.   http://www.youtube.com/watch?v=4j7yNeaLYt4

28.   http://www.youtube.com/watch?v=mdlzm96sLjU

Robert Fuller in Laramie: Ride On! [29]
https://www.youtube.com/watch?v=qcklPinqM4 .

Robert Fuller in The Hard Ride
https://www.youtube.com/watch?v=EWPWKTU_ixI .

Robert Fuller ~-Jess Harper
https://www.youtube.com/watch?v=oT15cV8TcI0 .

Robert Fuller (Jess Harper) Blue Eyes, Windows to the Soul
www.youtube.com/watch?v=ioMGw4s9rXl [30] .

Robert Fuller - John Smith - Forever young
https://www.youtube.com/watch?v=eOZ0XIyftlw .

Robert Fuller ... Just The Same ♥ ♥
https://www.youtube.com/watch?v=q9W9TrLI4e8 .

Robert Fuller - Let the Cowboy Dance [31]
https://www.youtube.com/watch?v=SMwsJ8gZoC4 .

Robert Fuller - Man On Fire
https://www.youtube.com/watch?vb-X9FkiBRs0 [32] .

Robert Fuller ("Mercy") (is birthday greeting)
https://www.youtube.com/watch?v=T2C1d1dbeMY .

Robert Fuller-MyBlueMountains
https://www.youtube.com/watch?v=n6QOVc-QGmY .

---

29. https://www.youtube.com/watch?v=qcklPinqM4k

30.   http://www.youtube.com/watch?v=ioMGw4s9rXl

31. https://www.youtube.com/watch?v=SMwsJ8gZoC4

32.   https://www.youtube.com/watch?v=b-X9FkiBRs0

Robert Fuller ... My Destiny ♥ ♥
https://www.youtube.com/watch?v=_J00fFvYn9A .

Robert Fuller - One Mans Courage
www.youtube.com/watch?v+DRCXgLtrpN4[33] .

Robert Fuller—One and Only for Jess
https://www.youtube.com/watch?v=Ig0QYy0H_SM .

Robert Fuller - One and Only for Jess
https://www.youtube.com/watch?v=Ig0QYy0H_SM .

Robert Fuller – Open Arms
https://www.youtube.com/watch?v=cecAyiofrCY .

Robert Fuller Part 2. !!!!!
https://www.youtube.com/watch?v=n1ZYnOs8Bdc .

Robert Fuller Phantom Hill
https://www.youtube.com/watch?v=vs_ReWOZka0&list=RD0bizY20UIDg&index=6 .

Robert Fuller - Phantom Hill
https://www.youtube.com/watch?v=vs_ReWOZka0&list=RDezH2zmZaqRM&index=2

Robert Fuller Raging On Emergency! (Reupload) [34]
https://www.youtube.com/watch?v=TLZa7iZ95LM .

Robert Fuller SCHÖNE MÄDCHEN SIND WIE BLUMEN (Beautiful Girls are like Flowers)
https://www.youtube.com/watch?v=5b9rgJ1HUfA .

---

33.   http://www.youtube.com/watch?v+DRCXgLtrpN4

34. https://www.youtube.com/watch?v=TLZa7iZ95LM

Robert Fuller – "Small Man"
   https://www.youtube.com/watch?v=10K6qo8GwQ0 .

Robert Fuller ("Spirit of Champions")
   https://www.youtube.com/watch?v=grgwGr8pvN0 .

ROBERT FULLER STAYING ALIVE [35] (as Jess Harper)
   https://www.youtube.com/watch?v=0rcW1-XXOrM [36] .

Robert Fuller - The Legend Begins (foreign)
   https://www.youtube.com/watch?v=Zetm1D9MNA0 .

Robert Fuller - The Nearness of You
   https://www.youtube.com/watch?v=v6erxSBiSu4 .

Robert Fuller - The River
   https://www.youtube.com/watch?v=KOqYFM-l3Kk .

Robert Fuller - There but for the Grace of God.
   https://www.youtube.com/watch?v=GkKI_mByAXE .

Robert Fuller This is Cooper Smith https://www.youtube.com/watch?v=So0fL82c4sw&list=PL2YYPNORBEDaIuUEOpYIQxjYsldrjwxU2&index=5&t=0s .

Robert Fuller ("Time is Time") - To Judycram - Happy Birthday Laramie
   https://www.youtube.com/watch?v=T2u860MBZ-U .

Robert Fuller - Topic [37]
   https://www.youtube.com/channel/UCf1InKw4wdmn2H9hR9—4Yw [38] .

---

35. https://www.youtube.com/watch?v=0rcW1_XXOrM

36.   https://www.youtube.com/watch?v=0rcW1_XXOrM

37. https://www.youtube.com/channel/UCf1InKw4wdmn2H9hR9_-4Yw

Robert Fuller - Under Your Spell [39]
    https://www.youtube.com/watch?v=zbPXeWq3JhU .

Robert Fuller ... When I See Your Face ♥ ♥
    https://www.youtube.com/watch?v=EHS7dK7aFH4 .

Robert the Greatest Cowboy
    https://www.youtube.com/watch?v=d04OAe2JUvk .

Roller Coaster
    https://www.youtube.com/watch?v=SxmCJyr5gT4 .

Say Nothing
    https://www.youtube.com/watch?v=b-VBBDMhdus .

Sharp Dressed Man
    https://www.youtube.com/watch?v=4MR9LtQlHBA .

Sharply Dressed Man
    https://www.youtube.com/watch?v=-Fk-a-ho5gg .

She's like the Wind. Coop Smith . Wagon Train
    https://www.youtube.com/watch?v=AdpnDarwSEQ .

Should Have Been a Cowboy
    https://www.youtube.com/watch?v=B3T5H7l1kQU .

Slim Sherman, Jess Harper. He's My Brother
    https://www.youtube.com/watch?v=fpfgjg87MrY .

38.	https://www.youtube.com/channel/UCf1InKw4wdmn2H9hR9_-4Yw

39. https://www.youtube.com/watch?v=zbPXeWq3JhU

Slim Sherman/Jess Harper ~ I'm Alright!
    https://www.youtube.com/watch?v=hwEfef0HCwg .

Slim & Jess - Kings of the West
    https://www.youtube.com/watch?v=P8ixcz8zhEg .

Staying Alive
    www.youtube.com/watch@v=OrcWl-XXOrM[40] .

Sunrise - A Tribute to Jess Harper
    https://www.youtube.com/watch?v=5pD-esOCVac&list=RDezH2zmZaqRM&index=4 .

Take Me to the Station
    https://www.youtube.com/watch?v=WencCGe0y1Y .

The Champion
    https://www.youtube.com/watch?v=J7SF4zT6Or4 .

The Days of Jess Harper
    https://www.youtube.com/watch?v=GNwr0I5JvTk .

The Different Faces of Robert Fuller
    https://www.youtube.com/watch?v=LYCWimHBtsM .

The Faces of Robert Fuller.mov
    www.youtube.com/watch?v=EJxylvtZ6VY[41] .

The Hard Ride Tribute - Robert Fuller
    https://www.youtube.com/watch?v=hxTvSBu1uzE .

---

40.   http://www.youtube.com/watch@v=OrcWl_XXOrM
41.   http://www.youtube.com/watch?v=EJxylvtZ6VY

The Sherman Ranch, a Place Called Home
    https://www.youtube.com/watch?v=ngtPU_ZKiKI .

The Sound of Silence
    https://www.youtube.com/watch?v=bLfNgOz2124 .

♫ The Thousandth Man (Laramie, 1959–1963)
    https://www.youtube.com/watch?v=g35KAldWj0c .

There You'll Be Millie
    https://www.youtube.com/watch?v=5J4l2jTJ8BA .

This is Jess Harper / Your Heart Will Beat Again
    https://www.youtube.com/watch?v=ljOZPGjdk3I .

To My Wife, Tribute to Robert Fuller.mpg
    www.youtube.com/watch?v=CLYBNcSpdsm[42] .

to the TV Man " Robert Fuller.wmv
    https://www.youtube.com/watch?v=ae3aSz9SSMw .

Tribute Getting Started Then
    https://www.youtube.com/watch?v=zghOOluOh9I .

Tribute Robert Fuller - Circle in the Sand (as Dr. Brackett)
    https://www.youtube.com/watch?v=Lb_2J8d_wTQ .

Tribute to Dix and Kel
    https://www.youtube.com/watch?v=LT3SruCIThc .

---

42.   http://www.youtube.com/watch?v=CLYBNcSpdsm

Tribute To Jess Harper

    https://www.youtube.com/watch?v=22Im5NOgOF4 .

Tribute to my wife tribute to Robert Fuller.mpg

    https://www.youtube.com/watch?v=CLYBNcSpdSM .

Tribute to Robert Fuller

    https://www.youtube.com/watch?v=HgXYLdbXZbw .

Tribute to the Man/Robert Fuller

    https://www.youtube.com/watch?v=vqeX0tR9UfY .

U Smile-Dedicated to Robert Fuller (Spanish)

    https://www.youtube.com/watch?v=xA8jC64fyHQ .

Unbreakable , Jess Harper

    https://www.youtube.com/watch?v=nkKQiZiRhBc .

Vin – Robert Fuller ("Silverado Theme")

    https://www.youtube.com/watch?v=MvE7lJoQqJQ .

Wasn't That A Party

    https://www.youtube.com/watch?v=5wbOL-IHPIE .

Watch Me Try. Phantom Hill

    https://www.youtube.com/watch?v=JmnFSsxI5e4 .

Where Am I Going Today - Bob Moline

    https://www.youtube.com/watch?v=kYVUxiNYiSY .

Who Do You Think You Are (Jar Of Hearts)

    https://www.youtube.com/watch?v=TELR679uDzY .

Wild Hearts Can't Be Broken

https://www.youtube.com/watch?v=kf_vZ7SPhfU .

You are my inspiration

https://www.youtube.com/watch?v=Qc_CcUREBO8&list=RDQc_CcUREBO8&start_radio=1&t=15 .

You Came for Me . Jess Harper

https://www.youtube.com/watch?v=yn7aB1taW0Q .

You Go to My Head, A Tribute to Robert Fuller

https://www.youtube.com/watch?v=2ZOzS0tTF4Y

You Pretty Wild Thing

https://www.youtube.com/watch?v=fz4eabwB70M&list=RD1GbnrdcV3Us&index=4 .

You Raised Me Up

https://www.youtube.com/watch?v=duMRc_W6MQg .

You Raise Me Up Jess and Slim

https://www.youtube.com/watch?v=I1YIyLsIaIc&list=PLfWh5Ru5N5_Ga79yWyqmVjCerKvCOmODt .

Fans can also check into www.interviews.televisionacademy.com/shows/laramie[43] . You will find Hal Needham, stuntman, mentioning Robert in his Laramie interview. His other programs (Wagon Train, Emergency) have interviews about the program but might not talk about Robert.

---

43. http://www.interviews.televisionacademy.com/shows/laramie

MISCELLANEOUS

CELEBRITY SHOWS

There are probably more but here are a few.

Cowboy Way Jubilee in June at Ardmore, Oklahoma. *See www.cowboywayfest.com[1] .*

Hollywood Collectors Show. They are in several states (California, Chicago and Las Vegas) and dates vary. *See www.hollywoodshow.com[2] .*

Mid Atlantic Nostalgia Convention in September at Hunt Valley, Maryland. *See www.midaltanicnostalgiaconvention.co[3]m .*

Mid South Nostalgia Festival in mid June. *See www.midsouthnostalgiafestival.com[4] .* (Formerly Memphis Film Festival).

Western Legends Roundup in August in Kanab, Utah. *See www.westernlegendsrundup.com[5] .*

Williamsburg Nostalgia Film Festival in Virginia. *See www.williamsburgnostalgiafest.com[6] .*

COLLECTIBLE ITEMS AVAILABLE FOR PURCHASE

Items that can be found on eBay include booklets like Western TV Heroes (mini Laramie pictures), Christmas cards, key chains, magnets, movie /TV magazines and decorative signs. Playing cards are in English and foreign languages for places like Argentina. There is a Cooper Smith action figure and Wagon Train fiction book. Comic books, games and lunch boxes were created for all three of Robert's television series Laramie, Wagon Train and Emergency. Fans may also find real / replica scripts along with other items or photos tied to his movies, television, events, etc.

You can focus on a favorite television series, movie or other event to see what is currently selling. As older fans die, more collections may become available enabling younger generations to own something special from Robert's career.

---

1.   http://www.cowboywayfest.com

2.   http://www.hollywoodshow.com

3. http://www.midaltanicnostalgiaconvention.co

4. http://www.midsouthnostalgiafestival.com

5. http://www.westernlegendsrundup.com

6. http://www.williamsburgnostalgiafest.com

One site to look is http://www.briansdriveintheater.com/robertfuller.html .

COMMERCIALS / PUBLIC SERVICE ANNOUNCEMENTS
Friskies Cat Food - Robert was national spokesman.

AOC (National Aviation Officer Candidate Program).

Robert did a 30 second public service announcement on poison prevention. *See FDA Poison PSA at https://www.youtube.com/watch?v=qjIlhecvEOs* and **https://www.youtube.com/watch?v=qjIlhecvEOs&list=PL146FBF24B1CE210C**

Robert did some voiceover work and commercials in the late 1960's to supplement his income. He may have earned $65,000 a year for this type of work.

DVD's
With fans around the world, fans will find many choices of where to purchase genuine legal copies of his movies and television programs. Most of Robert's movies and television programs are available in DVD format. With the release of more 1950's and 1960's television programs, you can find Robert in some very early roles. You can find them at your favorite local store or Internet site. Local used or discounted bookstores can save you money too.

If you are looking to hear Robert's own words the Memphis Film Festival's panel discussions and evening entertainment can be purchased. The main contact person is Terry Swindol at swindol@bellsouth.net or you can contact the festival, (new name is MidSouth Nostalgia Festival) at www.midsouthnostalgiafestival.com[7] .

In 1999 Robert joined Shirley Eaton (1/12/1937- Goldfinger) promoting the Memphis Film Festival on television's On Cable Tonight. Robert's responses are listed briefly below.

<u>1999 TV Interview</u>
That Robert's three series on now seen on TVland

Laramie's Hoagy Carmichael playing piano on set (Robert playing spoons) and writing the song "Marry me, Marry me in Laramie" in several episodes. Another great song Hoagy wrote "The Nearness of You"

A scene from Return of 7 movie is shown
>   Working with Yul Brynner a great experiences, stayed in touch, friends
>   A scene from color 1 ½ hour Wagon Train with Ronald Reagan

Knew Ronald as actor and executive in 1957 GEE. (General Electric) Theater at Republic. (Worked together in The Castaways which aired 10/12/1958).

Later Ron was President of the Screen Actor's Guild. Robert helped him for both governor and Presidential campaigns. A nice man, not well now.

Laramie was his favorite TV role
>   Return of 7 was a favorite movie – 4 months in Spain
>   Emergency's Bobby Troop played piano on set, Julie would sing at home.

Jack Webb, former husband of Julie and Bobby Troop got along since he was helping raise his children.

Julie London was his favorite leading lady.
>   Talks about Memphis Film Festival activities including watching films
>   Oldest this type of festival – 1972 – dealers too
>   Worked with Richard Boone as acting teacher for 4 years – a great man
>   A lobby card from The Brain from Planet from Arouse shown
>   Ends abruptly

Another DVD available that Terry has is Robert at the Knoxville Film Festival in 2004.

<u>2004 Knoxville Film Festival Panel #1</u>
>   Robert's parents were dancers – his dad died recently
>   Stuntman in early movies
>   His parents traveled world wide and appeared before President Harry Truman
>   He was 16 or so when moved to California

Worked at Grumman's Chinese Theater, costumed doorman, for 30 cents an hour

Drafted at age 19
    Chuck Courtney worked on Lone Ranger
    Richard Boone a great teacher – 20 students – each taught differently

Jimmy Dean style was looking down – to get Robert to face up Richard had him do Shakespeare's Hamlet. He cried he couldn't do. Richard said do or don't come back.

Robert bought albums, read book and learned how to do
    Met William Smith (also a panel guest) on Wagon Train - a great actor
    His big break was Laramie seen Tuesday nights for 30 million people

Life did change when people recognized but also grateful for fans and liked fans

Screen Actor's Guild had 4,000 people in when he joined vs. so many more today
    As a stuntman wore a wig as Jerry Lewis
    Doubled for Steve McQueen
    He did 99% of stunts himself

Only accident was on Wagon Train when he broke his right leg and ankle in 4 places

First vacation in 10 years
    Hal Needham was in scene with him

Redid scene and rushing because 10 minutes left and didn't recheck chairs – one was solid vs. breakaway

3 months to heal
    Happy studio paid him ½ salary

Debbie ? - older stunt woman (doubled for Kim Darby also on panel)
    No least favorite moments
    Liked working with Yul Brynner
    The industry has changed so much

Executives 20 or 30 years old and know nothing about business
Writers still good – TV worse, movies better
If weren't an actor, work for Fish & Game Dept – a nice game warden
Hosted fishing shows and paid to do something he loved
Scene he was injured in reshoot after healed
After 1 ½ months he sat on ladder with cast on (vs. horse)
Advice to those wanting to get into business
Competition - 3,000 people a week coming to California – very difficult

99% dedication, determined and must ask for help at least 10 times before Robert would take seriously

People can make a difference to get TV better - spread the word, write letters, etc.

Joel McCrae his very favorite - best horseman
Next week will be in Texas bass fishing

He has done his dream roles – westerns – if anything maybe a matador role with costume, bull

Rhonda Fleming his 2nd favorite with Julie London as first
Laramie shot 5 days vs. movies at 3 weeks otherwise no real difference

Robert got into westerns since grew up with, watched as kids and played cowboys

Great do play cowboys as adult
He was ready to get into business knowing how to ride, had clothing, etc.
Westerns had simple messages - good vs. bad - morality
Today's are too violent

The DVD's below summarize very briefly Robert's topic areas while on Memphis Film Festival panel discussions. Most topic areas are listed as they happened. If you haven't heard a story, here's your chance to see and hear him talk about it or fans can hear a favorite story again.

2009 Panel #4

How Robert got Emergency role
Blind Wagon Train episode
Laramie seduction scene redone to remove saddle blanket

Parties with James Stacy (known since 1952 when both were extras working 5-6 days a week)

Living in Texas and other stars like Alex Cord, Gary Clarke, and Buck Taylor

Being in Elvis' dressing room in Las Vegas, Nevada for about one half hour after show - discussed gun draw

Japan trip and Laramie being #1 show there in 1960's, 20,000 people at airport, later 500,000 people

Japanese awards, fundraising ($100,000 for Japanese Red Cross)
Brain from Planet Arous
Meeting and working with Julie London

2009 Panel #5

How he got part of Jess Harper in Laramie
Got a percentage of merchandise for Laramie, Emergency from Universal

Doing scene, seeing dailies with two producers and redoing scene with Rhonda Fleming

Working with Spring Byington

Hoagy Carmichael repairing prop piano and living on Thunderbird golf course in Palm Springs

7:30 or 8 a.m. was usual call, Hoagy often late, one year only
Being in Korea 17 months 1953-1955 time
Going into bar at 5 p.m. for beer and seeing Julie London perform

Meeting Julie and Bobby Troop and working with Julie later in Laramie and Emergency

Incident of Phantom Hill premier delayed his start of The Return of Seven in Spain

Meeting Yul Brynner in his dressing room while being made up, 3 hour time together before filming started

Warren Oates – both in an early Rin Tin Tin

Old values important like in Texas kids being allowed to be cowboys (guns and all) for Halloween

Saw other celebrities at western bars, magazine photo shoots
    Filmed in Utah and Colorado
    Universal didn't use stock footage

After working with Peter Brown in Lawman Robert was offered contract but already had Laramie, more money, etc.

Meeting Ward Bond in earlier Bette Davis Wagon Train - Ward removing and throwing prop hat he chose to ground

Ward Bond has his own private locked refrigerator with beer
    No scenes with Ward Bond

Second Wagon Train Robert showed Ward Bond worst hat he could find and was told t would do, Robert wore hat he wanted

Frank McGrath liked to start fights and go to Terry Wilson to finish them – both started as stuntmen

Frank in his 60's did saddle fall end of season, had a fifth of gin daily so shot his scenes early in day

Wagon Train Blind episode female co-star
    Bette Davis professional and nice to newcomer Robert
    John Smith and Robert's dressing rooms - shouted back and forth
    Whiskey Row (John, Robert, Ward, Frank, Terry and Lee Marvin)

Playing cards in evening

Frank and other tired of shouting and complained of noise and one evening Frank and John broke down wall

Crumbled walls on Robert's side vs. John's

Assistant director took Robert and John to explain to Lew Wasserman (not first time he and John in trouble)

After explaining dressing rooms were rebuilt with more perks and joined by sliding door

2011 Panel #2:
When he saw Robert Crawford, Jr. and Dennis Holmes last - Both Bobby Crawford and Dennis share stories

Laramie - Hoagy
Fan magazines - lies vs. truth
Dennis Holmes staying with Robert and his roommate Chuck Courtney
Trip to Japan - extended 10 to 30 days
Glen Ford and Buffalo Bill Historic Museum dedication with flying buffalo
How he got Laramie
How he got Emergency
Dennis Holmes' mom's story - Munster's set
Laramie - Camera man
Why Laramie ended
How he got Wagon Train - cast and costume changes
Mustang Country - Joel McCrae
Laramie script writers
How Robert did 99% of his own stunt work
Wagon Train - leg and ankle breaks
Laramie and Wagon Train - riding horses he owned
Laramie - Riding a horse across a deep river and on a bucking horse
Walker Texas Ranger
Retirement
How Westerns changed over time and why they are not on today

2011 Panel #3:
Stories about James Stacy

Stories about Chuck Courtney and David Nelson dirt biking
Fan Magazines - Kathy Nolan
House in North Hollywood
Italy trip
John McIntire and Jeannette Nolan
Chicken death and joke on Laramie
Peter Brown stories
Jock Mahoney story

2013 Panel #4

Buckskin
Richard Boone school stories including kittens inprov
Chuck Courtney
Extra and Dancers pay
Moving to Texas
John Intire and Jeannette Nolan
Robert plays spoons
Weekend shows with Chuck Courtney
First trip to Japan
Donner Pass movie
German movie
Israel movie
Demonstration of fighting techniques with Tony Gill

2014 Panel #2

Early Wagon Train role with Ruta Lee
Wagon Train - Rhonda Fleming story
Meeting Yul Brynner
Demonstration of fighting techniques with Tony Gill

2014 Panel #6

Father's career and pay
Robert's early musicals
Leaving school
Chuck Courtney and Richard Boone classes - kitten story, costs
Teenage Thunder - How he got part
Change in action in movies - script changes
Ellen Colby at Golden Boot Award
He is Jess
Mustang Country with idol Joel McCrae

Hollywood Square questions

Robert also did radio show - DVD titled <u>2014 Memphis Radio Show.</u>

2015 #4 Panel (sound quality issues)
Bob's recent ranch rainstorm damage
How he got Laramie
John Gavin test with Robert
Wagon Train - leg and ankle breaks
Early State Trooper role with Charles Bronson
Korea
Charles Bronson - kitten story
Friendly Persuasion
Chuck Connors - soldier role
Invite and refusal to Hollywood Collector's Show for Emergency reunion
How he changed character - Jess to Coop
Robert demonstration of fight scene with Tony Gill

2016 Panel #2
Graham Theater Job
Screen Actor Guild including pay
Chuck Courtney
Richard Boone encouragement, school costs and kitten story
Alex and Suzanne Cord's wedding
Mustang Country
Tyrone Power fan

2017 #1
Celebrity Tennis Tournament in Tucson, Arizona
How he met Jennifer and proposed marriage
His gun collection
Ranch
War Lords story extra during Laramie
Robert Pine limo story during filming of Bob Hope Chrysler Theater show
Getting Doug McClure's Hollywood Walk of Fame star
Being on Cimarron and how he got Laramie role

2017 #4 Panel

Ranch hay cutting
Grand Nation Club in Oklahoma
Little Joe role
Cameraman - Gone With The Wind
Early Buck Taylor painting while on Colorado River Adventure series
Dan Duryea
His new car
Hunting
Laramie - Germany #1 Show
German album story
Airport movie stunt
Getting paid for reruns
Special effects
Fast Draw
His horses
Wagon Train - broken leg and ankle
Hal Needham

2018 Panel #3

Proposal to Jennifer
How he got Emergency
MGM early start
Tennis tournaments (one was in Tucson, Arizona)
Saturday galas playing spoons
Fear of spiders
Paramedics on Emergency set
Learning to ride by Chuck Courtney
Steve McQueen story
Robert being an acrobat as kid

2018 Panel #4

Weekend act with Chuck Courtney
Japan Visit
Donner Pass movie
Filming in Germany
Filming in Israel
Stories involving James Stacy, Jock Mahoney, Peter Brown
Fight demonstration

2019 Panel #3

Robert's parents
Coming to Hollywood

Wanting to become a Game Warden since could do with High School education

Fan magazine lies
    How he got Emergency job
    How he met Julie London
    One Emergency accident
    Talked Raymond Mantooth into coming to event
    Working on Emergency
    Rattlesnake joke
    Parties
    John Smith
    Raymond Mantooth joke
    Getting on horse hop
    Stunt work
    How Emergency saved real lives
    Directors
    Afraid of spiders

Fans can find magazines at several Internet sites.

FEARS
    Spiders

INTERESTS
    Fishing. One of many places he enjoyed bass fishing was at Lake Ray Roberts reservoir near Denton, Texas.

Fund raising celebrity charity events
    Gardening
    Golfing

Gun Collection. Robert is a responsible and skilled gun owner. Many photos include Robert with his weapons.

Hiking
>Horsemanship / Horseback Riding
>Hunting
>Marksman (awards) - trap and skeet

Playing spoons entertaining friends – *See Robert Fuller Playing Spoons "Ragtime Cowboy at www.youtube.com/watch?v=a0tU2tWnio[8] .*

Rodeo - bull dogger
>Sailing

Tennis in charity tournaments and with Doug McClure (5/11/1935-2/5/1995) and Michael Landon (10/31/1936-7/1/1991).

Traveling
>Wildlife Way-Station. *See www.wildlifewaystation.org[9] .*

The Wounded Warriors Project. *See www.woundedwarriorsproject.org[10] .*

LIKES
>Brownies - dessert

MARKETING
>Colouring books (? Australia, Canada or England)

Each television program and movie would have had press releases, publicity, posters, etc. both in English and foreign languages.

MUSIC
>See songs on his website: *www.robertfuller.com[11]*

---

8. *http://www.youtube.com/watch?v=a0tU2tWnio*

9. *http://www.wildlifewaystation.org*

10. *http://www.woundedwarriorsproject.org*

Singles from his one German album include:
    A Horse and No Saddle
    Beide Heissen Jenny
    Blue Mountains (German)
    I Remember Asking Grandpa
    Texas Heartless
    Uberall Auf Der Wett
    What is a Fisherman
    What is a Quail Hunter

OFFICIAL WEBSITE - *www.robertfuller.com[12]*

Robert's site is constantly growing. A few of its topic areas are:

Awards, Biography, Blog, Career, Commercials (and Public Service Announcements), Fandom, Emergency, Fun and Games. Guest Book, Hot News, Laramie, Movie Theater (some episodes can be viewed), Music, Past Personal Appearances, Photo Gallery, Press Articles (interviews too), The Army, Theater and Wagon Train.

Movie sound tracks include Brain from Planet Arous, Mittsommernacht, The Gatling Gun, The Hard Ride and Return of Seven. Fans can listen to songs from his German album.

Fans original stories can also be read. I found out I was but one of many who wrote stories. I recently reread my Laramie story created over 50 years ago. I had no memory of the story line on those 64 handwritten one sided lined paper sheets (along with squeezed in edits after I made changes based on my English teacher's comments). The end continued on 9 tightly typed pages (remember this was long before "cut and paste" or easy correction options). Can you imagine how many hours I spent on this? A quick summary of my story was:

Girl with many male talents (bronco riding) is hired by Slims while Mike and Daisy are gone (she cooks too)

Mike and Daisy return and Mike finds she can trick ride (previous circus experience)

She overhears they have run out of work for her to do and leaves and Jess and Slim look for her during rainstorm

She gets her leg caught in trap and is found by Jess

---

11.   *http://www.robertfuller.com*

12. *http://www.robertfuller.com*

She goes fishing with Mike and she has a dress made and Daisy helps her make-over and she is popular at a dance

They celebrate Christmas

Secret gold shipment and arrival of four to steal - some are girl's relatives and one who isn't tries to rape her

Fights and shooting occur and Jess is wounded

Slim gets doctor who reports suspicious incident to sheriff so sheriff and posse return and come to their rescue
    Jess and girl marry

I was surprised how descriptive parts were but yes, it needed lots of work and maybe a script but not a novel. I also had created very simple drawings of story's main characters.

Western television programs and characters like Jess and Slim inspired other story tellers / writers to create their own stories. Check out their "finished" versions.

Another part of Robert's official site there is a fan club, Fandom, which started in 2004. Members share personal information to join and communicate through Facebook. Fandom has over 700 members. Membership perks include spending extra time with Robert at events he attends where 150 to 200 members may be present.

Fandom Presentation to Robert Fuller at Memphis Film. See www.youtube.com/watch?v=KWUiMebKtUg[13] .

Robert   Fuller   Fan   Party   -   See   https://www.youtube.com/ watch?v=1VgeAEVRZrw&list=PLF683D699AC8A04E4&index=4 .

Robert Fuller Fandom Party - Laramie Audition #1 of 3. See https://www.youtube.com/watch?v=cc8HL4r_sVQ . (?8/ 2012 in Utah).

---

13. *http://www.youtube.com/watch?v=KWUiMebKtUg*

Robert Fuller Fandom Party - Laramie Audition # 2. See https://www.youtube.com/watch?v=0Ymwyhky4FM .(? 8/2012 in Utah).

Robert Fuller Fandom Party - Laramie audition #3. See https://www.youtube.com/watch?v=gc5q6kiAddk . (? 8/2012 in Utah).

Robert Fuller Fandom Party. Robert with Doug McClure in Utah. See www.youttube.com/watch?v=C19swTERCk[14] .

OTHER CELEBRITIES ROBERT KNEW NOT MENTIONED ELSEWHERE

Robert's career enabled him to meet and know many of the movie and television personalities popular from the 1950's on. Fan magazines show him with many people at staged publicity events and at award ceremonies. Living and working in California offered him many opportunities to know people we also admire. Two are listed below.

Frank Brendel (11/24/1914-6/20/1992). Frank worked with Robert on Laramie doing special effects. Frank won a shared Academy Award for 1974's Earthquake movie visual effects.

Johnny Mack Brown (9/1/1904-11/14/1974). Johnny played football in high school and college in the 1920's and was inducted into the College Football Hall of Fame in 1957. After seeing his likeness on Wheaties cereal boxes, he was offered a screen test and got a five year contact. Over forty years, ending in 1966, Johnny made over 165 movies. From 3/1950 to 2/1959 he had a comic book series and in 6/1952 he also appeared in 21 Dell Giant Series Western Roundup comics. Johnny received awards during his lifetime and afterward. He and his wife Cornelia "Connie" Foster were married about 48 years. See https://obscurehollywood.net/johnny-mack-brown.html .

Anne Francis (9/16/1930-1/2/2011). A fine actress and dancer that Robert danced with.

Along with Terry Wilson from Wagon Train Robert was also photographed with Iron Eyes Cody (4/3/1904-1/4/1999). *He always claimed to be a Native American Indian but was Sicilian. He almost always played Indians and had over 300 roles in movies and television from 1927 to 1990. Iron Eyes Cody is also known for playing a crying Indian in anti-pollution ads. He and his wife Bertha Carter were married 42 years.*

OTHER PLACES TO CHECK OUT

Robert Fuller fans might also enjoy

2Wranglers - Puzzles - Jigsaw Planet at https://www.jigsawplanet.com/2Wranglers?rc=upuzzles&ts="robert fuller" .

---

14. *http://www.youtube.com/watch?v=C19swTERCk*

PERSONALIZED ITEMS FOR PURCHASE

Via Robert's official website. Robert has provided many options for fans. They can get signed photos, personalized audio messages, voice mail messages and birthday and congratulations messages.

His site store carries many items including ball caps, books, bumper stickers, buttons, clipboard, clock, coin, door knob hanger, jar opener, jewelry, keepsake box, mouse pads, note pads, patches, pens, pillow cases, seat covers, tea shirts, Laramie ranch model, pens, playing cards, posters, sticky note holder, sweat shirts, watches and water bottles. *See www.robertfuller.com*[15] - Gift Gallery. Another great place to find unique Robert related items for yourself or other fans are at www.duds-odd-n-ends.com[16]. You can find Robert's image on many items like clothing, hats, jewelry, luggage tags, ornaments, playing cards, puzzles, wrapping paper, etc. I often wear one of my Laramie long sleeve shirts to celebrity signings since they can be an icebreaker as I walking or meet celebrities that know Robert. My Emergency bag carries my newly purchased signed photographs, wallet, cameras, etc.

If you can't find what you want at Robert's official site, items can be found on Internet sites like eBay. Robert's autograph can be found on photos, signed cards, Award events and playbills. With items from 1959 to the present, fans have thousands of items to choose from including a 1 ¼ x 6 ½ name plate. Some items for sale include a Certificate of Authenticity. Several companies offer this service.

PHOTOGRAPHS

During Robert's career thousands of publicity photos for movies, television programs and events he participated in were taken. Candid shots were also taken. With developing technology now any scene from any movie or television program, video, slide, etc. can be turned into a photo. This means there are millions of choices to pick from but the best starting point is Robert's official website at *www.robertfuller.com*[17].

Robert's official site offers autographed photos. Fans can pick their favorite photos and this is one place you know his signature is real. If Robert continues to attend celebrity events, there is often a time to meet Robert, purchase photos and get them signed.

A few other places to find other photos (signed and unsigned) include:
www.westernclippings.com[18]
www.ebay.com[19] (old and newer candid, studio)

---

15. *http://www.robertfuller.com*

16. http://www.duds-odd-n-ends.com

17. *http://www.robertfuller.com*

18. http://www.westernclippings.com

19. http://www.ebay.com

https://www.pinterest.com/pin/471048442258780962/[20] and https://www.pinterest.com/pdianecm52/robert-fuller/ and https://www.pinterest.co.uk/lizapril55/robert-fuller/ [21](

100+ Robert Fuller ideas in 2020 | robert fuller, robert fuller actor, fuller at) [22]and https://www.pinterest.co.uk/lizapril55/robert-fuller/ . Photos can be viewed without signing in.

Some old movie magazines also have great photos.

PRESS RELEASE PHOTOS, ETC.

The studios took press photos for all his movies and television shows, etc. Fans can see or buy them at many Internet sites.

STUNT WORK

Robert has only been doubled twice during his whole career.

TONY GILL (www.tonygill130@gmail)

In Britain Tony oversees Robert's official website. He attends events with Robert organizing fan visit times, interviews, etc. Tony also helped Robert demonstrate how fight scenes are done. When Tony stays at Robert's ranch he enjoys shooting with Robert's shotgun, 9mm and 44. (Britain has no 2nd Amendment gun rights).

Robert Fuller Fan Club - Mr. Gill Goes to Stunt School or See Bob Fuller&Tony Gill stunt fight demonstration MemphisFilmFestival 2014 at https://www.youtube.com/watch?v=afLbAvM_M90 .

Robert Fuller Fan Party. Robert with Tony Gill. See www.youtube.com/watch?v=1VgeAEVRZrw[23] .

The Robert Fuller Fandom ambushes Tony Gill! See https://www.youtube.com/watch?v=COScziv4BWY .

VIEWING ROBERT'S WORK

20. https://www.pinterest.com/pin/471048442258780962/

21. https://www.pinterest.co.uk/lizapril55/robert-fuller/

22.   https://www.pinterest.co.uk/lizapril55/robert-fuller/

23. *http://www.youtube.com/watch?v=1VgeAEVRZrw*

If you don't own copies of Robert's television series or movies there are places you can see his performances. Some of his guest shot ones may be only in our memories. Others, like westerns might be found on oldie TV or Western focused channels.

Choices and costs will vary depending on where you live and if you have an outside antenna, cable provider, etc. Some options are www.grittv.com[24] (most U.S. states), www.inspire.com[25] (Southeast U.S.), www.metv.com[26] (U.S. and Canada) and www.thewesternschannel.com[27] (fee). One site Starz Encore Westerns can be found is www.directv.com/Channels/Encore-Westerns-[28] (fee).

Try sites like https://obscurehollywood.net/ or https://www.get.tv/shows/westerns. Search the website to see other sites that allow you to view a movie or television episode you haven't seen. Some can be found on www.youtube.com[29] . Another great place to find for free is to make a request from your library's Inter-library loan program. Local bookstores and resale shops also carry movies and television programs and music.

SINGING COWBOYS AND COWGIRLS

Rex Elvie Allen (December 31, 1920 - December 17, 1999), was known as "the Arizona Cowboy", and was also a songwriter.

Lester Alvin Burnett (March 18, 1911 – February 16, 1967), known as Smiley Burnette, besides being a comedic sidekick was a songwriter who might have played over 100 musical instruments. He performed from 1934 into the 1960's.

Carolina Cotton (*Helen Hagstrom*; October 20, 1925 - June 10, 1997) was known as the "Yodeling Blonde Bombshell", the "Girl of the Golden West" and the "Queen of the Range".

Eddie Dean (born Edgar Dean Glosup, July 9, 1907 - March 4, 1999). His singing talents were admired by both Gene Autry and Roy Rogers.

Dale Evans Rogers (Lucille Wood Smith 10/31/1912-2/7/2001) was known as "Queen of the West". Dale was also an actress, performer and songwriter.

---

24. http://www.grittv.com

25. http://www.inspire.com

26. http://www.metv.com

27. http://www.thewesternschannel.com

28. http://www.directv.com/Channels/Encore-Westerns-

29. http://www.youtube.com

Kenneth Olin "Ken" Maynard (July 21, 1895 – March 23, 1973) was an early silent star who in 1929 becomes a singing cowboy. He was active from the 1920s to the 1940s.

Woodward Maurice "Tex" Ritter (January 12, 1905 – January 2, 1974) was popular from the mid 1930s into the 1960s.

Roy Rogers (born Leonard Franklin Slye, November 5, 1911 - July 6, 1998) was known as the "King of the Cowboys", appearing in radio, television and movies. Too many to list but a few great books about Roy and Dale are Growing Up with Roy & Dale by Roy Rogers, Jr. and Karen Ann Wojahn; Cowboy Princess by Cheryl Rogers-Barnett and Frank Thompson; Cowboy Princess Rides Again by Cheryl Rogers-Barnett; Roy Rogers and Dale Evans Toys and Memorabilia by P. Allan Coyle and The Roy Rogers Book (reference trivia scrapbook) by Daniel Rothel).

James Clarence Wakely (February 16, 1914 – September 23, 1982) was a songwriter, country Western music vocalist popular in the 1930's to 1950's.

One early popular western song vocal group was the Sons of the Pioneers. In the 1930's and 1940's members were:
    Leonard Slye /Roy Rogers (1933–37) lead vocals, guitar
    Bob Nolan (1933–49) baritone vocals, bass
    Tim Spencer (1933–36, 1938–49) tenor and lead vocals
    Hugh Farr (1934–59) bass vocals, fiddle
    Karl Farr (1935–61) lead guitar

Lloyd Perryman (1936–43, 1946–77) tenor and lead vocals, guitar, 1st Trail Boss

Pat Brady (1937–43, 1946–49, 1959–68) bass
    Ken Carson (1943–47) tenor vocals, guitar
    Deuce Spriggens (1943, 1954–55) bass
    Shug Fisher (1944–46, 1949–53, 1956–59) bass
    Ken Curtis (1949–53) lead vocals (July 2, 1916 - April 28, 1991)
    Tommy Doss (1949–63) baritone vocals

Sons of the Pioneer members who started in the 1950's through 1970's include:
    Dale Warren (1952–2008) lead and baritone vocals, bass, 2nd Trail Boss
    George Bamby (1959–60) accordion
    Roy Lanham (1961–86) lead guitar

Wade Ray (1961–62) fiddle
Rusty Richards (1963–66, 1974–84) guitar, singer
Billy Armstrong (1966–72) fiddle
Bob Minser (1967–68) tenor vocals, bass

Luther Nallie (1968–74, 1980–2004, 2007–2014) vocals, guitar, bass, 3rd Trail Boss

Billy Liebert (1974–80) accordion, arranger
    Rome Johnson (1970's) vocals, guitar
    Sons of the Pioneers who started in the 1980's and 1990's include:
    Doc Denning (1980) fiddle
    Dale Morris (1981-83) fiddle

Tommy Nallie (1983-88, 2010-present) vocals, guitar, bass, drums, 4th Trail Boss

Sunny Spencer (1984-2005) vocals, multi-instrumentalist
    Jack Nallie (1984-86) bass
    Gary Foster (1986) vocals
    Gary LeMaster (1986-2006, 2008-2012) tenor vocals, lead guitar
    Daryl Wainscott (1987-1993) keyboards
    David Bradley (1989-1993) vocals, guitar
    John Nallie (1993-2000) lead vocals, keyboards, drums
    Roy Warhurst (1994-1997) fiddle
    Ken Lattimore (1998 to present) tenor vocals, fiddle

Sons of the Pioneers members who started in the 2000's include:
    Randy Rudd (2001-2017) lead vocals, guitar, MC
    Preston Eldridge (2001-2006) bass
    Jarrett Dougherty (2001-2002) drums, comedy
    Waylon Herron (2004-2006) vocals, guitar
    Justin Sifford (2006) vocals, guitar
    Ricky Boen (2006-2014) fiddle
    Mark Abbott (2006-2017) bass vocals, bass
    Justin Branum (2016-2017) fiddle, mandolin

Roy "Dusty" Rogers Jr. (2018-present) lead vocals, emcee. His father was founder.

John Fullerton (2018-present) vocals, rhythm guitar, bass guitar
    Paul Elliott (2018-present) fiddle, Chuck Ervin (2019-present) bass

You can listen to The Sons of the Pioneers' songs at www.sonsofthepioneers.org[30] . Riders of the Sky, another western song vocal group, started in 1977 and their songs can be found at www.ridersofthesky.com[31] . All members sang and included "Ranger Doug" Green on guitar, "Too Slim Fred LaBour on bass and "Windy Bill" Collins for one year on guitar. From 1978 to 1979 Tumbleweed Tommy" Goldsmith played guitar. "Woody Paul" Chrisman also joined in 1978 and still plays the fiddle. The last member "Cow-Polka King" Joey Miskulin played accordion in 1988 but wasn't an official Riders in the Sky member until the early 1990's.

WESTERN ACTORS AND ACTRESSES

    Western TV and movie info can be found at:
    www.ccvideo.com[32] . This site or its catalog sells many Western movies and TV programs.

www.fiftiesweb.com[33] . The 1950's and 1960's television programs.

www.grit.com[34] . This television station plays great western TV programs and movies.

You can also visit places like:
    Moab Museum of Film and Western Heritage at Red Cliffs Lodge, Miles Post 14, Highway 128 in Moab, Utah

The Museum of Western Film History at 701 S. Main Street / (P.O. Box 111) in Lone Pine, California 93545 with telephone number 760-876-9909 – See www.musuemofwesternfilmhistory.org[35] .

The Paley Center for Media (formerly the Museum of Television and Radio) at 250 West 52nd In New York, New York. *See www.paleycenter.org[36] .*

---

30. http://www.sonsofthepioneers.org

31. http://www.ridersofthesky.com

32.   http://www.ccvideo.com

33. http://www.fiftiesweb.com

34. http://www.grit.com

35. http://www.musuemofwesternfilmhistory.org

36. *http://www.paleycenter.org*

Other helpful and interesting research options and a few Internet websites are:

<u>www.b-westerns.com</u>[37]

<u>www.biography.com</u>[38]

<u>www.glamourgirlsofthesilverscreen.com</u>[39]

<u>www.imdb.com</u>[40]

<u>www.tvguide.com</u>[41]

www.westernclippings.com[42] created by Boyd Magers.

www.wikipedia.org[43] - type in Robert Fuller, actor and get details including his connection with co-workers and friends.

Your local library is another source to request old TV and movies via their inter-library loan program.

Your local ½ price or discounted bookstores may sell used or new DVD's and music.

Books I own and recommend include:

Another Side of Hollywood - An Autobiography by Actor House Peters, Jr.

Pat Buttram - The Rocking Chair Humorist by Sandra Grabman

Candid Cowboy by Neil Summers

Candid Cowboy - Vol. 2 by Neil Summers

Classic TV Westerns by Ronald Jackson

Dick Jones Where the Action Was by Ann Snuggs

Heroes, Heavies and Sagebrush: A Pictorial History of the 'B' Western Players by Arthur F. McClure and Ken D. Jones

Horses in the Movies by H.F. Hintz

37.   http://www.b-westerns.com

38.   http://www.biography.com

39.   http://www.glamourgirlsofthesilverscreen.com

40.   http://www.imdb.com

41.   http://www.tvguide.com

42.   http://www.westernclippings.com

43. http://www.wikipedia.org

Stars I Have Met - What They Were Really Like by Terry Swindol. *See Terry on Mississippi Authors and Artists with guest Terry Swindol on Hill Country Network at https://www.youtube.com/watch?v=sI_AaiFVYLg . Terry has created several other celebrity books. Terry also created several documentaries focusing on Mississippi or Sothern topics. Contact Terry at www.swindol@bellsouth.net .*

The All-American Cowboy Grill by Cheryl Rogers-Barnett, Ken Beck and Jim Clark

The Official TV Western Book – Vol. #2, Vol. #3 and Vol. #4

The Round-Up - A Pictorial History of Western Movies & Television Stars Through the Ages by Donald R. Key

Way Out West by Jane and Michael Stern. *In the Route 66 section, it tells how Bobby Troup came to write the song "Get Your Kicks on Route 66" in 1946.*

Another resource to help fans find more about their favorites celebrities is your library's Inter-library loan program. If you can't find an autobiography, is there a biography that got good reviews? Is there The Films of .... book?

Don't forget some celebrities have their own museums.
Rex Allen is in Wilcox, Arizona. See www.rexallencowboymuseum.org[44] .
Tom Mix is in Dewey, Oklahoma. See www.tommixmusem.com[45] .
Jimmy Stewart is in Indiana, Pennsylvania. See https://jimmy.org .

WESTERN MOVIE AND TELEVISION MEMORABILIA

Some fans are collectors. They may have saved magazines and newspaper articles or bought marketing merchandise. Items like posters, signed and unsigned photographs and many other items are sold at all Celebrity appearance events by vendors. *See Western show section below.*

Boyd Magers is an author and sells articles, books, lobby cards, photos, posters, etc. Find him at www.westerncliippings.com[46] .

44.   http://www.rexallencowboymuseum.org

45.   http://www.tommixmusem.com

46. http://www.westerncliippings.com

Look for your local Toy and Collector shows. For instance, Kane County Fairgrounds at 525 South Randall Road in St. Charles, Illinois (www.kanecountyfair.com[47]) has one twice a year and you never know what you will find. Fans can find books, comics, plastic cowboys and Indians, games including Laramie, Roy Rogers and Gene Autry holsters, action figures, toy guns, clothing and lots more. Vendors and items vary show to show and state to state. As with any purchase, do some investigation to determine typical asking prices.

Several Internet sites sell Robert Fuller items. Fans just need to type in what they are looking for and see what comes up. Ebay Japanese fans often sell items by the page (clipping) vs. whole magazine.

For anyone looking for replica badges, guns, holsters, plastic cowboys and Indians along with real BB guns check www.wildwesttoys.com[48] located in Azle, Texas. Their site also has Western Channel Theater.

---

47. http://www.kanecountyfair.com

48. http://www.wildwesttoys.com

WESTERN LIFE

Many of Robert's earliest fans fell in love with Robert playing a cowboy. There were lots of cowboy movies and television programs then and many were in black and white. We wore cowboy boots and hats and wore toy guns and holsters.

With reruns we can share our favorites with our children and grandchildren. VHS tapes and DVDs allow us to see performances over and over again. Although few westerns are being made and plastic cowboys and Indian toys are rare in stores, there are places to experience the cowboy world. Older fans can pass on western way of life and cowboy values to younger generations who really don't know what a cowboy is. Younger fans can become cowboys or cowgirls like we did. Yes, older fans can also go back in time. There are so many ways fans can have fun learning about western life.

The resources mentioned in this section are given only as examples. Some were found as recommended via Internet website topic area searches. Others mentioned I have personally visited or experienced. Each suggestion gives fans a starting point to do their own investigation. I did exclude a few Internet websites that forced cookies since I disagree with this.

As the author, I have three ebooks fans might enjoy reading. THE WORLD OF YOUR ANCESTORS - DATES - VOLUME TWO that covers the 1800's. It includes books, inventions, occupations, songs, sports, what things cost, what people ate and many more topic areas.

Facts and events of the past lets fans step back in time in THE WORLD OF YOUR ANCESTORS - GENERAL INFORMATION - VOLUME 1 that starts in Europe but continues in the Americas up to the early 1800's. Find out what it was like to be a Native American Indian, fur trader or mountain man. See what a typical day was.

THE WORLD OF YOUR ANCESTORS - GENERAL INFORMATION - VOLUME 2 continues to Victorian and Western times and then life in the early 1900's to the present. Find out about history, religion, holidays, transportation, diet, clothing worn and influential people. Learn things you were never taught in school or get a fresh perspective. Find the truth vs. highly fictionalized movies or those today trying to rewrite or reinterpret the past. Each topic area can give history buffs or genealogists valuable facts about reality back then.

Three western topic books I own and recommend are Days of the West by Mike Flangan, The Book of Buckskinning by the Muzzleloader Magazine and The Old West Quiz & Fact Book by Rod Gragg.

Below I chose a variety of western topic areas since personal interests vary. What are you curious about? What areas excite you? Exploring can be attending an event, visiting a historical site or museum. Fans can observe or participate. Do you want to travel to see new places or explore from home? Your library can find you books on most topics. Internet sites also offer fans places to read more or take a peek inside somewhere you can't visit now.

You can attend rodeos or shooting competitions. You can tour homes built and furnished in the period. Some of these homes may be connected to someone you know from history. You can visit birthplace and life event locations. One example is Buffalo Bill Museum and Grave in Golden, Colorado. See them at www.buffalobill.org[1] .

Fans can also see relocated real buildings representing a particular time. Here's your chance to enter a church, school house or store. The parched summer ground clearly shows that any chicken feed was only going to disappear underground. Seeing these places can really help fans imagine living then. One example is South Pass City Museum in Fairplay, Colorado.

It was hard to choose the best topic area since so sites overlap. Most locations mentioned have detailed websites with photos fans can check.

ANNUAL WESTERN THEMED FESTIVALS
A few to check out include:
Bishop Mule Days in Bishop, California - April or May. See www.muledays.org[2] .

Chief Joseph Days Rodeo - Joseph, Oregon - July. See www.chiefjosephdays.com[3] . This site also has a year round store.

Chuck Wagon Festival at the National Cowboy & Western Heritage Museum at 1700 NE 63rd Street in Oklahoma City, Oklahoma – May. See https://www.visitokc.com/event/chuck-wagon-festival-2021/15370/ .

Laramie Jubilee Days in Laramie, Wyoming - July. See www.laramiejubiliedays.org[4] .

Lone Pine Film Festival - Day of the Cowboy - July. See www.lonepinechamber.org[5] or www.seecalifornia.com/festivals[6] . Rodeo too.

---

1. http://www.buffalobill.org

2.   http://www.muledays.org

3. http://www.chiefjosephdays.com

4. http://www.laramiejubiliedays.org

National Cowboy Poetry Gathering in Elko, Nevada - late January to early February. See www.nationalcowboypoetrygathering.org[7] .

Nebraskaland Days in North Platte, Nebraska – June. See www.nebraskalanddays.com[8] .

Red Steagall Cowboy Gathering and Western Swing Festival in Ft. Worth, Texas – October. See www.redsteagallcowboygathering.com[9] .

Spirit of the Western Cowboy Gathering in Ellensburg, Washington – February. See www.ellensburgcowboygathering.com[10] .

The World's Oldest Rodeo in Prescott, Arizona - late June to early July. See www.worldsoldestrhodeo.com[11] .

United Tribes International Powwow in Bismarck, North Dakota – September. See www.unitedtribespowwow.com[12] .

BUFFALO AND ANIMALS OF THE WEST

Wagon Train featured buffalo in the 1964 episode The Hide Hunters. Buffalo were also the focus on a 1961 episode titled Clyde. Fans can see live buffalo at:

Cooks Bison Farm at 5645 East 600 South in Wolcottville, Indiana (www.cooksbisonranch.com[13]). They also offer chuck wagon meals.

Terry Bison Ranch at 51 125 Service Road / Frontage Road in Cheyenne, Wyoming (www.terrybisonranch.com[14]). They also offer horseback riding and a restaurant.

---

5. http://www.lonepinechamber.org

6. http://www.seecalifornia.com/festivals

7. http://www.nationalcowboypoetrygathering.org

8. http://www.nebraskalanddays.com

9. http://www.redsteagallcowboygathering.com

10. http://www.ellensburgcowboygathering.com

11. http://www.worldsoldestrhodeo.com

12. http://www.unitedtribespowwow.com

13. http://www.cooksbisonranch.com

Wild Winds Buffalo Preserve at 6975 North Ray Street in Fremont, Indiana (www.wildwindsbuffalo.com[15] and www.visiteubencounty.com[16]).

Other animals associated with Out West like the bears, prairie dogs, deer and elk can be seen in many western states especially in state and national parks. Animals are wild so keep a safe distance.

An animal book to check is Grizzlies in the Wild by Kennan Ward.

COWBOYS
Three books I own and recommend are:
Cowboy & The Trapping of the Old West by William Manns and Elizabeth Clair Flood

Cowboy Cultures: The Last Frontier of American Antiques by Michael Friedman

The Cowboy Boot Book by Tyler Beard

CRAFTS
Daisy from Laramie was shown doing cooking, cleaning, painting and shopping. I don't recall scenes where she was sitting down or doing any craft projects. However before her arrival, the episode A Sound of Bells from 12/27/1960 has characters making ornaments and gifts. The 1800's were a time when most people made everything they needed or they traded and bartered with others. Girls learned the art of sewing since clothing was mended and reused. Younger children often had hand-me-downs.

Craftwork skills created items of necessity, gifts and things to amuse children. Popular craft materials were beads, lace, paper and ribbons. Early dolls were made out of apples, clothespins, cornhusks or yarn. With fewer chores in the winter, quilts were often created. Visiting mid and later 1800 furnished homes that survive today can show fans the creativity of homestead women.

One book I own and recommend that includes a few 1800's items is Nostalgia Crafts Book by Phyllis Fiarotta.

---

14. http://www.terrybisonranch.com

15. http://www.wildwindsbuffalo.com

16. http://www.visiteubencounty.com

EDUCATION

Laramie showed Andy studying and then leaving home to go to school. Mike was also shown studying at home. Daisy taught school and Mike taught a boy to read in the 1/23/1962 episode The Runaway. As towns grew, schools were built. Time actually spent in school varied with the sex of the child, distance from the school and the season. Many historic school houses can be seen by themselves or as a part of restored / relocated towns. Fans can go inside and imagine sitting there in these one room school houses.

For Laramie fans, you can learn more about Wyoming schools at sites like: http://wyomingalmanac.com/buffalo_bones_stories_from_wyomings_past_1978-   2015/public_schools_in_territorial_wyoming[17]   and www.wyoachs.com/laramies-living-history-buildings-1/2018/4/15/a-high-school-for-laramie-takes-shapein-1876[18] .

For curious teachers or fan interested in seeing what 1800's students were taught, find Old Favorites From the McGuffey Readers by the American Books Company. This particular book combines the first through sixth readers (1836-1936). The 1880's New Normal Fourth Reader book is 351 pages and like McGuffey has notes to the teacher with exercises on the principles of reading including pronunciation.

At least two companies were publishing Fifth Readers in the 1880's. Harper's Fifth Reader has 510 pages with stories by well known people like F. Fenimore Cooper, Benjamin Franklin, Nathaniel Hawthorn, Oliver W. Holmes, Patrick Henry, Thomas Jefferson, Herman Melville, George Washington, Daniel Webster and Walt Whitman.

Swanton's Fifth Reader and Speaker with 475 pages has a totally different format. Each section has words to review and homework or follow up assignments. Swinton also has an 1872 Word Book of English Spelling that is 154 pages long and covers two years of material.

An 1880 book, The Methods of Teaching, by John Swett with 326 pages explains ethics, training (physical, moral, intellectual), school government and class room management. Actual teaching topics are arithmetic, composition, drawing, geography, grammar, punctuation, spelling, language, natural sciences, reading, spelling, U.S. history and writing. Teachers are using games, oral and written exercises.

Warren Colburn's First Lessons Intellectual Arithmetic written in 1849 and the revised 1884 version has 216 pages. It asks hundreds of questions and again shows a different teaching technique. Another great source for learning what is was like to be both a child and a teacher is to read Laura Ingalls Wilder books. See www.littlehouseontheprairie.com[19] .

---

17. http://wyomingalmanac.com/buffalo_bones_stories_from_wyomings_past_1978-%202015/public_schools_in_territorial_wyoming

18. http://www.wyoachs.com/laramies-living-history-buildings-1/2018/4/15/a-high-school-for-laramie-takes-shapein-1876

19. http://www.littlehouseontheprairie.com

FORTS

Both Laramie and Wagon Train had episodes with forts and the military. Which ones to you remember? Forts may be restored, reconstructed or persevered for western fans to see what fort life was like in the 1800's. You can also step back into time while attending reenactments which are sometimes held at forts. People participating are in period costume and are eager to share their knowledge with attendees. Some of these forts are in open more isolated locations with no modern things in view making the visit truly more enjoyable. Can you get into costume to join in on the fun?

Fans can learn more about forts on Internet websites like www.wickipedia.org[20] or for National Historic sites see www.nps.com[21] or www.nationalparks.org[22] . A few historic forts are included below.

Bent's Old Fort National Historic Site in La Junta, Colorado - reconstruction

Fort Abraham Lincoln State Park in Mandan, North Dakota - replica Indian village too

Fort Abercrombie State Historic Site in Abercrombie, North Dakota - original and reconstruction

Fort Bowie National Historic Site in Wilcox, Arizona

Fort Bridger State Historic Site near Evanston, Wyoming - See www.travelwyoming.com[23]

Fort Buford State Historic Site near Williston, North Dakota

Fort Caspar Museum and Historic Site in Casper, Wyoming - reconstructed buildings- See www.travelwyoming.com[24]

Fort Davis National Historic Site in Davis, Texas

---

20. http://www.wickipedia.org

21. http://www.nps.com

22. http://www.nationalparks.org

23. http://www.travelwyoming.com

24. http://www.travelwyoming.com

Fort Garland Museum and Cultural Center in Fort Garland, Colorado. See www.historycolorado.org[25] .

Fort Gibson Historic Site in Gibson, Oklahoma – reconstruction - See www.okhistory.org[26] .

Fort Griffin State Historic Site near Albany, Texas. Huge acreage and events are also held.

Fort Laramie National Historic Site near Torrington, Wyoming - See www.travelwyoming.com[27] .

Fort Larned National Historic Site near Bend, Kansas - See www.kansastravel.org[28] .

Fort McKavett State Historic Site in Mc Kavett, Texas - restored. See www.thc.texas.gov/historic-sites[29] .

Fort Phil Kearney State Historic Site in Banner, Wyoming - See www.travelwyoming.com[30] .

Fort Scott National Historic Site in Fort Scott, Kansas - See www.kansastravel.org[31] .

Fort Smith National Historic Site in Fort Smith, Arizona

Fort Stanton Historic Site in Stanton, New Mexico - See www.newmexicoculture.org[32] .

Fort Stevenson State Park in North Dakota - reconstruction

Fort Supply Historic Site in Fort Supply, Oklahoma - See www.okhistory.org[33] .

25. http://www.historycolorado.org

26. http://www.okhistory.org

27. http://www.travelwyoming.com

28. http://www.kansastravel.org

29. http://www.thc.texas.gov/historic-sites

30. http://www.travelwyoming.com

31. http://www.kansastravel.org

32. http://www.newmexicoculture.org

Fort Totten State Historic Site in Fort Totten, North Dakota - original buildings

Fort Union Trading Post National Historic Site in Williston, North Dakota

Fort Vancouver National Historic Site in Vancouver, Washington

Fort Vasquez Museum is near Greeley, Colorado. See www.historycolorado.org[34] .

Fort Verde State Historic Park is in Camp Verde, Arizona. See www.azstateparks.com[35] .

GHOST TOWNS

Locations will vary in size and deterioration. A few to consider are listed below. Other ghost towns and lesser known places can be found on Internet website like www.ghosttownaz.info/hisotric-sites[36] .

Ashcroft, Colorado is near Aspen – See www.undercovercolorado.com/ghost-towns[37] .

Bannack State Park in Dillon, Montana - See www.bannack.org[38] .

Bodie, California – not reconstructed - See www.bodie.com[39] or www.parks.ca.gov[40] .

Garnet, Montana is near Missoula – See www.garnetghostown.org[41] or www.visitmt.com/listings/general/ghost-town[42] .

33. http://www.okhistory.org

34. http://www.historycolorado.org

35. http://www.azstateparks.com

36.   http://www.ghosttownaz.info/hisotric-sites

37. http://www.undercovercolorado.com/ghost-towns

38. http://www.bannack.org

39. http://www.bodie.com

40. http://www.parks.ca.gov

41. http://www.garnetghostown.org

42. http://www.visitmt.com/listings/general/ghost-town

Mystic, South Dakota is near Hill City. See www.ruralresurrection.com/shots-towns[43] .

Virginia City, Montana – restored and touristy - See www.virginiacity.com[44] .

Vulture Mine in Wickenburg, Arizona – restoration - See www.vultureminetours.com[45] or www.ci.wickenburg.az.us[46] .

GUEST RANCHES

These facilities can give you a chance to 'go back in time'. Some offer horseback riding, herding cattle, roping and guests can even help do common 1800's chores. Some ranches have replica stagecoaches. You may be served traditional western foods. Countless songs have been written about cowboys and your visit may include a show or sing-along.

Some ranches may let you stay in the time period while others combine old time ranch activities with more modern options. Recommended ones I found on the Internet that appear to have less modern options are listed below. Each can give you a starting point to do your own investigation based on your preferences.

Bonanza Creek Guest Ranch is in Martinsdale, Montana. See www.bonanzacreekcountry.org[47] .

Circle Z Ranch is in Patagonia, Arizona. It is a former sheep ranch and western TV and movies have been filmed here. See www.circlez.com[48] .

Hideout at Flitner Ranch / Hideout Lodge and Guest Ranch in Shell, Wyoming. See www.thehideout.com[49] .

JJJ Wilderness Ranch is in Augusta, Montana. See www.triplejranch.com[50] .

---

43. http://www.ruralresurrection.com/shots-towns

44. http://www.virginiacity.com

45. http://www.vultureminetours.com

46. http://www.ci.wickenburg.az.us

47. http://www.bonanzacreekcountry.org

48. http://www.circlez.com

49. http://www.thehideout.com

50. http://www.triplejranch.com

Medicine Bow Lodge Adventure Guest Ranch is near Saratoga, Wyoming. See www.medicinebowlodge.net[51].

Rancho de la Osa Guest Ranch in Sasabe, Arizona. See www.ranchodelaosa.com[52].

Tombstone Monument Guest Ranch in Tombstone, Arizona. See www.tombstonemonumentranch.com[53].

GUNS

Robert learned how to draw and shoot many kinds of firearms both on film and in personal life. He is a skilled and responsible gun owner. In the 1800's children were taught gun safety and used guns at very young ages. Guns were not to be feared but used when needed whether for hunting or protecting themselves. Some better known gun museums include:

Cody Dug-Up Guns Museum in Cody, Wyoming - old found guns vs. those in more pristine condition - See www.codydugupgunmuseum.com[54].

Cody Firearms Museum: Buffalo Bill Center of the West, Cody, Wyoming[55] – See www.centerofthewest.org[56].

J.M. Davis Arms and Historical Museum at 330 North J.M. Davis Blvd. in Claremore, Oklahoma. *See www.thegunmuseum.com*[57].

The N.R.A. (National Rife Association) Fire Arms Museum is at 11250 Waples Mill Road in Fairfax, Virginia – See www.nramuseum.org[58].

The N.R.A. (National Rifle Association) National Sporting Arms Museum is at 1935 South Campbell Avenue in Springfield, Missouri – See www.nramuseum.org/museums/national-sporting-arms-museum[59].

---

51. http://www.medicinebowlodge.net

52. http://www.ranchodelaosa.com

53. http://www.tombstonemonumentranch.com

54. http://www.codydugupgunmuseum.com

55. https://centerofthewest.org/explore/firearms/

56. http://www.centerofthewest.org

57. *http://www.thegunmuseum.com*

58. http://www.nramuseum.org

59. http://www.nramuseum.org/museums/national-sporting-arms-museum

Sanders Museum at 115 East Madison Avenue in Berryville, Arkansas. It contains a gun collection. *See* *www.berryville.com*[60] .

Books that I own and recommend are:
Black Powder Revolvers - Reproductions and Replicas by Dennis Adler
Colt - An American Legend by R.L. Wilson

The Peacemakers - Arms and Adventures in the American West by R.L. Wilson

The Treasury of the Gun by Harold L. Peterson

MAGAZINES
American Cowboy - See www.americancowboy.com[61]
Arizona Highways - See www.arizonahighways.com[62]
Cowboys & Indians - See www.cowboysindians.com[63]
True West - See www.truewestmagazine.com[64]

MAIL
As more and more settlers moved West, communication was limited until the 1860's. For less than two years stations were built about ten miles apart and single young men took on the job of being a pony express rider. Buffalo Bill's pony express rider's experiences are in his autobiographies - See the Museum section below.

Here are two museums I enjoyed.
Pony Express Barn Museum at 106 South 8the in Marysville, Kansas. See www.marysvillemuseumsks.org[65] or www.visitmarysvilleks.org[66] .

Pony Express Museum at 914 Penn Street in St. Joseph, Missouri. See www.ponyexpress.org[67] .

---

60.   *http://www.berryville.com*

61.   http://www.americancowboy.com

62.   http://www.arizonahighways.com

63.   http://www.cowboysindians.com

64.   http://www.truewestmagazine.com

65.   http://www.marysvillemuseumsks.org

66.   http://www.visitmarysvilleks.org

MILLS

Converting grain crops into bread or useful food items was done in mills using water. Other mills were used in making clothing. Old grist mills can be found in many states and can be fun and informative places to visit. See www.scenicusa.net/Historic-Mills[68] .

A few western examples are:

Alley Spring Mill Historic Site is on Highway 106 in Eminence, Missouri. See www.nps.gov[69] .

Bollinger Mill State Historic Site is at 113 Bollinger Mill Road in Burfordville, Missouri. There is also a covered bridge here. See www.mostateparks.com[70] .

Benson Grist Mill is at 325 State Road 138 in Stansbury, Utah. See www.bensonmill.org[71] .

Cedar Creek Grist Mill is at 43907 Northeast Grist Mill Road in Woodland, Washington. There is also a replica covered bridge here. See www.cedarcreekgirstmill.org[72] .

Hollands Grist Mill in on Flynn Drive in Milbank, South Dakota - restoration. See www.scenicusa.net[73] .

Lidtke Mill Historic Site is on Mill Street in Lime Springs, Iowa. See www.visitiowa.org[74] .

Nielsen Grist Mill is on State Route 24 in Bicknell, Utah. See www.scenicusa.net[75] .

Thompson's Mills State Heritage Site is at 32655 Boston Mill Drive n Shedd, Oregon. See www.stateparks.oregon.gov[76] .

---

67. http://www.ponyexpress.org

68.   http://www.scenicusa.net/Historic_Mills

69.   http://www.nps.gov

70. http://www.mostateparks.com

71. http://www.bensonmill.org

72. http://www.cedarcreekgirstmill.org

73. http://www.scenicusa.net

74. http://www.visitiowa.org

75. http://www.scenicusa.net

War Eagle Mill is at 11045 War Eagle Road in Rogers, Arkansas - an operating reproduction. See www.wareaglemill.com[77] .

Watkins Woolen Mill State Historic Site at 26600 Park Road North in Lawson, Missouri. In the 1870's sheep were made into wool here. See www.watkinsmill.org[78] or www.mostateparks.com[79] .

MINING

Some story lines for Robert's television and movies featured bank robberies (real silver and gold shipments), prospectors and hunting for lost ore. There were mines that held missing cattle, mines blown up or rotting away.

The exploration and settlement of the West grew based on where silver and gold were found. Native American Indians had land stolen from them because it contained precious metals.

Many towns were founded because an ore strike was made and some of today's ghost towns are old mining towns. For more information see Internet websites like www.westernmininghistory.com[80] . A few other places to learn about mining include:

AMMNRE Mineral Collection is tied to the University of Arizona at 115 North Church Avenue in Tucson, Arizona (www.ammnre.com[81] or www.uamineralmuseum.com[82]) .

Geology / Mines Museum at 501 East St. Joseph Street in Rapid City, Missouri (www.sdsmt.edu[83]).

Queen Mine is at 478 Dart Road in Bisbee, Arizona (www.queenminetour.com[84]).

Western Museum of Mining and Industry at 225 North Gate Boulevard in Colorado Springs, Colorado (www.wmmi.org[85]).

---

76. http://www.stateparks.oregon.gov

77. http://www.wareaglemill.com

78. http://www.watkinsmill.org

79. http://www.mostateparks.com

80. http://www.westernmininghistory.com

81. http://www.ammnre.com

82. http://www.uamineralmuseum.com

83. http://www.sdsmt.edu

84. http://www.queenminetour.com

MUSEUMS

Museums are great places to see real items and learn about Western expansion and life. Museums can be more specialized or contain a little bit of everything. Many of those listed below I have personally visited. Others sounded good and fans may know others. You can often peek inside by checking out their websites. Museums an also be great places to find books you won't find anywhere else.

Autry Museum of the American West at 4700 Western Heritage Way in Los, Angeles, California. *See www.theautry.org[86]* .

Boot Hill Museum in Dodge City, Kansas[87] – See www.boothill.org[88] .

Buckhorn Saloon and Museum at 318 East Howard Street in San Antonio, Texas www.buckhornmuseum.com[89] .

Buffalo Bill Center of the West in Cody, Wyoming – See www.centerofthewest.org[90] . Two books I own and highly recommend are his autobiographies, the 1917 version titled The Life and Adventures of Buffalo Bill and the 1978 version titled The Life of Hon. William F. Cody. Although there is some overlap each contains different material.

Don King's Western Museum / King's Saddlery and Museum at 184 North Main Street in Sheridan, Wyoming. *See www.kingssaddlery.com[91]* . This is also a great place to see real cowboys shopping.

Frank Brownell Museum of the Southwest at 34023 64 West in Raton, New Mexico and is part of the NRA Whittington Center. See www.nramuseum.org[92] .

Harold Warp Pioneer Museum at 138 East US Highway 6 in Minden, Nebraska. *See www.pioneervillage.org[93]* .

---

85. http://www.wmmi.org

86. http://www.theautry.org

87. http://boothill.org/

88. http://www.boothill.org

89. http://www.buckhornmuseum.com

90. http://www.centerofthewest.org

91. http://www.kingssaddlery.com

92. http://www.nramuseum.org

93. http://www.pioneervillage.org

LaPorte County Historical Society Museum at 2405 Indiana Avenue in LaPorte, Indiana. It includes an antique firearms collection. *See www.laportecountyhistory.org*[94] .

National Cowboy and Western Heritage Museum at 1700 NE 63d Street in Oklahoma City, Oklahoma. *See www.nationalcowboymuseum.org*[95] .

Prairie Homestead Historic Site on the Badlands Loop in Interior, South Dakota www.prariehomestead.com[96] .

Texas Ranger Hall of Fame and Museum at 100 Texas Ranger Trail in Waco, TX 76706 with telephone number 254-750-8631 - See www.texasranger.org[97] .

The Superstition Mountain Museum at 4087 E Apache Trail in Apache Junction, AZ with telephone number 480-983-4888 - See www.superstitionmountainmuseum.org[98] .

Western Spirit: Scottsdale's Museum of the West at 3830 N. Marshall Way in Scottsdale, Arizona 85251- See www.scottsdalemuseumwest.org[99] .

Wyoming Pioneer Museum in Douglas, Wyoming – See www.travelwyoming.com[100] .

NATIVE AMERICAN INDIANS

During Robert's early extra and stuntman career he may have been an Indian. In earlier times, actors were allowed to show their talents playing different nationalities than what they were. Robert could play Mexicans. Both Laramie and Wagon Train episodes featured Indians. Robert also made many western movies where Indians were a part of the storyline.

---

94. *http://www.laportecountyhistory.org*

95. *http://www.nationalcowboymuseum.org*

96. http://www.prariehomestead.com

97. http://www.texasranger.org

98. http://www.superstitionmountainmuseum.org

99. http://www.scottsdalemuseumwest.org

100. http://www.travelwyoming.com

Indian museums show house building types including teepees and what was inside them. Museums (some run by Indians and located on reservations) also contain elaborate beadwork, clothing, moccasins and decorated buffalo skins. Every day life and hunting techniques are illustrated. You can find National Historical Site information at www.nps.com[101]. Fan can learn much about Native American Indians at places like:

Canyon De Chelly National Monument in Chine, Arizona

Fort Apache Historical Park & Apache Cultural Center in Apache, Arizona

Hubbell Trading Post National Historic Site in Gunado, Arizona

Nez Perce Historic Park has locations in Idaho, Montana and Washington

Real Native American made items can be found in many Indian owned shops too. Some items may truly be from the 1800's while others are more modern. You will find more in states where there are Indian Reservations. Some shops I have visited include:

Cherokee Trading Post at 1590 Winfield Dunn Parkway in Sevierville, Tennessee. (This is a popular shop name and can found in many areas including several in Oklahoma).

InterTribal Designs at 1520 North Portland Avenue in Oklahoma City, Oklahoma www.okitd.com[102].

The Prairie Edge Trading Post and Gallery at 606 Main Street in Rapid City, South Dakota. www.prairieedge.com[103].

There are many non-fiction books about Indians and ones I own and recommend are:
    Bury My Heart at Wounded Knee by Dee Brown
    Circles of the World by Richard Conn
    Fighting Indians of the West by Dee Brown and Martin F. Schmitt
    Indian Sign Language by William Tomkins
    North American Indian Arts by Andrew Hunter Whiteford

---

101. http://www.nps.com

102. http://www.okitd.com

103. http://www.prairieedge.com

Ottawa Quillwork on Birchbark by Harbor Springs Historical Commission

The Battle of the Washita (Sheridan and Custer Campaign 1867-1869) by Stan Hoig

The Native Americans - The Indigenous People of North America by the Smithsonian Institution

The Techniques of Porcupine Quill Decoration Among the Indians of North America by William C. Orchard

Books more autobiographic include:
    Apache Agent - The Story of John P. Clum by Woodworth Chum

Black Elk Speaks: Being the Life Story of a Holy Man of the Oglala Sioux by Black Elk

Captured by the Indians – 15 Firsthand Accounts 1750 -1870 by Frederick Drimmer

Empire of the Summer Moon: Quanah Parker and the Rise and Fall of the Comanches, the Most Powerful Indian Tribe in American History by S.C. Gwynne

Geronimo: My Life by Geronimo
    Lakota Woman by Mary Crow Dog
    Lame Deer, Seeker of Visions by John Fire Lame Deer

Memoirs of a White Crow Indian - Thomas Leforge told by Thomas B. Marquis

Mourning Dove: A Salishan Autobiography by Mourning Dove

No Turning Back: A Hopi Woman's Struggle to Live in Two World by Polingaysi Qoyawayma

The Dark Horse Speaks by Little White Bird

The Sacred Pipe: Black Elk's Account of the Seven Rites of the Oglala Sioux by Black Elk

Where White Men Fear to Tread: The Autobiography of Russell Means by Russell Means

Pow Wow's demonstrate modern Indian's craftsmanship in clothing creation. You can see traditional dancing talents and see and hear drummers performing songs. Indian vendors attending also may be selling unique traditional and modern items you will not find anywhere else. Don't forget to try some a favorite of mine, fry bread. Here is a place to look for buffalo or elk meat on the menu. There are many states where you can see Pow Wow performances. One pow wow is the Gathering of Nations Pow Wow in Albuquerque, New Mexico - April. See www.gatheringofnations.com[104] . You might have more luck finding pow wows in states with higher Indian populations like Arizona, California, Idaho, Michigan, Minnesota, Montana, New York, North Carolina, North Dakota, Oklahoma, South Dakota, Utah, Washington and Wisconsin.

REAL PEOPLE IN HISTORY

Readers can use the Internet or the library to search for both well known and every day people's stories or autobiographies. Curious readers can find trail blazers, explorers, cowboys, outlaws, sheriffs, politicians and travelers. There are also wagon train diaries and women's perspectives. Pick a name, pick a topic area and real western era fans can find many interesting stories.

Other than ones mentioned elsewhere three more I own and recommend are The Life of Hon. William R. Cody from 1879 or another version from 1917 titled The Life and Adventures of Buffalo Bill from 1917. Another is Davy Crocket's Own Story.

REAL PLACES IN HISTORY

Robert played real characters. Donner Pass located 9 miles west of Truckee, California can be visited and info can be found at www.eyewitnesstohistory.com[105] . The Fetterman Massacre site can also be visited near Banner and Sheridan, Wyoming. The actions that occurred there are still controversial - See www.wyohistory.org[106] . Fans can dig deeper in the real history of Laramie, Wyoming and stage stops. Fans can visit many places some special event occurred. Walking around battlefields or historic locations can be a fun way to relive history.

All National sites can be found at www.nps.com[107] . Several other Western historical locations include:

---

104. http://www.gatheringofnations.com

105.   http://www.eyewitnesstohistory.com

106.   http://www.wyohistory.org

107. http://www.nps.com

Independence Rock State Historic Site in Alcova, Wyoming

Little Bighorn Battlefield National Monument in Crow Agency, Montana. [108]Books I own and recommend are Apsaalooka - Survive Custer by Ottie W. Reno, Keep the Last Bullet for Yourself by Thomas Marquis, They rode with Custer by John M. Carroll and Troopers With Custer by E.A. Brininstool.

Sante Fe National Historic Trail has locations in Colorado, Kansas, Missouri, New Mexico and Oklahoma.
  Tombstone, Arizona
  Yuma Territorial Prison State Historic Park in Yuma, Arizona
  Wyoming Territorial Prison in Laramie, Wyoming

RESTAURANTS - COOK OUTS

Do you remember Robert's scenes in the kitchen or outside grilling during Laramie? What about scenes eating on the trail or in town? How about all the jokes made about cooking while on Wagon Train? Museums can show you real cooking utensils.

Your travels may take you to areas that have restaurants with a western theme. There are also outdoor chuck wagon or cookout type restaurants with entertainment (singing cowboys). See books like Stella Hughes' book Chuck Wagon Cookin'. Fans can enjoy hearing western singers and storytellers, both in person and on albums, cassettes or CD's.

STAGECOACHES AND WAGONS

Robert rode in or drove stagecoaches and wagons during his career. Real ones can be found in museums. Fans can ride a replica stagecoach experiencing the bumps and dust. Fans can visit real stagecoach stops and envision sleeping there with a bunch of strangers. One stagecoach location is Point of Rocks Stage Station Site in Rock Springs, Wyoming.

Fans who enjoy reading can find many books with personal accounts of people while traveling west on wagon trains. Two books I own and recommend are A Lady's Experience in the Wild West in 1893 by Rose Pender and The Gentle Tamers - Women of the Old Wild West by Dee Brown. Museum stores are great places to find reading material. Another Internet website to learn more is www.wyomingtalesandtrails.com[109] .

---

108. https://www.nps.gov/libi/index.htm

109. http://www.wyomingtalesandtrails.com

A few places to see wagon ruts or experience the Oregon Trail are Alcove Spring in Blue Rapids, Kansas, Big Hill in Montpelier, Idaho, California Hill in Brule, Nebraska, Columbia River Gorge in Biggs Junction, Oregon, Guernsey Ruts in Casper, Wyoming, Red Bridge Crossing in Kansas City, Missouri, Rock Creek Station in Fairbury, Nebraska and Virtue Flat in Baker City, Oregon.

Two other places fans might enjoy are:

California Trail Interpretive Center in Elko, Nevada – See www.californiatrailcenter.org[110] .

Overland Trail Museum at 1110 Overland Trail in Sterling, Colorado. *See www.sterlingcolo.com[111]* .

Do you want to travel by wagon train? Two places advertising wagon train rides are Teton Wagon Train and Horse Adventure in Jackson, Wyoming (www.tetonwagontrain.com[112]) and Western Legends Roundup in Kanab, Utah (www.westernroundup.com[113]).

A book I own and recommend about transportation options is Wheels Across America by Clarence P. Hornung.

STEAM RAILROADS

How many scenes can you remember Robert's character riding on a steam train? What about the 1960 Laramie episode, The Protectors, when Jess gets thrown off? Steam train rides can be found in many states but the list below focuses on those in Western U.S.

1880 Train in Hill City, South Dakota - See www.1880train.com[114] .

Cripple Creek & Victor Narrow Gauge Railroad in Cripple Creek, Colorado - See www.cripplecreekrailroad.com[115] .

Cumbres & Toltec Scenic Railroad in Antonito, Colorado - See www.cumbrestoltec.com[116] .

---

110.   http://www.californiatrailcenter.org

111. http://www.sterlingcolo.com

112. http://www.tetonwagontrain.com

113. http://www.westernroundup.com

114. http://www.1880train.com

115. http://www.cripplecreekrailroad.com

116. http://www.cumbrestoltec.com

Durango & Silverton Narrow Gauge Railroad Train in Colorado - See www.durangotrain.com[117] .

Georgetown Loop in Georgetown, Colorado - See www.georgetownlooprr.com[118] .

Grand Canyon Railway in Williams, Arizona - See www.thetrain.com[119] .

Nevada Northern Railway in East Ely, Nevada - See www.nnry.com[120] .

Railtown 1897 State Historical Park in Jamestown, California - See www.railtown1897.org[121] .

Roaring Camp Railroads in Felton, California - See www.roaringcamp.com[122] .

Skunk Train in Fort Bragg and Willits, California - See www.skunktrain.com[123] .

V&T Railway in Carson City, Nevada - See www.vtrailway.com[124] .

Books I own and recommend are:
    History of the Western Railroads by Jane Eliott
    Train Wrecks by Robert C. Reed

TRADE

America's discovery and exploration often started with fur trappers and traders encouraging the Native American Indians to supply items they could resell. Two places to learn about this are:

---

117. http://www.durangotrain.com

118. http://www.georgetownlooprr.com

119. http://www.thetrain.com

120. http://www.nnry.com

121. http://www.railtown1897.org

122. http://www.roaringcamp.com

123. http://www.skunktrain.com

124. http://www.vtrailway.com

Fort Cody Trading Post at 221 Hallingan Drive in North Plattt, Nebraska. *See www.fortcody.com*[125].

Museum of the Fur Trade at 6321 Highway 20 in Chadron, Nebraska. *See www.furtrade.org*[126].

A book I own and recommend is Kit Carson's Own Story of his Life - (December 24, 1809 - May 23, 1868).

Two artists who focused on fur trade were Alfred Jacob Miller (1816-1874) and Charles Dees (1818-1867).

WESTERN ARTISTS

Many artists drew, painted and sculptured what they personally saw. Two museums dedicated to western artists include:

C.M. (Charles Marion) Russell (1864-1926) Museum in Great Falls, Montana – See www.cmrussell.org .

Fredric Remington (1861-1909) Art Museum in Ogdensburg, New York – See www.fredericremington.org[127].

The list of western theme artists is long but a few fans might want to check out are listed below. Some artists born in the late 1700's and 1800's include Albert Bierstadt (1830-1902), Maynard Dixon (1875-1946), W. Herbert Dunton (1878-1936), Earnest Martin Hennings (1886-1956), Frank Tenny Johns (1874-1939), Thomas Moran (11837-1926) and Olaf Wieghorst (1898-1988).

Three artists born in the early 1900's were Joe Beeler (1931-2006), Frank McCarthy (1926-2002) and George Phippen (1915-1956).

Two artists who mainly focused on Native American Indians were George Catlin (1796-1872) and Howard Terpning (1927-).

WESTERN WRITERS

125. *http://www.fortcody.com*

126. *http://www.furtrade.org*

127. http://www.fredericremington.org

There are thousands of books available on any topic imaginable and diaries and autobiographies are especially insightful. Here is your chance to read someone's thoughts at the time, in their words, in their perspective and not the untrue versions we usually hear today. Your local library or Internet search can answer questions you may have and give curious fans helpful resources.

There are many western theme fiction writers. A few authors fans might enjoy reading are listed below.
Andy Adams (1859-1935)
Willa Cather (1873-1947)
Ben K. Green (1912-1874)
Zane Grey (1872-1939). He has a museum in Lackawaxen, Pennsylvania.

Ron Hansen (1947-)
Mackey Hedges (1942-)
Will James (1892-1942). His books were made into movie too.
Elmer Kelton (1926-2009)
Alan Le May (1899-1964)

Louis L'Amour (1908-1988). His books were made in movies too – See www.louislamour.com[128] .

Larry McMurtry (1936 -)
Ralph Moody (1898-1982)
Jack Schaefer (1907-1991)

Luke Short (1908-1975). His books were made into 1940's movies too.

Walter Van Tilburg Clark (1909-1971)

Laura Ingalls Wilder (1867-1957). There are several sites and museums in places she lived. Her Iowa and Minnesota locations feature the 1870's, the same time period as Laramie. See www.littlehousebooks.com[129] and d www.littlehouseontheprairie.com[130] . Also see the author's ebook Laura's Family Tree.

---

128. http://www.louislamour.com

129. http://www.littlehousebooks.com

130. http://www.littlehouseontheprairie.com

Another writer's museum is Mark Twain Boyhood Home at 206 Hill Street in Hannibal, Missouri (www.marktwainmuseum.org[131]). The author, Mark Twain / Samuel Clemens was a character played by Dabbs Greer in a Laramie episode titled Company Man that aired 2/1960.

Fans of traditional western theme poems can attend annual events like National Cowboy Poetry Gathering held in Elko, Nevada in January – See www.nationalcowboypoetrygathering.org[132] . Another websites to check into is www.westernfolklife.org[133] .

WESTERN SHOPS

Some forts, museums, national historic sites have shops selling items about the West or period items. A few items you might find in these shops are animal hides and horns, artwork, bedding, books, boots, candles, clothing, cookbooks, crafts, day to day replica items, figurines, food, jewelry, knives, minerals, moccasins, rocks, ropes, saddles and toys. If fans live or travel in the Western states, you will know more than the few here I visited below.

Bass Pro Shops - Outdoor World at 1935 South Campbell Avenue in Springfield, Missouri. *See www.basspro.com[134] .*

Merlin's Hide Out at 626 Richard Street in Thermopolis, Wyoming. Hunters take their animals here. Free tours explain the process of preparing skins and shop sells buffalo hides, leather products and many other items. *See www.merlinshideout.com[135] .*

The Old Cabin Shop at 8010 Lafayette Road in Lodi, Ohio. *See www.logcabinshop.com[136] .*

For fans wanting to look the part, a few clothing stores / catalogs selling western items include:
Cattle Kate – See www.cattlekate.com[137] .
Pfi Western – See www.pfiwestern.com[138] .
Sheplers – See www.sheplers.com[139] .

---

131. http://www.marktwainmuseum.org

132. http://www.nationalcowboypoetrygathering.org

133. http://www.westernfolklife.org

134. *http://www.basspro.com*

135. *http://www.merlinshideout.com*

136. *http://www.logcabinshop.com*

137.   http://www.cattlekate.com

138.   http://www.pfiwestern.com

139.   http://www.sheplers.com

For fans looking for real antiques, research very carefully and take all precautions you are buying real items vs. clever fakes.

271

Robert and cowboys from the 1930's through 1960's gave many of us a love of the West. Enjoy exploring the world of real cowboys and the West.

CONCLUSION

The creation of Robert Fuller's timeline is meant as a thank you for being a part of our lives. For some of us who have 'known' him for over 60 years, he is family. Fans all over the world have memories of how he or his work impacted their lives. I'll admit I was crazy about him as a kid and I feel the same way today. I am just one of thousands who felt his 'magic'.

Technology has enabled his professional and personal life to be remembered. Fans like me have collected and saved photographs, fan magazines, TV Guides, playbills and newspaper articles. Fans have autographed photos and taken candid shots. Below is another one of me with Robert.

ROBERT AND THE AUTHOR

Thankful and admiring fans have created songs, birthday greetings honoring Robert and his career. The Internet contains some guest appearances, interviews and events Robert was honored with special awards. Sharing this timeline and your enthusiasm for Robert with others will also make sure he is not forgotten.

Years ago we saw 'good guys' win over 'bad guys'. Right and wrong and values were more clearly defined. Children learned valuable lessons. In 1949 The Lone Range program premiered. Its Creed included:

I believe that to have a friend, a man must be one.

That all men are created equal and that everyone has within himself the power to make this a better world.

That God put the firewood there, but that every man must gather and light it himself.

In being prepared physically, mentally, and morally to fight when necessary for that which is right.

That a man should make the most of what equipment he has.

That "this government, of the people, by the people, and for the people," shall live always.

That men should live by the rule of what is best for the greatest number.

That sooner or later. somewhere. somehow. we must settle with the world and make payment for what we have taken.

That all things change, but the truth, and the truth alone lives on forever.
I believe in my Creator, my country, my fellow man.

In 1950 Gene Autry's Code of Honor was:
Never go back on your word
Never betray a trust, a trust confident in you
Always tell the truth
Be gentle with children, the elderly and animals
Help people in distress
Be a good worker
The Cowboy is a patriot
Keep yourself clean in thought, speech and action
Never shoot first
Never hit a smaller man
Never take unfair advantage
Do not advocate racially intolerant ideas
Do not advocate religious intolerance

In 1951 if you were a Roy Rogers Rider member, rules included:

Be neat and clean
Be courteous and polite
Always obey your parents
Protect the weak and help them
Be brave but never take chances
Study hard and learn all you can
Be kind to animals and take care of them
Eat all your food and never waste any
Love God and go to Sunday school regularly
Always respect our flag and our country

These codes, creeds and rules are still relevant today. Fans may not be able to impact the world like Robert did but we can change our own little part of the world. You can thank those who inspired you by inspiring others. I hope going down memory lane or learning something new about Robert has been a fun adventure for everyone.

A special thanks to Robert. Thank you for your hard work entertaining us. Thank you taking time away from your own life, your own family to spend time with us fans. Thank you for giving so many of us a lifetime of joy and smiles from seeing your face or hearing your voice. We love you and wish you great health and all the best forever.

Fans can thank Robert by buying and spreading the word about both A Timeline For Robert Fuller Fans ebooks. Remember that a portion of the profits are going to one of Robert and Jennifer's favorite charities Wounded Warriors or later if needed split between this charity and keeping Robert's official website running. Thank you so much.

I have countless hours over many years creating this ebook for Robert Fuller fans. After contributing things I had saved for over 50 years to Robert's official website I soon found them being sold as magnets, etc. If you are selling items related to Robert, please consider donating some of your profits to Wounded Warriors. It is a great way to thank Robert and honor our military.

ABOUT THE AUTHOR

Carol A. Wirth is a 1950's kid growing up with western TV programs and by 4 years old Carol was wearing cowboy boots. She has been a fan of Robert Fuller's since Laramie. In 1970 she and her mom went to see Robert in the play Boeing, Boeing in St. Charles, Illinois. In 1999 Carol flew to Las Vegas, Nevada and then drove down to Laughlin to see him along with many western stars at her first celebrity event. In 2011 she found that he was appearing at the Memphis Film Festival and drove almost ten hours to attend. Carol has attended several times since but the first few times were the best letting her dress up and be a cowboy / cowgirl again. Carol is still a TV nut, owning old fan magazines and can recall many names from the 1950's and 1960's TV programs. She loves watching Robert and other classics on VHS tapes, DVD's and on TV.

Carol A. Wirth has been writing since childhood for fun, making up stories, writing television scripts, short non-fiction articles and poems. She has always liked reading and history. Carol A. has written articles for a local women's magazine and is the author of several ebooks.

FINDING YOUR ANCESTORS SIMPLIFIED is an easy way to research family tree data. Some topic areas discussed include cemeteries, census reports, churches, death notices, foreign and military records, newspapers, plats, social security and taxes. Do you know how dates, language and boundaries can complicate your investigation? Learn how names and surnames came to be. Discover what it was like to be an immigrant coming to America and applying for early naturalization. Review some pros and cons about DNA testing. You will also get ideas and advice about sharing and saving your history, evaluating your findings and keeping an open mind.

Are you are looking for some fun facts? Curious or have an interest in history? The author's genealogy research, love of reading and learning helped create these nine ebooks. THE WORLD OF YOUR ANCESTORS – GENERAL INFORMATION – VOLUME 1 is the first of three volumes. It covers history and life in Europe (mainly Austria, Britain, Germany and Italy). Data continues in the Americas up to the early 1800's. What was it like to be a Pilgrim, Puritan, Quaker, Colonial, Native American Indian, fur trader or mountain man? Do you wonder why your relatives came to America? Let the facts in all THE WORLD OF YOUR ANCESTORS series help you gain insight into the past. What was a typical day like? What opportunities were available? What choices were made or were forced upon people and how do they still impact our lives today?

THE WORLD OF YOUR ANCESTORS – GENERAL INFORMATION – VOLUME 2 covers Victorian and Western times and life in the early 1900's into the present. Data includes life in Michigan, Oregon, Wisconsin and Quebec, Canada. Find out about history, religion, holidays, transportation, diet, clothing worn and influential people. Learn things you were never taught in school or get a fresh perspective. Find the truth vs. highly fictionalized movies or those today trying to rewrite or reinterpret the past. Each topic area can give history buffs or genealogists valuable facts about reality back then.

THE WORLD OF YOUR ANCESTORS – GENERAL INFORMATION – VOLUME 3 is last in this series and covers life in the 1900's to the present. It contains data on banking, crime, diet, education, games and toys. It shares courtship and marriage rituals, tells about people's homes, occupations, clothing, religion and slang. It concludes with a section for family tree enthusiasts. Learn about history of names and dates. Find immigration records and discover other contact resources and areas of interest for your genealogy research.

THE WORLD OF YOUR ANCESTORS – DATES – VOLUME ONE is the first of six volumes. It starts at the beginning of time and goes until 1800 sharing highlights. Glimpse into the past. You may remember some events but much will be new, lesser known items. It includes famous people, inventions, wars and news. Dates are often more than just a date and event since background info is shared. You will get the bigger picture vs. localized or one topic history. See how different life was or how much really hasn't changed.

THE WORLD OF YOUR ANCESTORS – DATES – VOLUME TWO continues with the 1800's and includes songs, books, occupations, sports, what things cost, what people ate and many more topic areas. Read about facts and events and step back into time. What inventions changed people's lives? What was the Civil War really like? What was life like for Indians? What priorities and challenges did people face in the 1800's?

THE WORLD OF YOUR ANCESTORS – DATES – VOLUME THREE continues with 1900 through 1929. It gives news, political leaders, prices, sports and facts about World War I. It was a time of epidemics and world events that changed everyone's daily lives. It was a time when many immigrated to the U.S. When and why did you ancestors first arrive? What current events changed or complicated their plans or dreams?

THE WORLD OF YOUR ANCESTORS – DATES – VOLUME FOUR continues with 1930 through 1949. What was life like during the Depression, Prohibition and World War II? Find out what books were read, movies watched, slang spoken, songs sung, cars sold, medicine used, crime and a whole lot more. Details will tell you about day-to-day life of your relatives living during these difficult times.

THE WORLD OF YOUR ANCESTORS – DATES – VOLUME FIVE continues with 1950 through 1979. It shares information on baby boomers, the emergence of teenagers, the Korean and Vietnam Wars. Find Broadway plays, movies, television, prices, new products, books, sports heroes and weather events. Read some mini biographies of people who made a difference. Changes occurred that still impact us today. Here is your chance to go down memory lane or learn about life before you were born.

THE WORLD OF YOUR ANCESTORS – DATES – VOLUME SIX is the last volume covering the years 1980 through 2017. Read about events you forgot or never knew. See biographical information, news items, television programs, population numbers, inventions and prices. Find many reasons why our daily lives have changed. Let the facts in all THE WORLD OF YOUR ANCESTORS series help all of us better understand the world of our living friends and relatives.

Two of the author's poems have received recognition. A SYMPHONY OF LIFE contains 136 poems and verses taking readers along life's journey. Celebrate life with all its emotions, good and bad, like finding yourself, college, friendship, love, loss of love, being lonesome, being cheered up, thanking someone, celebrating special events and more. Let these poems give you insight into how others see the world or maybe you'll see yourself in these poems. Maybe these words can inspire you to write some original verse to give to someone special in your life.

HOW TO TAKE A VACATION – SAVE TIME, MONEY AND FRUSTRATION focuses on the basics of how to travel for the beginner and for those seeking up-to-date resources for travel in today's world. This ebook give readers access to hundreds of linked websites and data is viewable anywhere and any time. Helpful tips and suggestions in many topic areas can make traveling less expensive and more fun. Find out what to do before your trip, during your trip and afterward. Make better choices and don't be caught unprepared. If you would like to take a less stressful and more exciting vacation and save some time and money, check out her new ebook. Let the author share her enthusiasm exploring new places with you.

EASY TRIP PLANNING is Carol A.'s latest travel ebook. It contains some new info and focuses on very detailed topic areas. It is mainly for newer or returning travelers or travelers trying something different. Are you thinking about taking your first cruise or renting a RV or going to your first foreign country? Topics cover choosing destinations, modes of travel, what you'll run into at lodgings, flying, with car rentals, tours, etc. Each area includes questions to ask yourself and giving possible answers to allow better decision making before, during and after traveling.

Ebooks can be read without buying a device at websites like Adobe Digital Editions. You can read ebooks on your computer or other devices you may have.

Carol A. continues to write and tries to maintain a positive attitude and enjoy what life brings each day. She has lived in Wisconsin, New York, Michigan and is currently living in Illinois. Carol A. Wirth sincerely hopes each of you will be encouraged to take steps toward accomplishing your own dreams. She believes you can succeed in making some of your wishes come true and turn your dreams into reality.

Volume 3 of 3
The World of Your Ancestors - General Information - Volume 3

Standalone
A Symphony of Life (Poems)
How to Take A Better Vacation - Save Time, Money and Frustration
Finding Your Ancestors Simplified
Travel Made Easy
A Timeline for Robert Fuller Fans
Laura and Her Family Tree